SCOTT, FORESMAN
SOCIAL STUDIES

California History

THE STUDY OF OUR STATE

About the Cover Art:

The cover art is one of ten works handcrafted in such traditional American art forms as quilting, needlepoint, embroidery, and applique. This art was specially commissioned for the covers of this series by Scott, Foresman and Company. Designed by Patricia Lenihan-Barbee, this 10″ × 10″ needlepoint was embroidered by Patricia Legg and Dona Werder of Needlecraft Gallery, Wilmette, Illinois. Needlepoint is embroidery worked on open mesh fabric known as canvas. It has been used for centuries for upholstery and carpets. In America, needlepoint has been popular since colonial times and used for samplers and household objects.—Commentary by Barbara Lee Smith, Oak Park, Illinois

**SCOTT, FORESMAN
SOCIAL STUDIES**

California History
THE STUDY OF OUR STATE

Scott, Foresman and Company

Editorial Offices: Glenview, Illinois

Regional Offices: Palo Alto, California • Tucker, Georgia • Glenview, Illinois • Oakland, New Jersey • Dallas, Texas

California History: The Study of Our State was developed for Scott, Foresman under the direction of **American Learning Corporation**. The textbook was developed with the assistance of:

Scott, Foresman Social Studies Program Developers

Dr. Joan Schreiber
Professor of History
Social Studies Methods
Ball State University
Muncie, Indiana

William Stepien
Instructional Coordinator
for Social Studies
School District No. 300
Dundee, Illinois

Dr. John Patrick
Professor of Education
Indiana University
Bloomington, Indiana

Dr. Richard Remy
Director of the Citizenship
Development Program
Mershon Center
Ohio State University
Columbus, Ohio

Dr. Geneva Gay
Associate Professor
of Education
Purdue University
West Lafayette, Indiana

Dr. Alan J. Hoffman
Professor of Education
Georgia State University
Atlanta, Georgia

Program Development

Norris Hundley, Jr.
Professor of American History
University of California
Los Angeles
Managing Editor of
Pacific Historic Review

Lyn Steg
Educational Consultant
Member, Cadre for the
Implementation of the
California Framework for
the Social Studies

Teacher Consultants

Paul Apodaca
Artist in Residence
Bowers Museum
Santa Ana

Joyce Dash
Region Administrator
Region D
Los Angeles Unified
School District

Antonio Delgado
Instructional Advisor,
Los Angeles Unified
School District

Betty M. Takizawa
Reading Coordinator
Dacotah Street School
Los Angeles

ISBN: 0–673–13392–3

The Acknowledgments section on page 288 is an extension of the copyright page.

12345678910-RRW-929190898786858848382

Contents

Atlas

Facts About California

Glossary

Index

Acknowledgments

List of Maps

List of Globes

List of Charts

SCOTT, FORESMAN
SOCIAL STUDIES

California History

THE STUDY OF OUR STATE

Unit ①

The First People of California

California has always been a good place for people to live. In California's early days, many Indians lived here. Later, Spanish and Mexican people came and settled. Each group depended on the rich land of California. The different groups learned to live together and began to depend on people outside California.

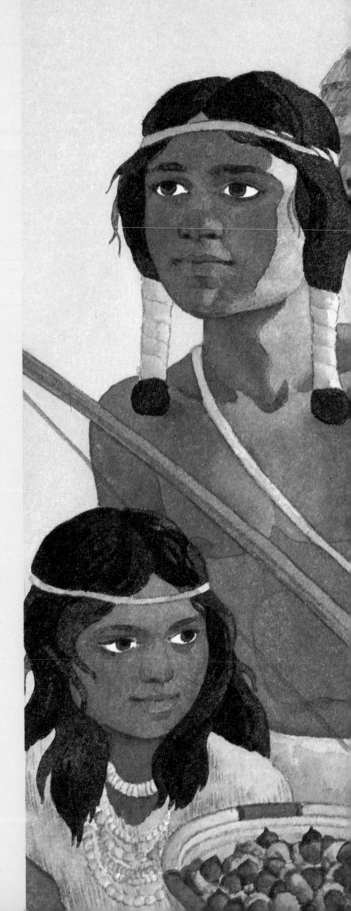

The Indians

When the California Indians hunted deer, they tried to look and act as much like deer as possible. In this way, they were able to get close to the animals without frightening them. Their bows and arrows worked better up close.

What do you see when you look out your window? Do you see houses, stores, schools, roads, or cars? It's hard to imagine life without these things. But there was a time when none of these things existed. What would the place you live in have looked like *before* there were any buildings or roads? How would people have lived then?

Lesson 1   Food from the Land

The first people who lived in California were American Indians. We know that they lived here at least eleven thousand years ago. Scientists think that they came from Asia. They may have walked across a land bridge that once joined Siberia and Alaska.

The Indians had no stores where they could buy food and clothes. They got everything they needed from the land.

Only a few groups of California Indians were farmers. Instead of planting seeds and growing crops, most California Indians simply used the animals and plants growing wild around them for food. Some Indians hunted deer, rabbits, and other small animals with bows and arrows. Some fished for salmon with nets and harpoons, or got shellfish from the sea. And most Indians gathered and ate insects, seeds, roots, and berries.

When they looked for food, the Indians took only what they needed. They did not waste food. Nor did they kill animals they were not going to eat. Sometimes a group of Indians would find only a few plants of a certain kind. When this happened, they would leave some seeds behind so more plants would grow. Other times a group of Indians would notice that there were not many of a certain animal. Then they would stop hunting that animal until its **population** grew again. In these ways, Indians made sure that there would always be plenty of food.

An important food for many California Indians was the acorn. They gathered acorns from the oak trees that grew nearby. Acorns contain a chemical called tannic acid. This acid tastes bad and makes people sick. The Indians had to get rid of the acid before they could eat the acorns.

The Indians developed a clever way to remove the tannic acid. First, they took off the acorn shell. Next, they ground the nut meat between two stones to make acorn meal. Then, they dug a hole in the sand and lined it with leaves. They spread the acorn meal on these leaves. Finally, they poured hot water over the meal. This hot water rinsed away the tannic acid.

To heat the water, the California Indians used baskets that they wove from grasses. These baskets were so tightly woven that they could hold water. But the baskets would burn if they were put on or near a fire. Instead, the Indians heated stones and dropped them into the water. In this way, they were able to warm the water without damaging their baskets.

Among the California Indians, everyone worked so everyone could eat. Most often, the children gathered acorns from the ground under the great oak trees. They carried these acorns in baskets Indian women had woven.

The most important food for many California Indians was acorns. Here, one woman uses a pestle [pes′əl] to grind acorns into meal in a mortar [môr′tər], or hard bowl. With wooden spoons, a second woman carefully drops a hot stone into a basket of water. The stone will heat the water. When the water is hot, it will be used to rinse the acorn meal and make it safe to eat.

Making acorn meal took a lot of time. Sometimes the Indians had to rinse the meal as many as ten times before it could be safely cooked and eaten. The Indians pressed the meal into pancakes or ate it as a hot cereal. Acorn meal did not keep, so fresh meal had to be ground and rinsed every day.

Acorns, berries, insects, fish, rabbits, and deer—the California Indians ate whatever food their land supplied. But they worked hard to get their food. The women spent long hours making acorn meal. The men spent days hunting and fishing. Children gathered seeds and berries. Everyone worked so that everyone had enough to eat.

Checking Up

1. Who were the first Californians? Where did they come from?

2. Name two animals the Indians used for food.

3. Name two foods California Indians got from plants.

4. What things did the California Indians depend on the land for?

5. Compare the ways in which the California Indians depended on the land with the ways in which *you* depend on the land.

Lesson 2 Many Ways of Living

California is large. It has many different kinds of land and several different **climates**. The climate of an area is the weather over a long period of time. Places with a cold climate have many days of cold weather, year after year. Places with a warm climate have many warm days.

Living in different places with different climates, each group of California Indians developed its own way of life. Indians in the valleys lived differently from Indians on the deserts or near the sea. Indians in colder places lived differently from those in warmer places. They built different kinds of houses and wore different kinds of clothes. They also made different kinds of baskets. And they spoke many different languages.

This map shows some of the different families of Indian languages. Which language was spoken where you live?

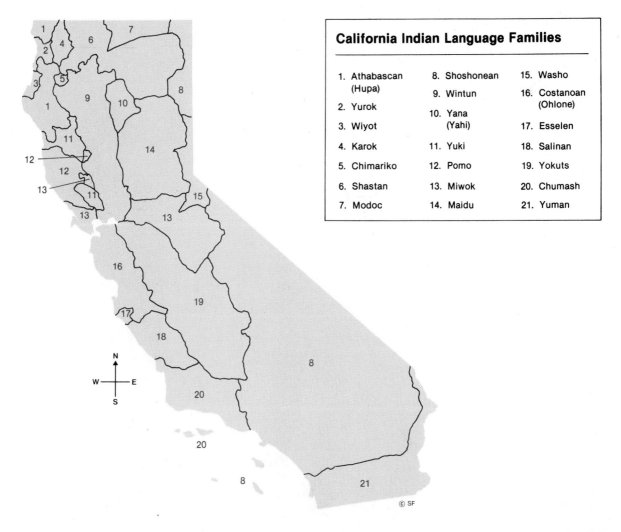

California Indian Language Families

1. Athabascan (Hupa)
2. Yurok
3. Wiyot
4. Karok
5. Chimariko
6. Shastan
7. Modoc
8. Shoshonean
9. Wintun
10. Yana (Yahi)
11. Yuki
12. Pomo
13. Miwok
14. Maidu
15. Washo
16. Costanoan (Ohlone)
17. Esselen
18. Salinan
19. Yokuts
20. Chumash
21. Yuman

© SF

Most California Indians lived in houses covered with brush, thatch, bark, or earth. These building materials were easy to find almost everywhere.

This Hupa [hü′pə] house was made of wooden logs. The Hupa lived in Northern California, where tall trees grew.

Indian groups that lived in warm places did not need as much clothing as those in cold places. This man is wearing an apron made of deerskin. And he isn't wearing shoes. In what kind of climate do you think he lived?

This woman has a blanket made of otter skins. She is wearing moccasins and leggings made of animal skins. Her snowshoes could help her walk in soft snow without sinking. In what kind of climate do you think she lived?

18

Most California Indians used the grasses that grew nearby to weave beautiful baskets. Each group of Indians had its own way of making and decorating baskets. The people of one village often traded baskets with the Indians in a neighboring village because they admired their designs.

One group of California Indians lived in the Mojave [mō hä′vē] Desert. They did not have much grass. They did have plenty of clay. They used this clay to make pots. The bowl on the top left was made from clay and baked in the hot desert sun.

Above is a Yokuts [yō′küts] basket decorated with feathers.

Below is a Pomo [pō′mō] basket decorated with shells, feathers, and beads.

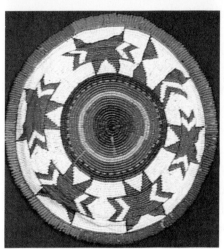

On the left is a Shasta [shas′tə] basket decorated with beads.

Checking Up

1. Why did different groups of Indians have different ways of life?

2. How would life have been different for most of the Indians if there had been no grasses growing in California?

3. How did climate affect the clothing of California Indians?

4. Which language was spoken at the southern end of California?

IN HARMONY WITH NATURE

During the winter months, a group of Indians called the Ohlone [ō lō ′ nē] lived near San Francisco Bay. Like the other California Indians, the Ohlone depended on the natural environment for everything they needed. They were lucky to be living in such a rich environment. There was plenty of water, and many different kinds of plants and animals lived in the area. Nature was good to the Ohlone. In return, the Ohlone lived in harmony with nature.

The Ohlone believed that everything in nature had a spirit. They treated these spirits with respect. They often gave names to special rocks, plants, and even parts of a trail. When they went by each of these things, they spoke to its spirit as they would to a friend.

The Ohlone treated nature carefully. They did not want to hurt the spirits. Also, they knew that, if they hurt nature, they would hurt themselves too. If they ate all the seeds of a plant or killed all the deer, there would be no plants or deer the next year.

The Ohlone admired animals and thought of them as brothers and sisters. They named their children after animals. In doing so, they hoped to give their children the special powers of the animals—the swiftness of the antelope, the courage of the bear.

The Ohlone sang about animals and nature. Here is part of an Ohlone song:

> I dream of you
> I dream of you jumping.
> Rabbit,
> Jackrabbit,
> Quail.

Do you ever sing or dream about animals? What animals do you admire? Do you, like the Ohlone, think of nature as your friend?

Write your answers on paper. Do not write in the book.

Using Key Words

From the list below, choose the word that best completes each of the sentences. Write it on your paper.

> climate
> population

1. The usual weather of a place is called its _____.
2. All of the deer that live in a particular place are a _____ of deer.

Reviewing Main Ideas

Choose the ending that makes each sentence true. Write its letter beside the question number on your paper.
1. To get their food, clothing, and houses, the Indians depended on
   a. harmony with other Indian villages.
   b. the environment around them.
   c. stores.
2. One reason the Ohlone treated nature with respect is that
   a. their winter home was in San Francisco.
   b. they believed that everything in nature had an evil spirit.
   c. they knew that, if they hurt nature, they would also hurt themselves.

3. The Indians of Northern California lived differently from those of Southern California because
   a. they faced different environments.
   b. they did not trade very much.
   c. they could not speak the same language.

Thinking Things Over

1. How do we depend on the environment today? List more than one way.
2. What lessons about use of the environment could we learn from the California Indians?

Practicing Skills

Study the picture below. On your piece of paper, describe the environment. Would life be easy or hard there? Why?

TIME OUT For Map and Globe Review

What Maps and Globes Show

Maps give us a view of the world like the one you get looking out an airplane window. Look at the picture and map on page 24. The picture was taken from an airplane. The map shows the same overhead view as the picture. If the photo and the map show the same view of a place, how are they different? The picture shows things as they really look. The map uses symbols to stand for real things such as buildings and roads. Symbols can be lines, dots, colors, or drawings.

Many maps have keys telling what the symbols mean. Before using a map, see if there is a key. Also, check the map title. It tells you what the map is about.

Can you tell what the photo below is? It is a picture of the earth taken from out in space. Next to the photo is a globe. Globes show you the world as you would see it from a spaceship. A globe is a small model of the earth.

A world map shows the same thing as a globe, but in flattened form. A flat world map is made by dividing the globe into sections. The drawing on page 25 shows how this is done.

Globes and world maps show all the continents and oceans. Look at the world map on page 26. Name the continents and oceans.

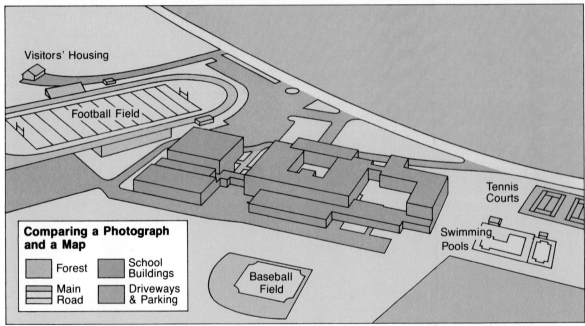

Visitors' Housing

Football Field

Tennis Courts

Swimming Pools

Baseball Field

Comparing a Photograph and a Map

Forest

School Buildings

Main Road

Driveways & Parking

Exploring with Maps. Find the key for the map above. What do the symbols in the key stand for?

Now make your own continent flashcards. Trace the shapes of the continents in a world atlas. Transfer your drawings to posterboard and cut out the shapes. Ask your classmates to guess the names of the continents from their shapes.

24

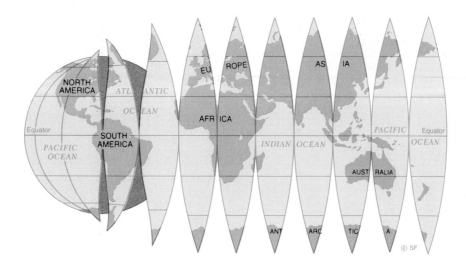

Where Is It?

If you invited friends to your house, you would have to tell them where you live. How would you do this? You probably would include the number of your house or apartment building, a street name, and maybe the name of your city or town.

In other words, you would tell your friends the *location* of your home. A location tells exactly where something is. You can locate any city by telling what state and country it's in. For example, Sacramento is in the state of California. Atlanta is in the state of Georgia. These cities are in the country of the United States. Locate these cities on the map on pages 272–273.

You can locate places on some maps by using a letter-number grid. The map on page 27 shows part of a city. Notice that there are blue lines going up and down and across the map. There are also letters and numbers along the edges of the map. You can tell where a place is by naming the letter and number of the square where the place is located.

Exploring with Maps. Refer to the city map on page 27. Find the library. It is in square A–4. In what square is the courthouse located? Is the baseball park located in square A–2? Where is the corner of First Street and Oak Street located? In which square is the Elm Street bridge located?

Which Way?

You can also use direction to find places on a map. There are four main directions—north, south, east, and west.

The direction north is toward the North Pole. The North Pole marks the point farthest north on the earth.

When you face north, you can find the other directions. East is on your right, west is on you left, and south is behind you. South is toward the South

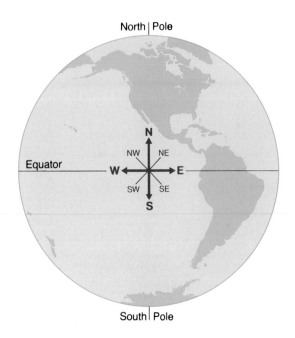

North | Pole

N
NW | NE
Equator   W ——+—— E
SW | SE
S

South | Pole

Pole, which is the point farthest south on the earth.

Most maps will have a direction symbol with an arrow pointing north.

The other directions may be given too. North is usually at the top of a map—but not always. Check the direction symbol to find north on a map. Then, you can find the other directions.

Sometimes a place is not exactly north or east of your starting point. In between, or intermediate, directions are northeast, southeast, southwest, and northwest. The college on the map, page 27, is southeast of the courthouse.

Exploring with Maps. Use intermediate directions to answer the following questions. Refer to the map on page 27.

1. What direction is the baseball park from the college?
2. The key for this map is located in the _____ corner of the map.
3. The college is located _____ of the dam.

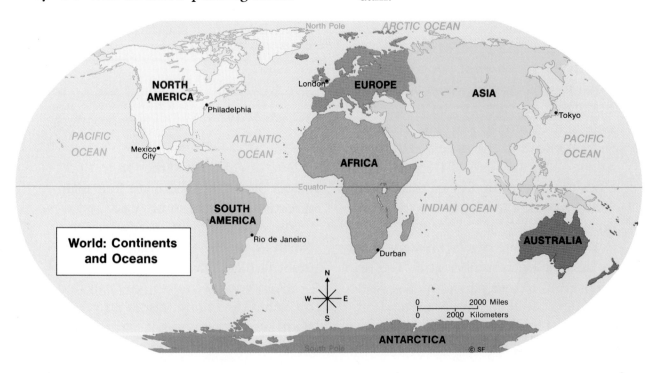

World: Continents and Oceans

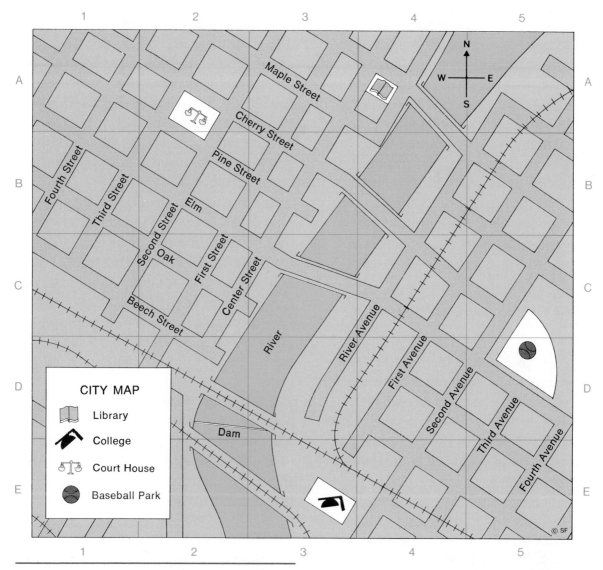

How Far?

Scale tells you about size. Drawing or making anything to scale means making a copy that is exactly like the real thing except for size.

Maps are scale drawings of places. The places and distances shown on maps must be smaller than their real size. A certain place may be many miles or meters in size on the earth. On a map made to scale, that same place may cover only a few inches or centimeters.

To find out how much distance on the earth is shown on a map, use the bar scale given on the map. The bar scale is a straight line with distances marked on it. Each mark stands for a certain number of miles or kilometers on the earth's surface. How many miles does each mark on the scale on the map at the bottom of page 26 stand for?

Exploring with Maps. Measure distance between cities on the map on page 30. Place a piece of paper along the bar scale. Mark the length of the unit that shows one hundred miles. Then, find the capital city and one other city. Place the unit of miles between the two cities. Is the distance more or less than one hundred miles? About how far is it?

What Causes Day and Night?

When you look at maps and globes, they are usually standing still. In real life, however, the earth is always moving. It is moving two ways at once.

The movement of the earth that causes day and night is called rotation. To rotate means to spin around. The earth spins around once every twenty-four hours, moving from west to east. Although the earth spins very fast, you cannot feel it spinning. But you can see the results! When the earth turns toward the sun, the sun seems to rise in the east. Then day occurs. As our part of the earth turns away from the sun, the sun seems to set in the west and it becomes night.

The earth spins around an imaginary pole called an axis. This imaginary pole runs through the center of the earth from the North Pole to the South Pole.

In addition to rotating on its axis, the earth moves, or revolves, around the sun. It revolves once around the sun every 365¼ days—one year. The earth's path around the sun is called its orbit.

Exploring Maps. Refer to the diagram on this page. Choose a partner and act out the rotation of the earth. One of you should be the sun; the other should be the earth. Show the motion that causes day and night.

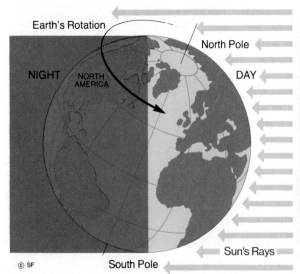

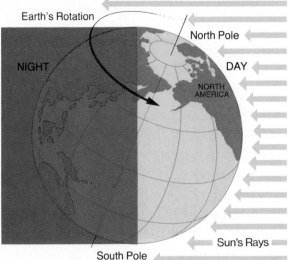

Lesson 1 Land and Water
Lesson 2 California's Climate

The Geography of California

Just as the Indians depended on nature to supply their needs, so people today depend on their environment. We all depend on the land, water, and climate around us. Let's see how these things affect where and how people live in California.

Lesson 1   Land and Water

California lies on the west coast of the United States. It's a very large state. Only Alaska and Texas are larger. California is also a very beautiful state. It is made up of many **landforms** and has many bodies of water.

Mirror Lake, Yosemite
[yō sem ′ə tē]

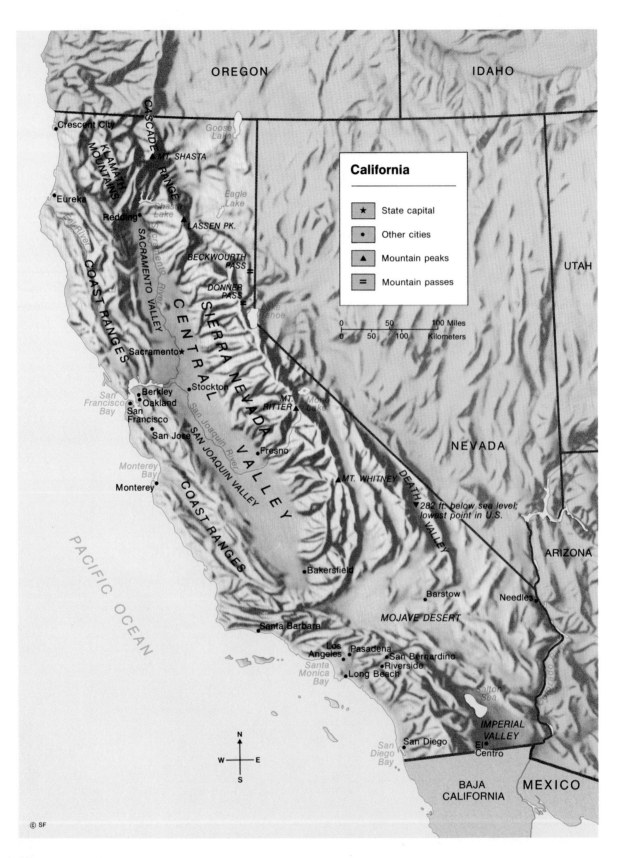

California

- ★ State capital
- • Other cities
- ▲ Mountain peaks
- = Mountain passes

0   50   100 Miles
0   50   100 Kilometers

OREGON

IDAHO

UTAH

NEVADA

ARIZONA

MEXICO

BAJA CALIFORNIA

PACIFIC OCEAN

Crescent City

KLAMATH MOUNTAINS

CASCADE RANGE

▲MT. SHASTA

Goose Lake

Eagle Lake

Eureka

Redding

Shasta Lake

▲LASSEN PK.

Kern River

Sacramento River

SACRAMENTO VALLEY

BECKWOURTH PASS

DONNER PASS

Lake Tahoe

COAST RANGES

CENTRAL

SIERRA NEVADA

VALLEY

Sacramento★

Stockton

Berkley

Oakland

San Francisco

San Francisco Bay

San Jose

San Joaquin River

MT. RITTER▲

Mono Lake

Presno

Monterey Bay

Monterey

SAN JOAQUIN VALLEY

COAST RANGES

▲MT. WHITNEY

DEATH VALLEY

▼282 ft. below sea level; lowest point in U.S.

Bakersfield

Barstow

Needles

MOJAVE DESERT

Santa Barbara

Los Angeles

Pasadena

San Bernardino

Riverside

Long Beach

Santa Monica Bay

Salton Sea

IMPERIAL VALLEY

San Diego

El Centro

San Diego Bay

Colorado River

N
W E
S

© SF

30

Mountains and Lakes

California has tall, jagged mountains. Its largest mountain ranges are the Sierra Nevada and the Coast Ranges. Within the Sierra Nevada stands Mount Whitney, the highest mountain in the United States outside Alaska. Mount Whitney is nearly three miles high! There are many other high mountains and ranges in California. Can you find some of them on the map on page 30?

Mountains are the highest, roughest form of land. Few people live in mountain areas because it is hard to build factories, homes, and roads there. It's also hard to grow food and raise animals on mountain land. However, many people visit mountains on their vacations.

Beautiful lakes lie in the California mountains. The largest and deepest of these is Lake Tahoe, which is in the Sierra Nevada. How many other lakes can you find on the map?

People use lakes in many ways. Some people live on the shores of lakes. Many other people visit lakes to fish, boat, swim, or water ski. Some lakes are used as a water supply for cities or to irrigate farmlands. Some lakes are even specially made by people to store up water for irrigation and for electric power. Shasta Lake is an example. It was made by blocking the Sacramento River.

Klamath [klam′eth] River

Valleys and Rivers

California has several wide valleys through which rivers flow. These valleys are smooth, not rough. Many people live in valleys. It is easy to build homes and roads on smooth land. Often the soil is good for farming or for raising cattle. Water from the rivers can be used on farms and in factories. The rivers are also used for travel and for shipping goods.

California's largest valley, the Central Valley, lies between the Sierra Nevada and the Coast Ranges. The Sacramento River flows through the northern part of this valley and empties into San Francisco Bay. The San Joaquin [san wä kēn′] River flows through the southern part of the Central Valley. It flows north to San Francisco Bay.

31

Windblown cypress trees cling to rocks along the California coast near Monterey.

The Coastline

Part of California's beauty is in its long coastline. Smooth, sandy beaches and tall, rugged cliffs line the edge of the Pacific Ocean. Bays and harbors offer shelter for fishing boats and cargo ships.

Many people live along the coast and especially in harbor cities. From many of these cities, fishing boats sail as far as South America to catch fish. And cargo ships come to California's harbors from all over the world. How many harbor cities can you find on the map?

California's mountains, lakes, rivers, valleys, and long coastline give us many places and ways to live. They also give us interesting spots to visit and beautiful sights to see.

Checking Up

1. Where do more people live, in mountains or valleys? Why?

2. Name three ways people use lakes.

3. Why do many people live in coastal California?

4. Using the map on page 30, name a California city that is on a river and one that is on the coast.

5. How do the landforms and bodies of water where you live affect your life?

Lesson 2 California's Climate

A very important part of the environment is weather. Everyone depends on weather. Farmers need rain and sunshine to grow their crops. Some industries, like the space industry, need certain kinds of weather. And weather affects how people everywhere dress, travel, work, and play.

Because weather is important to people, they watch it, report on it, and keep records of it. Weather scientists write down temperatures and wind speeds. They measure the amount of rain and snowfall. These records help to tell about the weather a place has over the months and years. Weather over a long period of time is called climate.

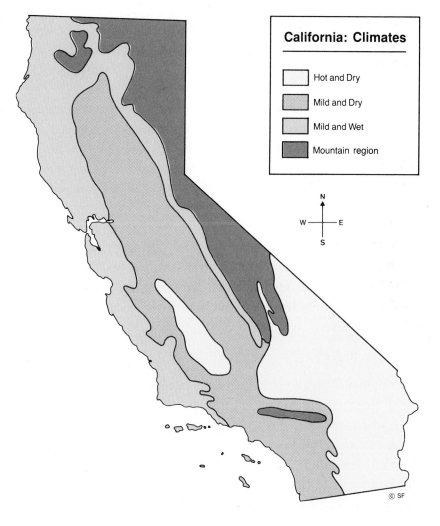

California: Climates

- [ ] Hot and Dry
- Mild and Dry
- Mild and Wet
- Mountain region

N
W — E
S

© SF

Find where you live on this map. What kind of climate does your area have? On the next two pages, you will read about the climates of California.

The Anza-Borrego [an ′ zə-bôr rā ′ gō] Desert, on the left, is hot and dry. The Sonoma [se nō ′ mə] Valley, on the right, has a mild, dry climate.

Different Kinds of Climate

California actually has three kinds of climate. These climates are based on temperature and the amount of rain or snow that falls during the year. The map on page 33 shows where these climates are found in the state.

Certain kinds of plants grow naturally in each climate. The plants that grow naturally in a place are called **natural vegetation**. For example, cactus grows where the climate is hot and dry, as in a desert. Cactus is one kind of natural vegetation of deserts.

Hot and Dry

Part of California is a desert. The climate there is hot and dry most of the year. Cactus and sagebrush grow in this climate. In a desert, there are large spaces between plants. There isn't enough water for the plants to live close together.

Mild and Dry

Much of California has a mild climate that is neither very hot nor very cold. Along the middle and southern parts of the state, summers are warm and fairly dry. Winters are cool with some rainfall. This climate is sometimes called Mediterranean. Grasses and oak trees grow in this climate, and some places are covered with forests of bushes.

Mild and Wet

Much of the coast of California has cool summers and cool winters. There is a lot of rain all year long. This climate is sometimes called Marine West Coast. Forests of pine trees, firs, and redwoods grow in this climate.

The Mountain Region

The mountain region of California has many climates. If you climbed a very tall mountain, the climate and vegetation would change as you got higher and higher. The lowest part of the mountain might be hot and dry like a desert. The top part of the mountain might be snowy and cold.

The different climates in California make it a pleasant place to live. People can spend warm summer days at the beach and cool summer days in the mountain forests. They can ski and play in mountain snows in the winter. People from other states and countries like California's climate too. Every year thousands of people visit California on their vacations.

California's climate is good for other reasons. Many crops—from oranges to grapes, from wheat to lettuce—can be grown here. And many industries have come to California because of its sunny weather. The aircraft industry came to California because planes could be built outside and flown all year. The movie industry came because movies could be shot outside.

The climate of the Muir [myür] Woods area is mild and wet.

Checking Up

1. What is climate?

2. What is the natural vegetation of the Marine West Coast climate?

3. What kind of climate do you like best? Why?

4. Look at the map on page 33. What is the climate of your area?

Building Social Studies Skills

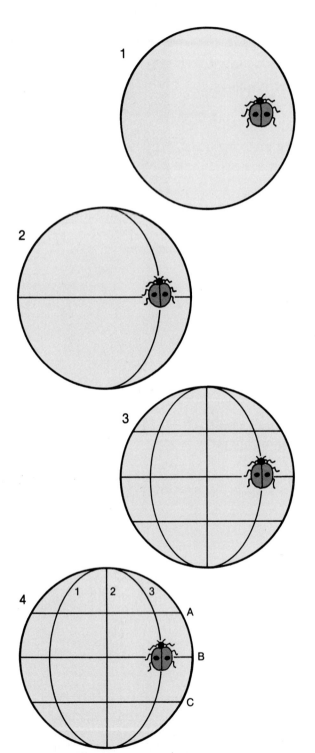

Using Latitude and Longitude

You know that the earth is like a ball. Finding a certain place on a ball can be hard. But there is a way to do it.

Here is a picture of a ball with a bug on it. Try to explain exactly where the bug is. It's hard to explain the bug's **location** because a ball has no top or bottom. It has no left or right side.

But if two lines are drawn on the ball, the job becomes easier. You can say that the bug is located where the two lines cross.

If more lines are drawn on the ball, explaining the bug's location is harder again. How do you tell one line from another?

You could give the lines names or numbers. Look at the ball marked 4. The lines that run one way are numbered, and those that run the other way are lettered. Can you give the bug's exact location?

Lines on Maps and Globes

How can we explain exactly where a place is on the earth? For example, how can we explain the location of a certain city? Mapmakers have imagined that there are lines on the earth. They have drawn these lines on maps and globes.

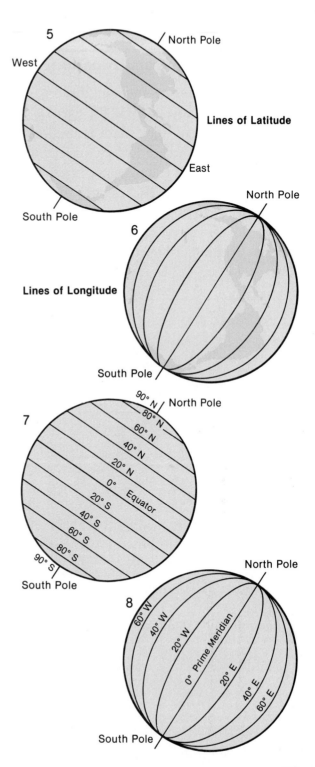

The lines that run east and west around the earth are called **parallels**, or lines of **latitude**. They never touch. The lines that run north and south around the earth are called **meridians**, or lines of **longitude**. Meridians meet at the North Pole and the South Pole.

Latitude

Lines of latitude and longitude are given number names. For example, the Equator, which is a parallel, is named 0° latitude. (We say *zero degrees latitude*.) The other parallels are numbered to show how far north or how far south they are from the Equator.

The Equator divides the earth into two halves, or hemispheres. The north half is called the Northern Hemisphere and the south half is the Southern Hemisphere.

Longitude

The line for 0° longitude is called the Prime Meridian. The other meridians are numbered to show how far east or how far west they are from the Prime Meridian. The earth can be divided into Eastern and Western hemispheres along a meridian.

37

Practicing Latitude and Longitude

Using both latitude and longitude, you can locate any spot on the earth. This map of forty-eight states is marked with lines of latitude and longitude. All of the parallels on the map are *north* latitude. All of the meridians are *west* longitude. Do you know why?

Four locations are listed below. Use latitude and longitude to find what city is near each location. Write the city's name on a piece of paper.

1. What city is near 40° N and 75° W?
2. What city is near 40° N, 90° W?
3. What city is near 30° N, 95° W?
4. What city is near 40° N, 105° W?

Find the locations of these cities. Write the latitude and longitude of each on a piece of paper.

5. Memphis
6. New Orleans

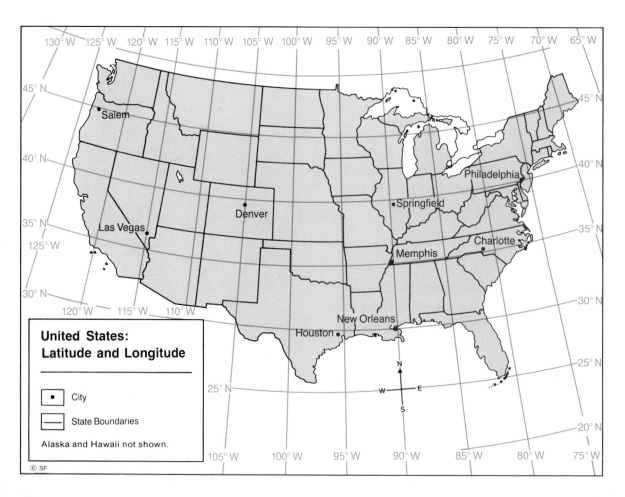

United States:
Latitude and Longitude

• City

State Boundaries

Alaska and Hawaii not shown.

© SF

Write your answers on paper. Do not write in the book.

Using Key Words

From the list below, choose the term that best completes each of the sentences. Write it on your paper.

landform
latitude
location
longitude

meridian
natural vegetation
parallel

1. A line of latitude is also called a _____.

2. A line of _____ runs from the North Pole to the South Pole.

3. The plants that grow naturally in a place are called _____.

4. Philadelphia is near 40⁰ north _____.

5. A city's _____ tells exactly where it is.

6. A line of longitude is also called a _____.

7. Mountains are the roughest and highest _____.

Reviewing Main Ideas

Write "true" for the sentences that are true. Write "false" for the sentences that are false.

1. People are affected by climate.
2. Many people live in the mountains because it's easy to farm there.
3. Grasses and oak trees grow in a hot, dry climate.
4. Landforms affect how people live.
5. Forests of redwoods often grow in a mild, wet climate.
6. People who live along rivers can ship goods to other places easily.

Thinking Things Over

Why does California's geography make it a popular place to live and visit?

Practicing Skills

Study this map. Write the latitude and longitude for each of these places.

1. Mount Maria   3. Matt's Mountain
2. Baker City   4. Hernandez Park
5. What is located at 34° N, 121° W?

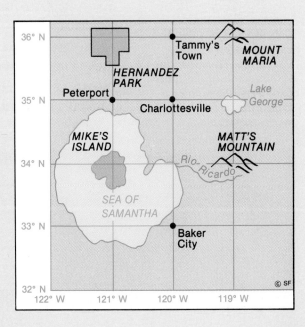

Lesson 1   Exploration
Lesson 2   Missions in California

The Spanish Arrive

About five hundred years ago, Spanish ships began coming to America. Fifty years later, the first Spanish ships explored California. This began a chain of events that changed California.

Read to find out what happened when the Spanish and Indians met during the first Spanish **exploration** of California.

Lesson 1   Exploration

On June 27, 1542, two ships sailed from the port of Navidad [nä vē däd'] in New Spain. New Spain was the area that today we call Mexico. The captain of the ships was Juan Rodríguez Cabrillo [kä brē'yō]. Cabrillo was born in Portugal, but most of his life he had been a sailor for Spain. Now he had been sent by the ruler of New Spain to look for a way to sail straight through North America.

As soon as Cabrillo and his sailors set sail, they had bad luck. First the winds were too strong, and the ships were blown off course. Then there was no wind. The ships rocked back and forth but went nowhere. Finally, three

Cabrillo was not the only explorer who visited California. This time line shows some of the other explorers who came to California. It also tells when they came.

Cabrillo lands in San Diego 1542 · Ferrelo explores Northern California 1543 · Drake lands in Northern California 1579 · Vizcaíno explores Monterey Bay 1602

1540   1550   1560   1570   1580   1590   1600   1610

months after the ships left New Spain, they reached what is now called San Diego. Cabrillo and his crew were the first Europeans to see California!

When the men landed in San Diego, they saw some Indians. Most of the Indians were frightened and ran away. Only a few stayed. Naturally, the Indians did not speak Spanish, and the explorers did not speak the Indians' language. So they used actions, not words, to talk to each other. The Indians told the Spanish why they were frightened. They had heard that men with beards—like the Spanish—had come to other villages from the East. These bearded men had killed many Indians.

Cabrillo didn't want to kill the Indians. He wanted their help. So Cabrillo gave the Indians presents of beads. In return, the Indians supplied the explorers with food and water.

Then Cabrillo's ships sailed on. They traveled past the bay where Santa Monica and Los Angeles now are. Because the smoke from Indian campfires hung in the air over this bay, Cabrillo called it the "Bay of Smokes."

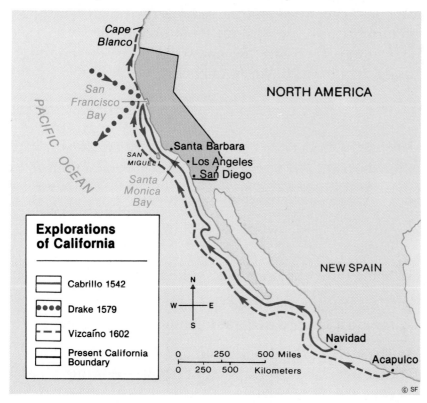

Which direction did Cabrillo's ships sail? Which direction did Drake's ship come from? Which explorer started from farther south? Which explorer traveled farther north?

41

The first English ship to land in California arrived thirty-seven years after Cabrillo's exploration. Sir Francis Drake was captain of this ship. Drake was on a voyage around the world. He stopped in Northern California to fix his ship. Some people believe that he left this brass plate near San Francisco to show that he had been there and to claim the land for England. Other people think the plate may have been made by someone else as a trick.

Near Santa Barbara, the sailors saw many Indians with well-built boats. The Indians used the boats to fish and to trade with other Indians on nearby islands.

Cabrillo's ships landed on the island that today we call San Miguel [san mē gel ']. The people there painted their faces in squares, like a checkerboard. Cabrillo had more bad luck on the island. He fell and broke his arm. But Cabrillo kept on exploring.

He and his crew sailed north to San Francisco Bay and farther. But they could never land because the sea was too rough. Finally, they sailed back to San Miguel. Cabrillo died there—his broken arm had never healed.

Before he died, Cabrillo made his sailors promise to keep looking for a water passageway across North America. They tried, but the sea was too rough. They had to turn back to New Spain without finding the passageway. Of course, we know today that there is no way to sail through North America.

Juan Rodríguez Cabrillo

Checking Up

1. Why did Cabrillo explore California?

2. How were the Spanish greeted by the Indians in San Diego?

3. Name three explorers who visited California.

4. What reasons might the Spanish have had for wanting to find a water passageway through North America?

5. Think about the dangers and unknown land that the explorers faced. What sorts of people must the explorers have been?

Lesson 2   Missions in California

Juan Cabrillo came to California in 1542. For more than two hundred years after that, Indian life in California did not change much. Only a few Spanish ships sailed along the coast.

The First Mission

Then, in 1769, the ruler of New Spain sent a group of people to live in California. The group was made up of soldiers, Indians from New Spain, and two Franciscan friars. Friars were religious men who traveled from place to place teaching people about the Catholic religion. They wanted to bring Christianity to the California Indians.

The group from New Spain first stopped in San Diego. One of the friars, Junípero Serra [ser´rä], started a **mission** there. The mission was more than a church. It was like a tiny town built inside walls. There was a church, but there were also rooms to sleep and work in.

Mission San Luis Rey, like all missions, was made of *adobe* [ə dō´bē]. Adobe is a brick made of sun-dried mud and straw. The bricks were laid one atop another to make thick walls. These walls formed rooms and enclosed a courtyard.

43

Outside the mission walls was land on which to grow food.

The Spanish people wanted the Indians to leave their villages and come to live in the mission. The Indians would be given all the food and clothes they needed. In return, they would work at the mission.

Some Indians liked this plan and came to live at the mission. These Indians learned the Spanish way of life. The men grew food in gardens and herded sheep and cattle. They also helped to build the mission. The women cooked, and they spun and wove wool to make cloth. The friars depended on the Indians' work for food and clothing.

The Indians brought their own skills to the mission. They brought their beautiful baskets. The Spanish were surprised that the baskets held water. Some Indians showed the Spanish how they polished shells. The friars liked the shells and had the Indians use them to decorate the church. The mission Indians also kept some of their own customs, such as their dances.

Junípero Serra went on to start other missions along California's coast. In all, he and his helpers started nine missions, and later Spanish friars started twelve more.

How We Know About Mission Life

Francisco Palou [pä lü '] was Junípero Serra's friend. They had both grown up on an island near Spain, and they had come to America together. After Serra had been in California for several years, Palou joined him and worked with him.

When Junípero Serra died, Palou was very sad. He felt that Junípero was a great man, and he wanted everyone to know about Serra's work in California. So Palou wrote books about Serra and about mission life. Most of what we know about this time comes from Palou's books.

We have to remember that Palou wrote about things as *he* saw them. Palou thought it was important for all Indians to become Christians and live in the missions. But some Indians did not want to live in a mission. They ran away or fought the Spanish. This made Palou very angry. He wrote that these Indians were bad.

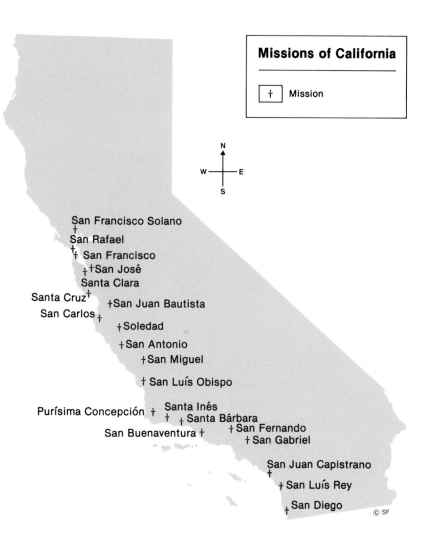

Missions of California

† Mission

San Francisco Solano †
San Rafael †
† San Francisco
† † San José
Santa Clara
Santa Cruz † † San Juan Bautista
San Carlos †
† Soledad
† San Antonio
† San Miguel
† San Luís Obispo
Purísima Concepción † Santa Inés
† † Santa Bárbara
San Buenaventura † † San Fernando
† San Gabriel
San Juan Capistrano †
† San Luís Rey
† San Diego

© SF

Twenty-one missions were built by Spanish friars in California. Each mission was about one day's walk from its neighbor missions. Later, cities that developed near the missions took the missions' names. Do you recognize any of these mission names?

However, many Indians had reasons to hate mission life. If an Indian ran away, he or she was often beaten. Many Indians died of new diseases the Spanish brought from Europe. And some Indians did not want to work for the Spanish. They didn't want to leave their own way of life. Francisco Palou did not write about these things in his book. They did not seem important to him.

How do we know how the Indians felt? It's hard to know because they did not have written languages. But they could tell stories. About eighty years ago, an old Indian man named Fernando Librado [lē brä ′ dō] told about mission life the way he, an Indian, saw it. His story is now a book.

By reading the words of Palou and of Librado, we can learn about two different views of mission life.

45

The first California Indian child was baptized on July 22, 1769.

Mission Life Ends

After more than 150 years, a change in the government of New Spain changed the missions. They became regular churches. The Indians no longer had to live and work in them. Half of the mission land was given back to the Indians, and the rest was sold to other people. Many of the Indians had their land taken away while others sold their land. Some went to work for the Californios, whom you will meet in the next chapter, but most went back to live in their own villages.

Checking Up

1. What things did the friars depend on the Indians for?

2. Name two things mission Indians learned from the Spanish.

3. Name two skills Indians brought to mission life.

4. Why is it important to read about or listen to more than one side of a question?

5. If you were telling someone about mission life, would you tell the story Palou's way, Librado's way, or some other way? Explain your answer.

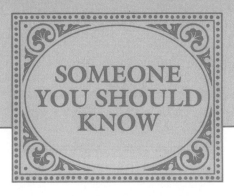

SOMEONE YOU SHOULD KNOW

Ishi

Many groups of California Indians have died out. One such group was the Yahi [yä ′hē]. They lived in Northern California. Some of the first white settlers in this area treated the Yahi badly. The Yahi fought back. For years, they were chased and attacked by settlers and soldiers. Finally, they disappeared.

People thought that the Yahi had died out, but there was one Yahi left. For two years this last Yahi man lived alone. But he couldn't keep up the Yahi way of life by himself. Hungry and weak, he came into the town of Oroville in August 1911.

He was treated kindly. Scientists at the University of California in Berkeley took him there to live. They called him *Ishi* [ē ′shē], which is the Yahi word for *man*.

The scientists and their families soon grew to love Ishi. He was eager to learn English. He was even more eager to teach the scientists how the Yahi lived. Ishi showed the scientists how the Yahi built houses. He taught them his language and more than sixty Yahi songs. The songs were about animals, hunting, and the weather.

Best of all, Ishi showed the scientists how he made arrowheads, bows, and arrows. Ishi taught his new friends to shoot arrows the Yahi way.

Ishi also taught the scientists important things about himself. They learned that he was a kind and intelligent man. He was thoughtful of others' feelings. Ishi was sad to be the last of his tribe. But he had a sense of humor, and he liked to laugh. Ishi was a good teacher and a good friend.

Ishi lived at the university for about five years. Then, he got sick and died. There were no more Yahi people in the world.

Write your answers on paper. Do not write in the book.

Using Key Words

From the list below, choose the word that best completes each of the sentences. Write it on your paper.

exploration

mission

1. A place where people live, work, and hold religious services is called a _____.

2. Traveling to little-known places in hopes of discovering something is _____.

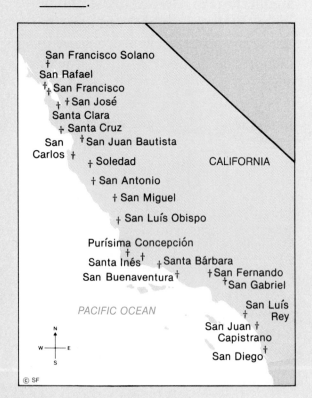

San Francisco Solano
†
San Rafael
†† San Francisco
†† San José
Santa Clara
† Santa Cruz
San   † San Juan Bautista
Carlos †
   † Soledad   CALIFORNIA
     † San Antonio
       † San Miguel
         † San Luís Obispo

Purísima Concepción
†
Santa Inés† † Santa Bárbara
San Buenaventura†   † San Fernando
                  † San Gabriel
PACIFIC OCEAN   San Luís
                  †   Rey
              San Juan †
              Capistrano
              San Diego †

N
W   E
S

© SF

Reviewing Main Ideas

Write "Spanish" for sentences that are true about the Spanish. Write "Indians" for sentences that are true about the Indians. Write "Both" for sentences that are true about both.

1. They did most of the work at the missions.
2. They slept in rooms at the missions.
3. They showed others how to weave baskets.
4. They taught others how to spin and weave cloth.
5. They had their own view of mission life.

Thinking Things Over

The Spanish and Indians began to live and work together. Explain the good and bad results of this.

Practicing Skills

Use this map to answer the following questions about the missions of California.

1. Which mission is farthest north?
2. If you traveled from San Miguel to San Antonio, you would travel
   a. north. **b.** south. **c.** northwest.
3. Which mission is farther south, Santa Cruz or Santa Clara?
4. Which mission is farther east, San Buenaventura or San Fernando?

Lesson 1   Hide and Tallow Trade
Lesson 2   Life on a Rancho

The Californios

The missions were not the only places where settlers from New Spain, or Mexico, lived in California. Soldiers built forts called **presidios** [pre sē ′ dē ōs]. These forts were armed with cannons and were supposed to defend Spanish California. Groups of settlers started **pueblos** [pü eb ′ lōs]. *Pueblo* is the Spanish word for *town*. Many of these settlers were farmers. They grew food for themselves and for the soldiers. Another group of settlers owned **ranchos** and raised cattle.

The settlers included blacks and Indians as well as Spanish people. Many of the settlers had mixed backgrounds because Spanish, black, and Indian people in New Spain often married one another.

As the years passed, the people born here in California came to call themselves Californios. Gradually, ranchos became very important to California and Californios. Read to find out how and why.

Indian Population in California

1745 Before the first mission	1845 During the rancho period

 = 50,000 Indians

This is what Los Angeles looked like as a pueblo. These buildings, like the missions, were made of adobe.

Lesson 1 Hide and Tallow Trade

Rancho owners raised
long-horned cattle.

Until 1822, California and Mexico were ruled by Spain.
But in that year, the Mexicans fought against Spain. In
this **revolution**, they won the right to rule their own
country. California became a part of the new country,
Mexico.

The Mexican Revolution meant that there were a lot of
changes in California. One of the most important changes
was in trade. The Spanish had tried to keep all of the
California trade for themselves. They had not wanted
people in Mexico and California to trade with any
countries other than Spain. But after the Mexican
Revolution, Mexicans and Californians decided to trade
with many countries. They traded with Russia, England,
America, and other nations.

With the new trade, Californians soon realized that
they could make more money raising cattle than they
could by growing crops. Both the English and the
Americans wanted the hides, or skins, and the tallow, or
fat, of cattle. In fact, they were prepared to sail all the
way around the southern tip of South America to get
hides and tallow from California ranchos.

Factories in America and England could turn hides and
tallow into useful things. Hides were made into leather
for shoes, clothes, and book covers. Leather was also
used for the belts that ran the machines in the factories.
Tallow was used to make soap and candles. People
needed many candles then. They used them to light their
houses because there were no electric lamps.

As the hide and tallow trade grew, more people wanted
to raise cattle. They wanted to buy mission land to start
ranchos. They also wanted the mission Indians to work
on their ranchos. These were some of the reasons the
Mexican government made the missions regular churches
and sold much of the mission land.

Californios became very **specialized**. They did not
make everything they needed and wanted. There were no
factories in California to make things like tools, fine cloth,
china, or shoes. The Californios depended on trade for
these things.

English and American ships came to California carrying all kinds of goods. The Californios often boarded these ships to pick out what they wanted to buy. They paid the traders with hides instead of money.

One rancho girl, Prudencia Higuera [ē ger ′ rä], wrote about trading with the Americans.

66 My brother had traded some deerskins for four toothbrushes, the first ones I had ever seen. I remember that we children rubbed them on our teeth till the blood came. Then we decided that, after all, we liked best the bits of willow root we had used for brushes before.

After the ship sailed, my mother and sisters began to cut out new dresses. On one of mine mother put some big brass buttons about an inch across, with eagles on them. How proud I was! I used to rub them hard every day to make them shine. One girl offered me a beautiful black colt she owned for six of the buttons. But for a long time I loved those buttons more than anything else I owned. 99

The hide and tallow trade changed California. Mission life came to an end, and rancho life blossomed. Also, people from other countries began to come regularly to California. Americans began to be interested in the area, and some even settled in California.

Checking Up

1. What is a presidio? Who built the presidios?

2. What is a pueblo?

3. What important change in California resulted from the Mexican Revolution?

4. Name one thing made from hides and one thing made from tallow.

5. Do people today specialize? Do we depend on trade for things we want and need? Explain your answers.

Facts and Figures

Some of the trading ships could carry thirty thousand hides. It sometimes took a year to save enough hides to fill such a ship! Loading the hides was difficult. The trading ship was anchored offshore. Sailors carried hides back and forth from land to ship in small boats. They had to be very careful not to let the hides get wet because salt water would spoil them. Sometimes tall waves and splashing water made their job even harder. Many Hawaiians, who were skilled sailors, worked in the hide and tallow trade.

51

Lesson 2   Life on a Rancho

The rancho owners became the richest and most powerful people in California. But there was much hard work to do on a rancho. One way we know about rancho life is through the words of a Californio named José del Carmen Lugo [lü ′ gō], who told about growing up on a rancho near Los Angeles.

José's day began at three o'clock in the morning, when the family got up and said prayers together. Then the women cooked breakfast. The men worked in the fields and took care of the animals.

For breakfast, the family usually ate beans and meat cooked with chilies, onions, and tomatoes. They also had chocolate milk and tortillas [tôr tē ′ yəs] covered with butter. They had to eat a large breakfast. They would not eat again until late in the afternoon.

After breakfast, everybody got to work. The cowhands, or vaqueros [vä ker ′ ōs], often rode around the rancho all day long. They had to round up lost cattle and protect them from danger. Many people worked in the fields.

Vaqueros on California's ranchos used their reatas to trap and hold the legs of their long-horned cattle.

To the left is a Californio in Spanish clothes. The woman above is making flour for tortillas. She is grinding corn for the flour with a heavy stone roller.

They grew foods like corn, beans, and pumpkins. Most women and girls on the rancho were excellent riders. But they were not allowed to be vaqueros. Instead, they prepared meals and made and cleaned clothes. They also made foods like cheese and butter.

Late in the afternoon, the family came together for dinner. This meal was often much like breakfast—beef, chilies, tomatoes, and tortillas. By eight o'clock the family was ready to say prayers and go to bed. José's parents slept in one room. His sisters slept in another. He and his brothers slept on hide beds on the outside porches.

In April, all of the Californios who lived near the pueblo of Los Angeles held a rodeo. The cattle were rounded up from the hills and counted. Then the young calves were caught and branded with the mark of their rancho. The vaqueros caught the calves with long strips of leather called reatas [rā ä ′ täs]. A vaquero had to swing the reata just right to circle and trap a calf's legs. Wild horses were also caught and tamed for riding at the rodeo.

Life on a rancho was not all work. The Californios held fiestas to celebrate weddings, baptisms, a good harvest, or a profitable hide sale. At fiesta time, work stopped. There was food, music, and dancing.

Several times a year, the Californios held fiestas [fē es ′təs]. These celebrations usually lasted two or three days. There were parades, food, music, dancing, and even bullfighting. Anyone could try his luck at bullfighting. Some young men like José came up to bulls from behind and tried to bring them down by twisting their tails until they fell. It was difficult and dangerous.

Many times, when Californios traveled, they did not take any food or money along. Instead, they were given rooms and food by the missions and ranchos they passed on the way. Travelers even left their own tired horses and took fresh horses for the next day's journey. The horses were traded again on the return trip.

Checking Up

1. What kinds of work had to be done on a rancho?

2. How was life on a rancho different from life at a mission?

3. How were the two ways of life the same?

4. Which would you have liked more—mission life or rancho life? Explain your answer.

Reviewing Chapter 4

Write your answers on paper. Do not write in the book.

Using Key Words

From the list below, choose the word that best completes each of the sentences. Write it on your paper.

presidio   rancho   specialized
pueblo   revolution

1. A large farm where cattle were raised was called a _____.
2. A country that grows only one crop for trade is very _____.
3. A fort in Spanish California was called a _____.
4. A fight for a new government is called a _____.
5. The Spanish word for town is _____.

Reviewing Main Ideas

Choose the ending that makes each sentence true. Write its letter beside the question number on your paper.

1. Under Spain's rule, Californians traded with
   a. Spain only.   b. many nations.
   c. any country that wanted to buy hides and tallow.
2. Mission land was sold so that
   a. the Indians could become rich.
   b. the Californians could grow their own food.
   c. more ranchos could be started.

3. We say that Californios became specialized because
   a. they raised only cattle for trade.
   b. they made everything they wanted and needed.
   c. they depended on the Americans for food.

Thinking Things Over

Tell two ways Californians today are like the Californios. Tell two ways they are different.

Practicing Skills

Use the graph to answer these questions.
1. What does each 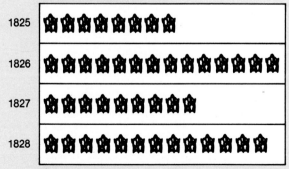 stand for?
2. In what year did the rancho have the most hides to trade?
3. How many hides were there to trade in 1825?

**Hides to Trade
Rancho Santa Marta**

1825	🐄🐄🐄🐄🐄🐄🐄🐄
1826	🐄🐄🐄🐄🐄🐄🐄🐄🐄🐄🐄🐄🐄
1827	🐄🐄🐄🐄🐄🐄🐄🐄
1828	🐄🐄🐄🐄🐄🐄🐄🐄🐄🐄🐄🐄🐄🐄

🐄 = 100 Hides

What Do You Know?

Write your answers on paper. Do not write in the book.

Words to Know

From the list below, choose the word that best completes each of the sentences. Write it on your paper.

climate   mission
meridian   parallel
longitude   specialized

1. A _____ is a line on a map that runs north and south.

2. Because the Californios traded only hides and tallow, we say they were _____.

3. A church that has rooms in which to sleep and land on which to work is called a _____.

4. A place's _____ is its usual weather over the years.

5. A _____ is a line on a map that runs east and west.

6. A place's _____ is its location east or west of the Prime Meridian.

Ideas to Know

Write "true" for the sentences that are true. Write "false" for the sentences that are false.

1. The Spanish were the first Californians.

2. Most California Indians depended on wild plants and animals for their food.

3. People often live in smooth, flat areas.

4. Most of California has a hot, dry climate.

5. People today are not affected by climate.

6. One reason people live in different ways is that they face different environments.

7. The Californios depended on trade for all of their food.

8. The Spanish friars depended on the mission Indians' work for their food.

9. "Sierra Nevada" is the name of California's Coast Ranges.

10. Cabrillo and his crew tried to find a water passageway through North America.

11. Most California Indians depended on trade for the things they wanted.

12. The rancho owners specialized in making leather shoes and belts.

13. The mission Indians depended on the friars for food, clothing, and baskets.

14. The Mexican Revolution resulted in less trade for Californians.

15. The Spanish friars came to depend on the mission Indians.

16. The hide and tallow trade brought mission life to an end and changed California.

Rainy Days in Los Angeles

Winter

Spring

Summer

Fall

= 2 Days of Rain

Using What You Know

Use the graph to answer the following questions.

1. Which season has the most rainy days?
2. How many rainy days does Los Angeles average in the spring?
3. How many rainy days does each stand for?
4. How many rainy days does stand for?
5. Which season has an average of seven rainy days?

Use the map to answer the following questions.

6. Name a state through which the 40° north parallel runs.
7. A city located 35° north and 110° west would be in which state?

8. A city located 40° north and 115° west would be in which state?
9. Name California's three neighbor states.

Unit 2

Settlers from the East

Chapter 5
The First Settlers

Chapter 6
The Gold Rush

Chapter 7
California Becomes a State

In the 1800s, Americans began to come to California from the East. They came slowly at first, a few people or families at a time. But when gold was discovered in California, they came by the thousands. As a matter of fact, people from all over the world joined the rush for gold.

Each group that came had its own way of life. The people in each group taught this way of life to their children. But all the settlers had to learn new ways too. They had to learn how to get along in a new environment. They had to learn how to get along with the different groups of people who lived in California.

The First Settlers

As you know, first Spain and then Mexico ruled California during the early 1800s. But other people were interested in this region too.

Russians wanted to search for sea otter furs along California's coast. In 1812, they built Fort Ross in Northern California. Neither Mexico nor the United States welcomed the Russians. Soon they left.

You have already read that Americans began coming to California from the East. For some time, they came only by sea, sailing around the tip of South America. No one came by land. Can you guess why?

Lesson 1 Mountain and Desert Barriers

California was cut off from the East by three kinds of barriers. One barrier was distance. About two thousand miles of wilderness lay between the settled parts of the eastern United States and California. There were no trails across this wilderness.

A traveler who made the long trip would face another barrier—the Sierra Nevada rising like a wall more than four thousand feet high. The only way over the Sierra Nevada would be through passes. A **pass** is a low place between two mountains in a mountain range. The Sierra Nevada would be most difficult to cross in winter.

A traveler who tried to go around the Sierra Nevada would be blocked by the third barrier—California's deserts. The traveler would face a stretch of hot, dry land as much as two hundred miles wide. It would take a week to cross this land on foot or on horseback. And there might be no grass to feed a horse and, even more important, no water to drink!

Reading Elevation Maps

This elevation map shows how high landforms in the western United States are. Looking at this map, you can see the mountain and desert barriers of California.

The **elevation** of a landform is its height above sea level. Sea level is the level of the surface of the water in the oceans. Land that is 10,000 feet in elevation is 10,000 feet above sea level.

The map uses different colors to stand for different elevations. The map key explains what elevation each color stands for. Red, brown, orange, yellow, and green stand for elevations above sea level. Purple stands for elevations below sea level.

What color shows land that is more than 10,000 feet high? What color is land that is between 700 and 3,000 feet high? How high is most of the Sierra Nevada? How high is most of the San Joaquin Valley?

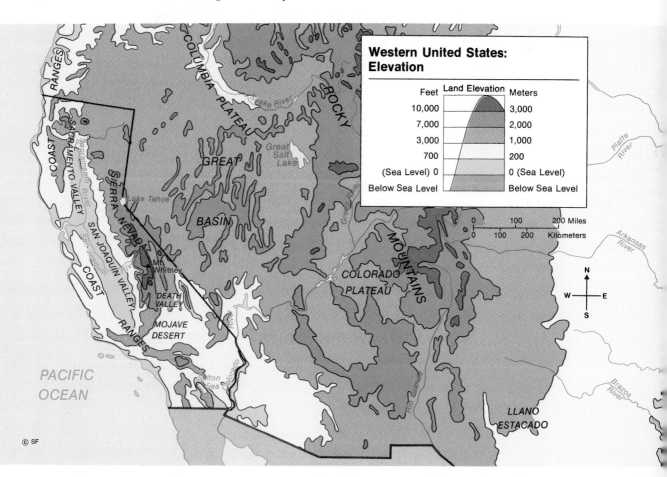

California's worst mountain barrier was the Sierra Nevada. These rugged mountains were hard to cross at any time of year. But they were most difficult to cross in winter. As much as thirty-seven feet of snow fell in some places. Cold winds howled through the passes. Temperatures fell as low as −30° Fahrenheit (−34° Celsius). The deep snow and bitter cold often made winter travel through these mountains impossible.

California's worst desert barrier was Death Valley. This desert had rough ground, steep cliffs, and dead-end canyons. It was *very* hot and dry. In summer, temperatures often rose as high as 125° Fahrenheit (52° Celsius). Most areas of the valley had only two inches of rain each year. Other areas had no rain at all for many years.

Checking Up

1. Name the three kinds of barriers that separated California from the East.

2. Why would climate be a problem for travelers in the Sierra Nevada? In Death Valley?

3. Why do trails and highways go through passes?

4. If you were a settler, would you have traveled to California by crossing the Sierra Nevada or Death Valley? Why?

5. Look at the elevation map on page 61. What color is land that is between 7,000 and 10,000 feet high?

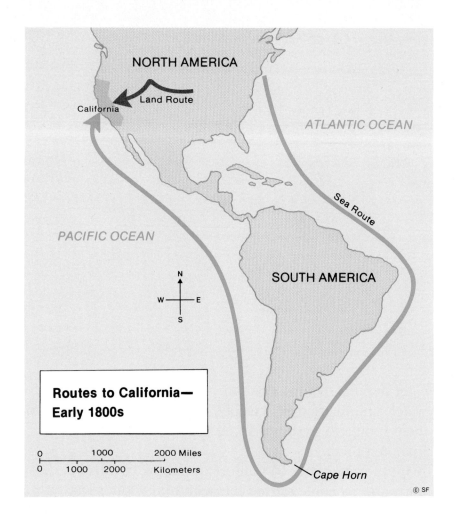

NORTH AMERICA

Land Route

California

ATLANTIC OCEAN

Sea Route

PACIFIC OCEAN

N
W — E
S

SOUTH AMERICA

Routes to California— Early 1800s

| 0 | 1000 | 2000 Miles |
| 0 | 1000 | 2000 | Kilometers |

Cape Horn

© SF

Lesson 2 The Trailblazers

As you can see in the map above, the land route to California seems much shorter than the sea route. But in the 1820s, traveling to California by land was difficult and dangerous. People had to pick their way over unknown and unmapped land. They had to find a way over or around California's rugged, snowy mountains and hot, dry deserts. No wonder people traveled by sea!

The first Americans to reach California by land were fur trappers looking for new places to trap beaver. At first, they followed Indian trails. Later, some of the trappers led parties of settlers along trails they had blazed.

One of these trappers was Jedediah Smith. He led a group of people from the Great Salt Lake in Utah to Mission San Gabriel in California. Their journey lasted

Frederic Remington was an American artist. He worked as a cowboy in the western United States. He painted pictures of things he saw and heard about. In this picture, Remington has painted trailblazer Jedediah Smith leading a group of people to California.

By the Way

Some members of Walker's party were the first Americans to see Yosemite. After their long and difficult journey, they were too hungry and tired to notice how beautiful it was.

eight months. During this time, they ran out of food and water, and many died. Luckily, some Mojave Indians gave them food and fresh horses. At Mission San Gabriel, the friars fed them.

Smith came twice to California. On the two trips, thirty-three people started out with him. Only seven of them made it. Obviously, Smith hadn't found a very good trail to California.

Many fur trappers who came after Smith found better trails. One of them was a black American named James Beckwourth. He discovered a good place to cross the Sierra Nevada. Today, it is still called Beckwourth Pass.

One of the best trappers and **trailblazers** was Joseph Walker. In 1833, he set out for California with forty men. Walker planned carefully, leaving nothing to chance. He told each man to bring one horse to ride and three other horses to carry supplies. He had the men prepare dried meat for the trip. And he asked Indians about the best trails in their areas.

Even with planning, the journey was hard. Walker and his men suffered crossing the desert. They wanted to turn back when they came to the Sierra Nevada. But they carried on, and not one of them died.

Once he arrived in California, Walker was polite to the Californios. In turn, he was treated well. He and his men were invited into people's homes and to fiestas. Six of his men liked California so much that they stayed.

Later, Walker led a group of settlers to California. But even though he was offered fifty square miles of land, he liked the wild country too much to settle down. A man who traveled with him wrote, "Mr. Walker was a man well hardened to the wilderness. To explore unknown regions was his chief delight."

Joseph Walker

James Beckwourth

Checking Up

1. When the first trailblazers came west, what were they looking for?

2. What problems and dangers did the trailblazers face in their travels?

3. Name two reasons Joseph Walker was successful as a trailblazer.

4. What kind of people must the trailblazers have been?

Lesson 3   Traveling the California Trail

After the fur trappers had found trails to the West, it wasn't long before groups of **pioneers** followed. People in the East began to hear about the wonderful land and climate of California. Many of them wanted to come here.

Some people came on foot or on horseback. Most came by wagon. They carried with them all of the supplies and belongings they thought they would need. As more and more wagon wheels carved ruts in the ground, the trail to California became well marked. In some places in the United States, you can still see this old wagon trail.

A boy named Elisha Brooks traveled on this California Trail with his family. When Elisha was eleven years old, he lived in Michigan with his mother, twin brother, older sister, and three younger brothers. His father had gone to California two years before. One day the family got a letter from Mr. Brooks. He wrote that California was wonderful. He said that he would like to stay, but he missed them. The family decided to join him. They sent Mr. Brooks a letter telling him they were coming, but they did not wait for him to answer. They knew it would take too long. Usually, it took four months for letters to travel just one way from Michigan to California.

Mrs. Brooks and her children prepared carefully for their long journey. They bought a wagon and filled it with supplies like bacon, flour, and beans. They had oxen to pull the wagon, cows for milk, and chickens for eggs. Mrs. Brooks also hired a man to drive their wagon. Then they set off.

By the Way

The trip across the United States was long and hard. Many people died from hunger and thirst in the deserts. Others died trying to cross the snow-covered Sierra Nevada. One group of pioneers, the Donner party, arrived to find early snow in the Sierra Nevada and were snowed in for nearly six months. They did not have enough food to last the winter. Thirty-four people died, and forty-seven lived.

The place where the Donner party crossed the Sierra Nevada is called Donner Pass. Today, it is still hard to cross this pass in winter.

66

After only one week, their driver got scared and went home. But the Brooks family kept on going. One day they saw a band of Sioux [sü] Indians on the trail ahead. Elisha was afraid. He felt sure the Indians would kill them. But the Sioux only wanted to trade. Mrs. Brooks traded a blanket and some sugar for a pony for Elisha. Years later, Elisha wrote about what happened next.

66 I mounted the pony bare backed. I never had been on a horse before, and he ran away with me. I clung to him for dear life as he hustled over the plain. Soon I was in the camp of the Sioux.

The Indians laughed hard over my bare back riding, but I was scared that I would be an Indian the rest of my life. However, after performing a dance around me and feeding me, several boys mounted their ponies and took me back to my family. We concluded that Indians were not so bad as they were painted. This turned out to be a very friendly tribe. 99

Another day, the Brooks family came to a place called Independence Rock. Here were carved the names of many pioneers who had passed that way. As they added their own names, the children were excited to find their

Some trails were so steep that no animal could drag a wagon up them. On the left, pioneers use a winch to pull a wagon up a steep trail.

On the right is the cover of a wagon guide printed in 1858. Books like this one held maps and tips for travelers. In some ways, they were like the tour guides we use today.

People

Juliette Briar and her three young sons traveled to California with the Manly party. This group tried to cross Death Valley. But they spent weeks trapped in dead-end canyons with very little food and no water. Finally, Juliette's boys couldn't walk any farther. She tied two large bags over the back of an ox. One boy rode in each bag. Juliette carried the third boy on her back. At last, after more than two months, the Manly party found a way out of Death Valley. Juliette Briar had saved her sons' lives.

father's name on the rock. It had been carved two years before!

The California Trail was quite busy. Sometimes the Brooks family joined a wagon train for a few days. Most of the time, they traveled alone. But they were not doing well. Their oxen were weak, and their food supply was getting low. Finally, there came a day when the food ran out. The family traveled on, trying to get as close to California as they could. As the day passed, they got hungrier and hungrier. Suddenly, one of the children saw someone coming toward them. It was a man riding a mule. The closer he got, the more familiar he looked. It was their father!

When Mr. Brooks had gotten his family's letter and learned that they were coming to California, he had been very worried. He knew how dangerous the wagon trail was. He packed his mule with food and set off to find them. As he traveled, Mr. Brooks asked each group of pioneers he met if they had seen his family. At last, he ran into some people who had, and ten days later he found them.

With their father's mule to help the tired oxen pull the wagon, the Brooks family made it across the Sierra Nevada before the snows came. It had taken them six months to travel to California.

Checking Up

1. Why were Americans interested in coming to California?

2. What were some difficulties Elisha and his family faced on the trail to California?

3. Describe some of the feelings Elisha and his family must have had as they left Michigan to travel to California. How would *you* have felt?

4. Elisha learned something about Indians on the way to California. What did he learn?

Lesson 4 Revolt and War

The first Americans who lived in California were adventurers who came on their own. Once they settled in California, they learned new ways of life. They became Catholics and Mexican citizens. They spoke Spanish and took Spanish names. Many of them married Californios and brought up their children as Californios.

The settlers who came in the 1840s were different. Most of them came with their families. When they arrived in California, they wanted to live as Americans and bring up their children as Americans. Because they would not become Mexican citizens, these settlers were not allowed to buy land. This made them very angry.

Like many Americans at this time, the settlers believed that the United States had a right to take over all of the land from the Atlantic to the Pacific Ocean. James K. Polk, the President of the United States, had tried to buy California from Mexico. But the Mexican government would not sell.

In 1845, an explorer named John C. Frémont led a group of armed Americans into California. Historians today think that Frémont encouraged California settlers to fight against the Mexican government. At any rate, in 1846 a small group of settlers took over a Mexican fort in Sonoma. They said that California was now **independent**, or free, of Mexico. They called it the "California Republic." They replaced the Mexican flag with one they had made. Because this flag had a grizzly bear on it, this event became known as the "Bear Flag Revolt."

Meanwhile, unknown to the Californians, the United States and Mexico had gone to war. Years ago, people in Texas had revolted against Mexico and become independent. Then, in 1845, Texas became part of the United States. Mexico was angered by this new move. Next the two countries couldn't agree where the **boundary**, or borderline, between Mexico and Texas should be. President Polk sent troops to the borderline in question, and war soon broke out. An American ship came to California with news of the Mexican War. The Bear Flaggers and Frémont immediately joined the

Facts and Figures

The idea that the United States had the right to take over all of the land from sea to sea was called "Manifest Destiny." People believed that it was America's destiny to grow—that this was what was meant to be for the American people.

John C. Frémont

69

The original Bear Flag was drawn on unbleached cotton. The star and grizzly bear were drawn in blackberry juice. Below the star and bear, the words CALIFORNIA REPUBLIC were written in black. A piece of red flannel was sewn across the bottom. The flag pictured here is a copy of the one made by the California settlers. That first flag was burned in the fire that followed the San Francisco earthquake of 1906.

American army. The California Republic had lasted less than a month.

The Californios fought bravely, but in the end the Americans took over California. By 1848, Americans had also won the war in Mexico and Texas. And Mexico had lost all the land that now makes up New Mexico, Utah, Arizona, Colorado, Nevada, and California.

Checking Up

1. How were later American settlers different from the first?

2. Who revolted in the Bear Flag Revolt? Against whom did they revolt?

3. How did the Mexican War change California?

4. Do you think that California would have become part of the United States if there had been no war?

Write your answers on paper. Do not write in the book.

Using Key Words

From the list below, choose the word that best completes each of the sentences. Write it on your paper.

boundary   pass
elevation   pioneer
independent   trailblazer

1. The height of land above sea level is its _____.
2. A person who marks new trails in an unknown land is called a _____.
3. A line or border between two countries is a _____.
4. Another word for *early settler* is _____.
5. A narrow opening between mountains is called a _____.
6. A country that is free of others' rule is _____.

Reviewing Main Ideas

Choose the ending that makes each sentence true. Write its letter beside the question number on your paper.

1. California's geography made it difficult to reach by land because
   a. everyone had to come through the same pass.
   b. travelers had to face tall mountains or dry deserts.
   c. California is below sea level.

2. The main reason some trappers and pioneers succeeded in coming safely to California was that they
   a. planned carefully for the trip.
   b. brought oxen to pull their wagons.
   c. were not afraid of the trip.

3. California became part of the United States because
   a. Mexico sold it to President Polk.
   b. American settlers took over a Mexican fort in Sonoma.
   c. Mexico lost a war with the United States.

Thinking Things Over

Why, do you think, did some Americans believe that the United States had the right to stretch from the Atlantic to the Pacific Ocean?

Practicing Skills

Use this map to answer the questions.

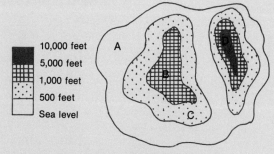

1. Which land is lower, A or D?
2. Which land is higher, B or C?
3. Which is lower than 500 feet?

The Gold Rush

In 1848, the year the Mexican War ended, an exciting event took place. Read about a discovery that changed California's population and way of life forever—a discovery that was talked about all around the world.

Lesson 1   Gold Is Found

John Sutter and James Marshall were partners. Sutter, who was born in Switzerland, owned land and a fort in the area where the American and Sacramento rivers meet. Marshall was a carpenter who was helping Sutter build a sawmill.

By January of 1848, Sutter's Mill was almost completely built. Then James Marshall made a discovery that shook the world. This is how Marshall told his story:

66 About half past seven o'clock on or about the 19th of January, I went down to the mill as usual, and there, upon the rock, about six inches beneath the surface of the water, I discovered the gold. I was entirely alone at the time. I picked up one or two pieces and examined them. I then collected four or five pieces and went up to Mr. Scott and said, "I have found it."

"What is it?" inquired Scott.

"Gold," I answered.

"Oh, no," returned Scott, "that can't be."

I replied positively—"I know it to be nothing else. 99

At first Marshall and Sutter tried to keep the discovery quiet. But it was impossible. Soon the workers building the mill wanted to look for gold. In March, a San Francisco newspaper reported the discovery. People were

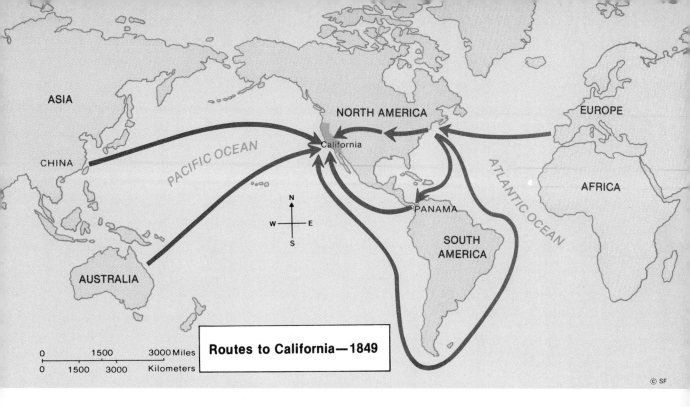

Routes to California—1849

slow to believe it. They thought it might be some kind of joke. Then Sam Brannan, who owned a store in Sutter's Fort, took action. Hoping his store would make a lot of money if gold miners came to the area, he brought a bottle filled with gold to San Francisco. He ran through the streets shouting, "Gold! Gold! Gold from the American River."

The Gold Rush was on! Most of the people living in San Francisco went to the "gold country." By June, both of the city's newspapers had closed down. There weren't enough people left in San Francisco buying newspapers.

By the following year, the news of the discovery had spread far and wide. People were coming from all over the world to find gold. Because most of the gold seekers came through San Francisco, that city began to grow again. As a matter of fact, San Francisco's population grew by thousands in just a few years.

The map above shows how the gold seekers came to California. Many people came by ship. Some came to California from the Far East, mainly China, by sailing across the Pacific Ocean. Some came from Europe and the east coast of America by sailing around the tip of South America. Others sailed to Panama. There the gold seekers got out and traveled by canoe and mule to the Pacific

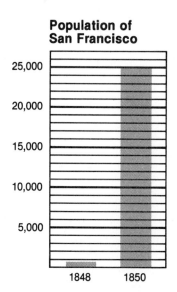

Population of San Francisco

73

When ships anchored in San Francisco Harbor, everyone on board, even the sailors, left to go look for gold. No one could be found to sail the ships away. Soon the harbor looked like a forest of ships' masts.

coast, where they got on another ship to sail to San Francisco. Most Americans came across the United States by wagon train. However they came, all the miners were in a hurry to get rich. One miner even saw people digging for gold in the streets. Everyone had caught gold fever!

Checking Up

1. Where was gold first discovered in California? Who discovered it?

2. How did the discovery of gold change California?

3. Tell four routes by which people came to the gold fields.

4. Look at the graph. What was the population of San Francisco in 1848? What was it in 1850?

5. Why did so many people come to California to look for gold? Would you have traveled three thousand miles for such a chance?

Lesson 2   Life in the Gold Fields

> On Selby Flat we live in style;
> We'll stay right here till we make our pile.
> We're sure to do it after a while,
> Then good-bye to Californy.

This was one of the songs that gold miners sang. It tells how they would have *liked* to have lived, but it wasn't true.

For one thing, miners did *not* live in style. They lived in badly made cabins. Most cabins had no windows, and some had only a leather curtain or blanket for a door. The miners had to work hard in every kind of weather and were often cold, wet, and tired.

Nor did most miners get rich, or make their pile, as it says in the song. It's true that some miners quickly became rich. There were stories about miners who dug up thousands of dollars' worth of gold in a single day. But most miners worked hard for weeks and found only

By the Way

Some people in California were lucky enough to find gold without hard work. One young girl found a seven-pound lump of gold while she was playing. And a man was chasing his cow when he stubbed his toe on a gold-bearing rock!

The first large numbers of people who came to California looking for gold were called forty-niners because they came in 1849. One of the most common ways the forty-niners separated gold from the sand and gravel in which it was found was by panning. Miners scooped up the sand and gravel from a riverbed in a shallow pan. They shook the pan under a stream of running water. The water washed away the lighter sand and gravel. The heavier gold settled to the bottom of the pan.

Some miners used a long trough called a sluice box to separate gold from sand and gravel. They shoveled sand and gravel into the box and piped water through it. The sand and gravel washed through the box, but the gold sank to the bottom and was caught there.

By the Way

Some people came to California to open stores, to work as doctors or blacksmiths, or to do other jobs for the miners. Other people who had come to find gold ended up being storekeepers instead. These merchants and workers made a lot of money during the Gold Rush.

a few specks of gold. Many found no gold at all. Neither John Sutter nor James Marshall—who discovered gold in California—could make any money from their discovery!

Many miners could not afford enough food. Bread that was five cents a loaf in the East cost fifty to seventy-five cents in the mining camps. Coffee was five dollars a pound, and eggs cost fifty dollars a dozen. With prices like these, it was mostly storekeepers, or **merchants**, not miners, who got rich.

Life in the gold fields was quite different for the miners than the life they were used to. Most of the gold miners were men who had come to California without their families. Many miners were lonely. Also, there were people from all over the world living in the gold fields. Mexicans, South Americans, Chinese, Europeans, Americans, Mexican Californians, and Indians—people from all these groups became gold miners.

At first, most of these groups of people got along well together. Everyone was too busy looking for gold to care what the others were doing. But as time passed, some groups were treated badly. In some mining towns, laws were passed to stop black Americans, Mexicans, and

Chinese from mining gold. In some places, Indian children were captured as slaves and made to work for miners.

Not all miners cared what color a person's skin was or what language a person spoke. Some were interested in learning about different ways of life. Here is a story about two groups of people who enjoyed living together and helping each other.

One day Obed Wilson, a miner in the Downieville area, came across a wounded Indian man. The Indian was afraid his two children would starve before he could hunt again. So Wilson and three other American miners took the Indian family to live with them.

Togie, aged twelve, and his ten-year-old sister, Tiny, were a great help to the miners. While their father was getting well, they kept a supply of dry firewood near the door of the cabin. They brought water from the spring. They also collected foods like wild plums.

The miners taught Togie and Tiny to speak English. In return, the children taught the miners their language. Soon the two groups were able to talk to each other in a mixture of the two languages.

When the father's wound had healed, he built a home for his family not far from the miners' cabin. The Indians continued to share food and meat with the miners. And whenever the miners went to the nearest camp, they brought back presents for the children. These miners and Indians were good neighbors to each other.

What's in a Name?

Levi's got their start in California during the Gold Rush. They were created by a German-born merchant named Levi Strauss. He came to San Francisco in 1850 and saw that the miners needed sturdy pants that would not tear easily. To make these pants, he used heavy blue denim. He sewed the seams twice and added copper rivets at points of strain. Strauss's long-wearing jeans became very popular with the forty-niners. The family-run business is still based in San Francisco. Today, it produces enough of the ever-popular Levi's to be sold all over the world.

Checking Up

1. Describe some ways in which miners' lives in the gold fields were different from what they expected.

2. Name five groups of people who became gold miners.

3. How did Obed Wilson and his friends help the Indian family?

4. How did the Indian family help the four miners?

This picture, painted in 1851, shows what life was like in a Chinese mining camp.

Lesson 3   The Chinese

In 1848, when gold was found, there were only about seven Chinese people in San Francisco. One was a trader named Chum Ming. He heard about the gold and set off for the hills to find some for himself. When he was successful, he wrote about it to a friend in China. Chum Ming's friend packed his bags and came too. The news that there was gold in California spread fast in China.

Times were hard in China. People were starving. Digging for gold in California seemed like a way out. So many Chinese people came to try their luck. By 1852, twenty-five thousand Chinese people had come to California. Most were working in the mines.

The Chinese were the largest group of people from another nation to come to the gold fields. Some American miners began to get angry that so many Chinese had come. These Americans seemed to feel that they had a right to all of the gold in California. You remember that some camps made laws that Chinese people could not mine gold. Also, Chinese miners in other places were made to pay a special tax. Some Chinese were even beaten up or killed.

This **discrimination** did not stop the Chinese miners from coming. Most of them did not want to stay in America forever. Thousands returned to China with the gold they had found. However, many more had to stay in California because they never made enough money to return.

Most Chinese people who were not living in the mines lived in San Francisco, in a section of the city that is still called Chinatown. As the gold ran out, more and more Chinese people came to live and work in Chinatown. It was usually the only place they were allowed to live in the city.

In Chinatown, the Chinese tried to keep their own way of life, or **culture**. They wore the kind of clothes they had worn in China, and the men wore their hair long, braided in one pigtail. The people put on bright-colored costumes and held parades to celebrate Chinese holidays, like the Chinese New Year. Chinese people continued to

These Chinese children lived in *Jim Shan*, which was the Chinese name for San Francisco. *Jim Shan* means Golden Mountain.

cook the way they had cooked in China, and they asked Chinese traders to bring special foods and goods from China. They tried to make their new homes in America like their old homes in China.

Rice and chopsticks are parts of the Chinese culture.

The Chinese also taught their culture to their children. The families spoke the Chinese language, and in special schools, Chinese children learned to read and write it. Parents taught their children the **customs** and ways of behaving they had learned in China.

Today, you can visit Chinatowns in San Francisco and Los Angeles. In them you will find stores that sell goods from China and restaurants that serve Chinese food. But today, most Chinese Americans don't live in a Chinatown. Chinatowns are places that everybody can visit, places where everybody can experience Chinese ways of life. They are places to remind Chinese Americans of some parts of their special culture.

Checking Up

1. Why did so many Chinese come to California's gold fields?

2. Where did most Chinese who came to find gold end up living?

3. Name two ways in which Chinese people were discriminated against during the Gold Rush.

4. What is *culture*?

5. Name three things that are part of the Chinese culture.

Building Social Studies Skills

Understanding B.C. and A.D.

Chinese Americans can be proud of their ancient culture. The history of this culture goes back more than 3,500 years. But how do we date that time? How do we show the dates of events that far back in history?

Here is a time line. The red part of the time line is marked **B.C.** The green part of the time line is marked **A.D.**

What do B.C. and A.D. mean? B.C. stands for *Before Christ*. A.D. stands for *Anno Domini* [an ′ ō dom ′ ə nī], which means "in the year of our Lord." All of the years *before* the birth of Christ are thought of as B.C. The year 1500 B.C. was 1,500 years before Christ's birth. All of the years *after* the birth of Christ are thought of as A.D. For example, A.D. 1848 was the 1,848th year after the birth of Christ.

As you know, a time line shows earlier dates and events on the left side, and later dates and events on the right.

Look at the time line and answer these questions.

1. Which happened earlier, the building of the Great Pyramid or Cabrillo's exploring of California?
2. Which started earlier, the Mayan or the Chinese civilization?
3. Which date is earlier in history, 1500 B.C. or 1000 B.C.?
4. As you move along the B.C. section of the time line, dates with smaller numbers are
   a. earlier in history.
   b. later in history.
5. Which date is earlier in history, A.D. 1500 or A.D. 1000?
6. Starting with the earliest date, write these dates in the correct order:
   A.D. 859
   1432 B.C.
   500 B.C.
   A.D. 1700
   A.D. 2000

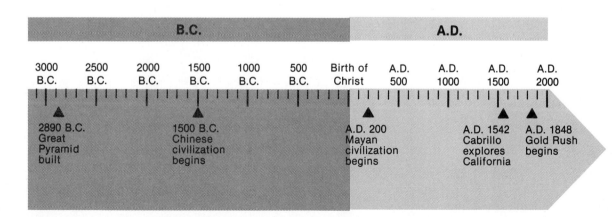

Write your answers on paper. Do not write in the book.

Using Key Words

From the list below, choose the term that best completes each of the sentences. Write it on your paper.

A.D.	culture	discrimination
B.C.	custom	merchant

1. A _____ sells things.
2. _____ is used to name the years after the birth of Jesus Christ.
3. A people's way of life is its _____.
4. Treating people unfairly because of their race is called _____.
5. One _____ of the Chinese is to hold a parade to celebrate the New Year.
6. _____ is used to name the years before the birth of Jesus Christ.

Reviewing Main Ideas

Choose the ending that makes each sentence true. Write its letter beside the question number on your paper.

1. The Gold Rush changed California. One of the biggest changes was that
   a. everyone became richer.
   b. Chinatown got smaller.
   c. the population grew larger.
2. Most American forty-niners traveled to California by crossing
   a. the Pacific Ocean.
   b. the Atlantic Ocean.
   c. America with wagon trains.

3. One reason miners' lives were so hard is that
   a. prices for food and tools were very high.
   b. everyone had to pay high taxes.
   c. there were no stores in which to buy tools.
4. The Spanish language, the Catholic religion, and fiestas were all parts of the
   a. Californio culture.
   b. gold miners' lives.
   c. discrimination against the Chinese.

Thinking Things Over

List five things that are part of your culture. Then tell how you learned about each thing. (Who taught you? Where did you learn about it?)

Practicing Skills

Number your paper from 1 to 6. Decide which point on the time line stands for each date below. Write the letter of each point next to the correct number on your paper.

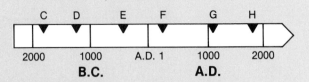

1. 1985 B.C.   4. 1313 B.C.
2. A.D. 1066   5. A.D. 1849
3. A.D. 356   6. 470 B.C.

Lesson 1   The Constitution
Lesson 2   Statehood

California Becomes a State

You know that Mexico lost California to the United States when it lost the Mexican War. Many Americans and some Californios living in California wanted it to become a state.

Lesson 1   The Constitution

Before California became a state, Californians wrote a **constitution**. A constitution is a law that tells how a state will be run. It explains how other laws will be made and what will happen when laws are broken. A constitution even says how people can change it.

All over California, people were chosen to go to a special meeting and write a state constitution. The people

Among those delegates who signed California's constitution of 1849 was Joseph Walker, about whom you have read. Others who signed included Antonio Pico, who once served as governor of California, and William Hartnell, who wrote the constitution in Spanish.

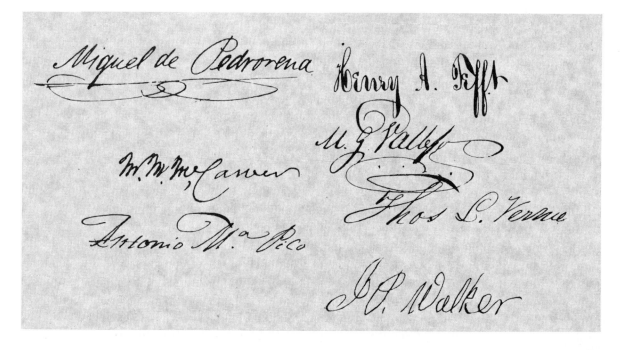

who were chosen were called **delegates**. These delegates met in Colton Hall in Monterey on September 13, 1849. You can still visit Colton Hall and see the room where they met.

Altogether, there were forty-eight delegates. Many of them were Americans. A few, like John Sutter of Sutter's Fort, were from other countries. Seven of the delegates were Spanish-speaking Californios.

Often, the Californios and Americans had different ideas about laws and the constitution. The Californios were used to the Spanish and Mexican laws that California had before the Americans arrived. The Americans were used to the English laws on which laws in the United States were based. California's constitution ended up with a mixture of both kinds of laws.

The delegates decided that California should have a government with three parts like the United States government. One part would be people elected to represent others in a state assembly and senate. They would write and change the state's laws. Another part would be the governor and other workers who would make sure that state laws were put into action. The third part would be courts that would decide if the laws were fair and had been broken.

The delegates had a harder time deciding who could vote in **elections**. At that time, many states allowed only white men to vote. Women couldn't vote anywhere in the United States. Most of the American delegates wanted to have similar voting rules in California. But many Californios had Indian blood, so their delegates wanted rules that made Mexican and Indian men voters too. In the end, the group decided that all white men could vote and that the state lawmakers could pass a law that would let men with Indian blood vote. Black men, Chinese men, and women of all colors were not allowed to vote for a long time.

The delegates decided that **slavery** would not be allowed in California. They also decided what rights women should have. In most states at this time, married women had to give all of their property to their husbands. But in California under Mexican law, married

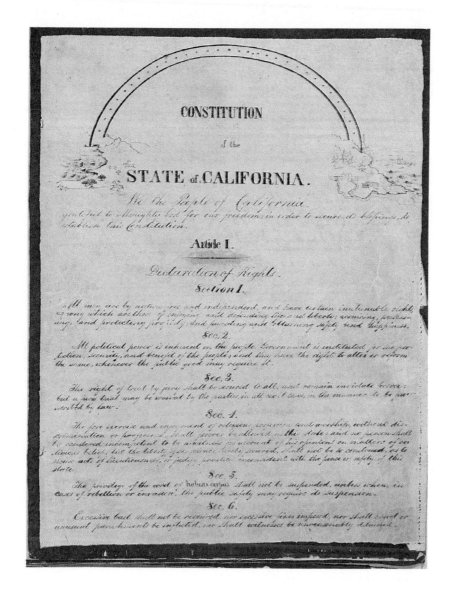

This is the first page of the California constitution written and approved in 1849.

women had the right to own property. The Californios persuaded the other delegates that the Mexican law was better, and California became the first state where married women had this right.

On October 13, the constitution was finished, and the meeting ended. Copies of the constitution were made in English and Spanish, and riders galloped off to give a copy to every pueblo, rancho, and mining camp. One month later, those who could vote agreed to accept the new constitution. The voters elected Peter H. Burnett as the first governor and chose lawmakers for the new state assembly and senate.

For the next thirty years, California was run under the 1849 constitution. Then, in 1879, a new, longer one was written. Although it has been changed many times, we still use the 1879 constitution today.

How Is the Constitution Changed?

California's 1879 constitution has been changed more than 350 times. There are three ways to change the constitution.

1. The state assembly and senate can vote to suggest a certain change to Californians. Then, during the next election, all the state's voters can decide if they like the suggestion.

2. Californians can suggest a certain change. If enough people want the change, the suggestion is voted on during an election.

3. A special meeting can be held to add to or rewrite the constitution. The voters of California then vote whether or not to accept the changes. This way of changing the constitution hasn't been used since 1879.

Checking Up

1. How was the California constitution like the United States Constitution?

2. List the three parts of government and tell what each part does.

3. What important idea from Mexican law was included in the California constitution?

4. Tell one way our constitution was different from other state constitutions.

5. Tell one way California's constitution can be changed.

Lesson 2   Statehood

Californian voters chose John Frémont and a man named William Gwin as their national senators. These two men went to Washington, D.C., hoping to persuade the United States Congress to let California join the Union.

But Frémont and Gwin had a hard time in Washington. They had arrived in the middle of one of the most serious clashes of opinion ever between Americans. The people of the fifteen states of the South wanted to keep slaves. The people of the fifteen states of the North thought slavery should be done away with. Neither side wanted to add any new states that would favor the other side.

As you know, California's constitution said that slavery wouldn't be allowed. So northern senators voted for California's statehood, and southern senators voted against it. Neither side could win a **majority** of votes.

Finally, after a year, Congress worked out a plan that both sides could agree to. And on September 9, 1850, California became the thirty-first state in the Union.

When news of statehood reached San Francisco, most people were happy. They marched in the streets. They waved flags and cheered. Why might some people have been unhappy?

Mariano Guadalupe Vallejo poses for a photograph with his five daughters and their dog.

News of statehood took two weeks to reach California. When the news arrived, San Francisco went wild. There were bonfires and firecrackers. People played drums, trumpets, and trombones. Many of the big buildings were lighted up. Everyone seemed to be pleased that California had become a state.

But not everyone was pleased. Many Californios were sad to see so many newcomers in their land. The Americans brought a new language and new customs. They took rancho land for farms, and some took cattle and horses that belonged to the Californios as well. Americans had even driven Californios away from many gold mines.

The Californios did not want the old way of life to change. Many of them left and went to Mexico. Others stayed but tried to keep their own culture. Mariano Guadalupe Vallejo [vä ye ′ hō] was one of the Californios who wanted statehood and stayed. He lost much land because of the Americans, but he was very generous. When he was an old man and had thought about the changes, Vallejo wrote that Californians "have no reason to complain of the change of government, for if the rich have lost thousands of horses and cattle, the poor have been bettered in condition."

Checking Up

1. Why did some senators vote against statehood for California?

2. When did California become a state?

3. How did most Americans react to the news of California's statehood?

4. How did many Californios react to statehood?

5. Do you think Californios had good reasons to be unhappy with the American takeover of California? Explain your answer.

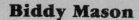

Biddy Mason

Biddy Mason was a black slave who came to San Bernardino, California, in 1851. She came with her master, Robert Smith, her three children, and another slave family. Because slavery was against the law in this state, the blacks became free servants. But Smith continued to act as if they were slaves.

A few years later, Smith decided to move to Texas, a slave state. He also decided to take the two black families with him, even though they would become slaves again in Texas.

Smith's move was reported to the Los Angeles County sheriff, who kept Smith from taking the families. He also kept Biddy Mason and her family under protection in Santa Monica. Later, a court declared Biddy Mason and the others "free forever."

After the court had freed her, Biddy Mason had no place to live. So Mr. and Mrs. Robert Owens, Sr., invited the family to stay with them in their Los Angeles home.

In Los Angeles, Biddy worked as a nurse. She used the money she saved to buy a few pieces of land, which later became quite valuable.

Biddy Mason also used her money to help other people. She worked in the jails and poor parts of the city. One time a flood washed away many peoples' homes. Biddy helped by inviting the homeless to buy all the groceries they needed and to put them on her bill.

Biddy Mason was highly respected. She is still fondly remembered. At the time of the United States Bicentennial, a plaque in her honor was given to the city of Los Angeles by the Association for the Study of Afro-American Life and History.

CITIZENSHIP

Two Flags Over California

Two flags fly over California's state building. One is the Stars and Stripes, the flag of the United States. The other is California's own state flag. Do you recognize it? It's very similar to the flag made and flown by the Bear Flaggers in 1846.

California's Bear Flag was designed by William Todd, a nephew of Mary Todd Lincoln, Abraham Lincoln's wife. The grizzly bear was chosen to stand for determination. This flag, a reminder of our history, was adopted in 1911.

America's Stars and Stripes was first adopted on June 14, 1772. Then it looked quite different, for it had only thirteen stars. Today, our flag's fifty stars stand for the fifty states. And the thirteen stripes stand for the thirteen original colonies that fought for independence.

One part of being a United States citizen is saying the Pledge of Allegiance to our American flag. It's the custom in many schools for students to say the pledge every day. At other schools, the pledge is saved for special days and assemblies. But did you know that saying the pledge as a regular custom began here in a California school?

The pledge was written by Francis Bellamy, an editor of *The Youth's Companion*. He wrote it in 1892 to celebrate the four hundredth anniversary of the discovery of America. Mary Fackler, a first-grade teacher in Redlands, California, heard it in a patriotic program. She began to use it in her classroom. This practice came to the attention of Joseph C. Breckenridge, a general of the United States Army. He visited Fackler's class to hear the salute.

The general liked the pledge and took it to Washington, D.C. There it was said by a group of children at a meeting of the Sons and Daughters of the American Revolution. The people at the meeting were moved by the beauty of the pledge. The general told them that the idea of saying the pledge came from California children.

Later, the Pledge of Allegiance was adopted by the Second National Flag Conference. It's now said all over America.

Reviewing Chapter 7

Write your answers on paper. Do not write in the book.

Using Key Words

From the list below, choose the word that best completes each of the sentences. Write it on your paper.

constitution majority
delegate slavery
election

1. A person chosen to speak for others at an important meeting is a _____.
2. A law that explains how a government will be run is a _____.
3. More than half is a _____.
4. A constitution tells who can vote in an _____.
5. The custom of owning people is called _____.

Reviewing Main Ideas

Choose the ending that makes each sentence true.

1. The 1849 constitution was written by
   a. the United States Congress.
   b. forty-eight Californios.
   c. delegates at a special meeting.
2. The 1849 constitution was like the United States Constitution in that
   a. slavery was not allowed.
   b. black men could vote.
   c. the government was divided into three parts.

3. Based on Mexican law, California's constitution said that
   a. married women could vote.
   b. married women could own property.
   c. all women could vote.
4. Statehood for California was held up because
   a. Congress couldn't decide what to do about the slavery problem.
   b. Northern senators didn't want California in the Union.
   c. the constitution was written in both English and Spanish.

Thinking Things Over

Write at least three reasons for having a state constitution.

Practicing Skills

Read about a black American woman. Write one paragraph to summarize what you read.

Mary Ellen "Mammy" Pleasant was born a slave in Georgia. She was very intelligent and was sent to Boston to be educated. There she became free.

Pleasant married a rich black man. When her husband died in 1849, she came to San Francisco. There she succeeded in business. She used her money to help runaway slaves and worked to end slavery everywhere.

What Do You Know?

Write your answers on paper. Do not write in the book.

Words to Know

In each group below, match the four words with their meanings.

> A.D.   delegate
> B.C.   pioneer

1. A person who represents others at an important meeting.
2. Used to name dates before the birth of Jesus Christ.
3. Used to name dates after the birth of Jesus Christ.
4. One of the first persons to settle in a new land.

> boundary   majority
> culture   slavery

5. More than half of a group.
6. The custom of owning other people.
7. A borderline.
8. The customs and ways of a group of people.

> constitution   elevation
> discrimination   pass

9. A low place in a mountain range.
10. The height of a place above sea level.
11. A law that describes how a government will be run.
12. Treating people unfairly because of their race or sex.

> custom   election
> independent   merchant

13. A way of behaving in a certain culture.
14. A person who sells things.
15. A means of choosing government officers.
16. Not ruled by another country.

Ideas to Know

Write "true" for the sentences that are true. Write "false" for the sentences that are false.

1. After the gold ran out, California was much like it was before the Gold Rush.
2. California became a state because it allowed slavery.
3. When people move to a new land, they often try to keep their own culture.
4. The heat made it hard for wagons to cross the Sierra Nevada.
5. Children learn about their culture from their parents.
6. To get to California, pioneers followed trappers' trails.
7. After the Mexican War, California became part of Mexico.
8. There was discrimination against black, Mexican, and Chinese gold miners.
9. 1246 B.C. was one year before 1245 B.C.

10. California's constitution was written by delegates representing both Americans and Californios.

11. Land travel to California was easier in the early 1820s because sea travelers had to go around the tip of South America.

12. California was the first state to allow married women to own property.

13. When California became a state many Californios who stayed tried to keep their own culture.

14. Some gold miners came to California by crossing Panama.

15. Most gold miners found gold without hard work.

16. Sea level is the level of the bottom of the oceans.

17. Biddy Mason was freed because California didn't allow slavery.

18. Death Valley was a barrier because it was so high in elevation.

19. In coming to California, some pioneers ran out of food or water.

20. The year A.D. 456 came *after* A.D. 463.

21. When California became a state, black people could vote everywhere in the United States.

22. Prices were very high in California during the Gold Rush.

23. Not all people in California were happy about statehood.

Using What You Know

1. Put the events below in order from the earliest to the latest. Number your paper from 1 to 5. Then, write the letter of the first event next to the number 1, the letter of the second event by the number 2, and so on.

    a. A.D. 1000   Leif Ericson sails to North America.

    b. 509 B.C.   The Roman Republic is set up.

    c. A.D. 1869   The Suez Canal opens.

    d. A.D. 1532   Pizarro lands in Peru.

    e. 206 B.C.   The Great Wall of China is completed.

2. Write a paragraph telling about the culture of one of these groups in the 1820s.

    Californios
    Chinese
    Americans

    Tell at least three things about the culture.

3. Certain events have changed ways of life in California. Write a paragraph describing how California changed as a result of one of these events.

    The Mexican War
    The Gold Rush
    Statehood

Unit ③

A Changing California

More and more American settlers came to California. They brought American ways of life and American ideas about land use. These new ways and ideas caused changes in California.

Other things changed California too. New ways of getting news, mail, packages, and people back and forth between California and the rest of the United States were found. New ways of traveling inside California were developed. As a result of all these changes, California grew in size.

Chapter

8

Lesson 1   The Californios and the Land
Lesson 2   The Indians and the Land

Changing Ideas About Land

As California's population began to change, so did ideas about the land. American settlers came to California looking for land to plow and farm. Many of them did not understand the ways in which the Californios and the Indians were already using the land. Because the land had not been farmed and did not look as if it had been changed in any way, the settlers thought it was free for them to use. Soon problems arose. People began to ask: Who owns the land? How should the land be used?

Lesson 1   The Californios and the Land

People who own land in America today have a piece of paper, called a **deed**, that describes exactly which piece of land they own. An official copy of the deed is kept in the county recorder's office. If there is any question about who owns a piece of land, it can usually be settled by checking the recorded deeds.

The Californios usually did not keep records as exact as these. They were often unsure about how much land they owned. They did not have **surveyors** to measure their land and figure out its boundaries. Instead, they used natural features to describe the outlines of their ranchos. A range of mountains might mark one side of a rancho; the skull of a cow just laid on the ground could mark one of the corners. With so much land to go around, the Californios had never been worried about proving who owned it. So there was usually no exact record of land ownership.

All of this changed when the American settlers came. The settlers were used to United States land laws. The Americans thought they could settle and farm any piece

surveyor, person who carefully measures land to decide its boundaries.

The sturdy Levi's pants that were popular with the miners of the Gold Rush quickly became a favorite of hard-working cowboys in California and throughout the West. They are still a part of western ranch tradition.

of land that was not fenced and being farmed. Sometimes the Californios were able to get the settlers off their land. More often, Californios could do nothing. The number of settlers became too large. Everyone was confused and angry about the land.

In 1851, the United States Congress tried to solve this **conflict** by passing a Land Act. Under this **act**, or law, Californios who wanted to get settlers off their land had to prove that the land really belonged to them. They had to take the settlers to court, and whether they won or lost, the Californios had to pay the court costs.

conflict, a disagreement or fight about a thing or idea.

Californios thought that this new law was unfair. The settlers thought that the act was a good thing. The Land Act did not clear up the conflict over land. The court cases often dragged on for years. One case took twenty-four years to settle. And proving land ownership in court took a lot of money. Even when the Californios won, they often had to sell as much as half of their land to pay court costs. Men like Mariano Vallejo and John Sutter, who had once been rich, lost most of their land and ended their lives poor.

In the end, most of the land was owned by Americans. Very few large ranchos remained. The way of life of the Californios had changed forever.

Checking Up

1. Compare how the American settlers and the Californios felt about land ownership.

2. Do you think that the Land Act was a fair way to solve the land problem? Explain your answer.

3. Why were the American settlers able to win most of the land in the end?

Indian Population

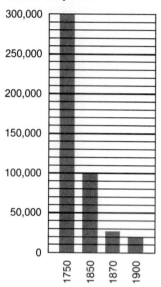

Thousands of Indians were killed by the American settlers and the diseases they brought. Many times, Indians were not killed over land. Some were attacked for no reason. And when things were stolen, settlers often blamed it on the nearest group of Indians. Without trying to find the thief, these settlers went to the Indian village and killed whoever was there.

ancestor, family member who lived in the past; person from whom one is descended.

Lesson 2   The Indians and the Land

The Indians had lived in California for thousands of years, but they did not have any deeds to prove they owned the land. They also believed the land could be shared. The Californios had taken Indians' lands. And, although there were some problems, it was possible for the Californios and the Indians to use the same lands. The Californios grazed their cattle on the same land that the Indians used to hunt and gather their food.

The American settlers, on the other hand, plowed up the land and built fences. They tore up the natural vegetation that the Indians used as food. The settlers also hunted or drove away the animals that the Indians hunted.

The Americans thought that the Indians did not use the land because they did not change it in any way. They thought that, because the Indians moved often, they did not care where they lived. But this was not true.

Many Indian groups did move from place to place in search of better hunting and food. But they didn't move just anywhere. They always stayed on the land that their **ancestors** had lived on. Each group knew where the land of their family ended and where the land of other groups began. They did not need fences.

When settlers moved onto Indian lands and began to farm, no one stopped them. The Indians did not understand this. One Indian chief said, "This is our country; why do the Americans come here? They are good and brave, but they come upon the land of my people. What do they intend to do?"

As the American settlers took more and more Indian land, it became harder and harder for the Indians to find enough food. Sometimes hungry Indians stole from the settlers. Sometimes fighting broke out between settlers and Indians. As a result, the United States government set aside special areas of land for the Indians. These areas were called **reservations**. The Indians were told to live on these reservations and learn to be farmers.

Most Indians found life on the reservations terrible. The lands they were given were lands the settlers did not

98

want. These lands were not usually good for farming. The Indians could not live in the way they were used to. Nor could they live like the Americans. They became very poor.

Not all Indians lived on the reservations. Some worked on the ranchos. A few gave up their own way of life and were accepted by Americans. Sometimes whole tribes were able to live far from the Americans and keep their own cultures alive.

Not all Indian groups who wanted to keep their old ways were able to do so. One group, the Modocs [mō′docs], tried and failed. The settlers wanted Modoc land, and fighting had broken out between the two groups. Then the government stepped in. It made the Modocs move to a reservation in Oregon. This reservation was on the land of their old enemies, the Klamaths. The Modocs found life there impossible, and they returned to California.

The government sent some soldiers to force the Modocs back to the reservation. These soldiers were led

For nearly twenty years, army soldiers chased and fought with the Modoc Indians in Northern California. While looking for bands of Indians, the soldiers slept in tents like these.

Chief Kientepoos
(Captain Jack)

By the Way

Not all Americans treated Indians badly. One pioneer woman in Shasta County had been helped by Indians and wanted to repay them. One day she had her chance. A group of settlers were hunting down and killing Indians. The American woman was able to hide an Indian mother and baby in the attic of her home.

Another American woman, Helen Hunt Jackson, wrote books about the Indians' suffering. One book, *Ramona* (rä mō′nä), became a best seller. Jackson's book helped to improve the way Indians were treated.

by General Canby. The leader of the Modocs was Chief Kientepoos [kē in′ tə püs], also known as Captain Jack. He had a plan to outwit the soldiers. He asked to talk to General Canby and other army leaders about peace. They agreed. Chief Kientepoos met with them in a camp set up between the army and the Modocs. Suddenly the Modocs brought out hidden weapons and killed General Canby. Then they ran off.

The Americans had been tricked. Angry, they chased the Indians. The soldiers and the Modocs fought for many months. Finally, some of the Modocs escaped back to the reservation in Oregon. The rest, still led by Kientepoos, gave up fighting.

The Americans had won the Modoc War. But it was their most expensive fight with the Indians. It cost half a million dollars and the lives of seventy-five soldiers. No one knows how many Modocs died.

The Indians no longer controlled the lands that had been theirs for thousands of years. In fact, it was not until the 1900s that Indians in California were again allowed to own any land at all. By 1900, there were only about 20,000 Indians left in the state—where 300,000 Indians had once lived.

Checking Up

1. Why were the Indians more able to share the land with the Californios than with the Americans?

2. Why did the settlers feel that they could claim Indian land?

3. How did Indians feel about life on the reservations? Why?

4. Why did the Modocs refuse to live on the government reservation in Oregon?

5. What was the cost of the Modoc War in lives and in money? Do you think the cost was worth it? Explain your answer.

Reviewing Chapter 8

Write your answers on paper. Do not write in the book.

Using Key Words

From the list below, choose the word that best completes each of the sentences. Write it on your paper.

act   deed
ancestor   reservation
conflict   surveyor

1. A paper that records who owns a piece of land is a _____.
2. A _____ is someone who measures a piece of land to set its boundaries.
3. An _____ is a family member who lived in the past.
4. A law passed by Congress is an _____.
5. A _____ is a piece of land that the government set aside for Indians.
6. A _____ happens when people cannot agree.

Reviewing Main Ideas

Write "true" for the sentences that are true. Write "false" for the sentences that are false.

1. The ways in which Californios kept track of land ownership resulted in their losing much of their land to the American settlers.
2. The Americans believed whoever farmed the land should own it.

3. Life on the Indian reservation gave Indians the chance they wanted to learn new skills.

Thinking Things Over

In the 1850s, conflicts over who could use the land were painful. How could the Californios, American settlers, and Indians have settled the problem in a friendly way?

Practicing Skills

Student Population of Lincoln School

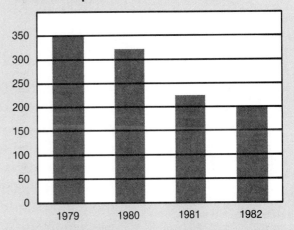

Use the graph to answer the following questions.

1. In which year were the most students at Lincoln School?
2. Between which two years was there the greatest drop in the number of students?
3. How many students were lost between 1979 and 1982?

Changes in Transportation and Communication

Californians wanted better links with the rest of the United States. They wanted to transport people and goods between the east and west coasts safely and quickly. They wanted to communicate more quickly too. Californians looked forward to getting letters from friends and relatives back east. And they were interested in news from the rest of the United States and Europe. Because mail, news, and packages took about three months to reach California, people in California felt like they were on a distant island.

Lesson 1   By Stage and by Steamer

In 1857, the United States Congress passed a bill to help California's communication problem. This bill promised money to anyone who would set up a fast **overland** mail service to California. A man named John Butterfield took up the challenge. He decided to use horse-drawn stagecoaches. He hired more than one thousand people to work for him and set up stations all the way from St. Louis, Missouri, to San Francisco, California. At these stations, the tired horses could be changed for new ones so that the stage could drive on.

The first stage ran in 1858. It took 24 days, 18 hours, and 26 minutes to travel the 2,800 miles from St. Louis to San Francisco. It was much faster than any other way.

Butterfield's stagecoach line carried people and packages, as well as mail, and made regular trips between East and West. Riding the stagecoach was dusty, bumpy, and boring. Passengers looked forward to station stops.

overland, on land, by land, or across the land.

Unfortunately, the food at the stations was bad. Another problem with riding the Butterfield Stage was the possibility of attack by Apache [ə pach ′ ē] Indians. Still, the stages ran for several years.

Other people tried to find faster ways across the country. Some people in the army had the idea to use camels to cross the desert in Southern California and Arizona. The camels were fast and needed little water. But they got sore feet from prickly cactus and other plants, and not many people knew how to drive them. The camels were not a success. In the end, most of them were sold to circuses.

Transportation within California was getting better too. Goods could be shipped more quickly. People could visit and do business in other parts of the state.

The first stage lines in California were started in 1849. One of them ran from Sacramento to Coloma and cost $32 one way. This was a lot of money for a fifty-mile ride. Before long, there were stages running all over California, especially in the gold country.

A quicker and more comfortable way to travel within California was by steamboat. Great paddle-wheel steamers

The Butterfield Stage ran twice a week from San Francisco to St. Louis, Missouri.

In the 1860s, the army tried using camels to carry people and packages. Although these animals moved fast and needed little water, they were difficult to manage. Horses and mules worked just as hard and were much easier to handle.

Stagecoaches such as this one carried people, packages, and letters back and forth over the rough trails between California and Missouri.

The steamship *Centennial*, built in 1876, carried passengers and freight along California rivers for twenty years. Here, she passes Telegraph Hill on her way to San Francisco wharf.

freight, goods transported, or carried, by train, truck, ship, or aircraft.

ran up and down the Sacramento, American, and San Joaquin rivers. These boats carried **freight** as well as people. The passengers could walk about the boats, meeting one another and watching the passing shore. Of course, this kind of travel could be done only on large rivers. Another problem with the steamers was that the captains liked to race one another. It was not uncommon for a steamboat engine to explode because it was traveling too fast!

Checking Up

1. Why did Californians want better links with the East?

2. How long did it take mail to go from East to West on the Butterfield Stage?

3. Only the Californians in some areas were able to use steamboats as transportation. Why?

4. What were some results of better transportation within California?

5. Tell what it was like to travel by stagecoach and by steamboat. Which one would you have liked better?

6. How do people travel within California today? How is freight shipped? How is mail carried?

Lesson 2 By Pony Express and by Telegraph

The Butterfield Stage delivered mail in about twenty-five days. Still, this was a long time to wait for a letter. On April 3, 1860, a faster way was found. The first Pony Express riders set off from Sacramento, California, traveling to St. Joseph, Missouri. Their journey was completed in just ten days. It had taken less than half the time needed to travel the same distance by stagecoach!

The Pony Express was more of an adventure than a business. A single rider set off across the country on a pony with saddlebags full of letters. Every ten to twenty-five miles, there was a station where the rider could change horses. Only two minutes were allowed for the change. Riders usually changed horses three times before they handed their saddlebags over to the next rider. Then, they waited in the station until the mail came in from the other direction so they could carry it back on their return trip.

Everything about the Pony Express was designed for speed. The ponies were the strongest and fastest mustangs

Facts and Figures

There were 80 riders and 500 horses used in the Pony Express. Each rider rode from 30 to 100 miles. Once, in an emergency, a rider carried the mail 280 miles!

Pony Express riders were allowed only two minutes to change horses. In his painting called *Changing Horses*, Frederic Remington shows what this quick change was like.

The Thomas Gilcrease Institute of American History and Art, Tulsa, Oklahoma

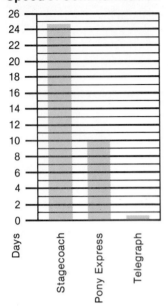

Speed of Communication

What does this graph tell you about the speed of communication?

What's in a Name?

Samuel Morse was an American artist and inventor who lived in the 1800s. He invented a code that uses dots and dashes to stand for each letter of the alphabet. This code is used to send telegraph messages. The dots and dashes become short and long sounds carried on the telegraph wire. In American Morse code, the first three letters of the alphabet are

A • —
B — • • •
C • • •

that could be found. The riders were usually young, small, and lightweight. The saddles were much lighter than most. And letters sent by Pony Express had to be written on paper as light as tissue paper. It cost ten dollars per ounce to send a letter by Pony Express.

The horses and riders of the Pony Express had to face many dangers. It was easy to miss the trail, especially after dark. There were wolves and stampeding buffalo to avoid. And sometimes Indians attacked them. But the riders were determined to get the mail through. In some instances, when a rider was knocked off his pony or killed, the pony still galloped on to the next station, carrying the mail. During the time the Pony Express ran, only one mail packet was lost.

This is how one rider, William Campbell, described a Pony Express adventure:

66 The hardest ride I ever had was when I had to spend twenty-four hours in the saddle, carrying the mail one hundred and twenty miles. The snow was from two to three feet deep along the Platte River. The temperature was down to zero. It was impossible to travel more than five miles an hour. Often I had to get off and lead my horse. I met no one on the trail, as even the stages had stopped running. The only way I could tell where the trail lay was to keep an eye on the tall weeds, which showed above the snowdrifts on either side.

There was no rider to go on with the mail when I reached my regular station. The station men refused to go out in such a storm. So I started for the next station, twenty miles away. I reached there at four o'clock in the afternoon, just twenty-four hours from the time I had started. I had used up four horses in making this ride. 99

Even while the Pony Express was running, the **telegraph** lines were slowly coming westward. The telegraph was a system of wires stretching from city to city. Messages in Morse code were sent across these wires using electricity. This kind of communication was very quick. But messages could be sent only to and from places connected by telegraph wires. Many people

106

believed that it was not possible for telegraph wires to cross the entire country, connecting East and West. Other people thought this could work.

In 1860, two companies began to set up telegraph wires between California and Nebraska. One worry was that the Indians might break down the wires. But a man named Edward Creighton [krī′ ton] had an idea. He invited a Shoshone [shō shō′ nē] chief to talk over the telegraph to a Sioux chief who was miles away. Neither chief really believed what was happening. They agreed to meet halfway to make sure they hadn't been tricked. Of course, they found out that the telegraph really worked, and they were impressed. This may be one reason that most Indians left the wires alone.

On October 24, 1861, the telegraph wires were finally completed, and a message was sent all the way from Washington, D.C., to San Francisco. It took the message only a few minutes to cross thousands of miles!

A few days later, after running only one year, the Pony Express was shut down. It was no longer needed. Regular mail went by stage, and fast messages came over the telegraph wires.

The new communication system meant that California was no longer cut off from the rest of the country. Californians got news in minutes instead of days or months. Business people could order goods and get messages to workers quickly. California was no longer an "island."

Holding a pencil in one hand and resting his other hand on the telegraph key, this telegrapher is ready to send or receive a message.

Checking Up

1. Why was the Pony Express started? How long did it take the Pony Express to go from California to Missouri?

2. Why was the Pony Express shut down?

3. Describe how messages were sent by telegraph.

4. How did the telegraph change life for Californians?

Building Social Studies Skills

Using an Encyclopedia

1 You want to find out more about the telegraph. You want to learn who invented it and how it works. Where do you start?

Follow the Reference Worm.

2 Telegraph begins with the letter T. Find the encyclopedia **volume**, or book, marked T.

3 **Key words** appear in the upper corners of encyclopedia pages. They help you find what you're looking for.

telegraph
telegram
Teheran

4 Here's the article on the telegraph. It's a long one. Where's the information you want?

telegraph

Telegraph

Invention

History

5 **Subheadings** help. They are these small titles in dark print. Where do you think you'll find information on who invented the telegraph?

telegraph

Telegraph

Morse
electric pulse
Invention
The telegraph
Samuel F

6 telegraph

The Telegraph Today

How It Works

Where do you think you'll find information on how the telegraph works?

7 You've found it! There's even a drawing that shows you how to make a telegraph set.

8 And there's a chart showing the code that's used to send telegraph messages.

9 You've learned a lot about the telegraph. But have you found *all* the information the encyclopedia has to offer about the telegraph?

10 No! There's more. And there are two ways to find it.

11 First, look for **secondary references**. "What," you ask, "is a secondary reference?"

12 Here's one kind of secondary reference.

One of the inventors of the telegraph was Samuel F. B. Morse. See MORSE, SAMUEL F. B.

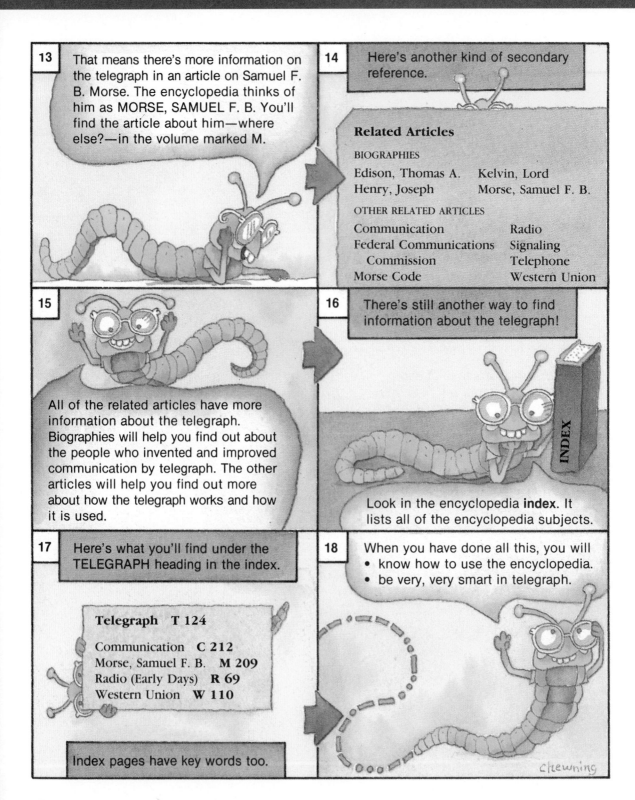

13 That means there's more information on the telegraph in an article on Samuel F. B. Morse. The encyclopedia thinks of him as MORSE, SAMUEL F. B. You'll find the article about him—where else?—in the volume marked M.

14 Here's another kind of secondary reference.

Related Articles

BIOGRAPHIES
Edison, Thomas A.   Kelvin, Lord
Henry, Joseph   Morse, Samuel F. B.

OTHER RELATED ARTICLES
Communication   Radio
Federal Communications   Signaling
  Commission   Telephone
Morse Code   Western Union

15 All of the related articles have more information about the telegraph. Biographies will help you find out about the people who invented and improved communication by telegraph. The other articles will help you find out more about how the telegraph works and how it is used.

16 There's still another way to find information about the telegraph!

Look in the encyclopedia **index**. It lists all of the encyclopedia subjects.

17 Here's what you'll find under the TELEGRAPH heading in the index.

Telegraph   T 124

Communication   **C 212**
Morse, Samuel F. B.   **M 209**
Radio (Early Days)   **R 69**
Western Union   **W 110**

Index pages have key words too.

18 When you have done all this, you will
- know how to use the encyclopedia.
- be very, very smart in telegraph.

Chewning

110

Write your answers on paper. Do not write in the book.

Using Key Words

From the list below, choose the term that best completes each of the sentences. Write it on your paper.

freight   secondary reference
index   subheading
key word   telegraph
overland   volume

1. A book in a set of encyclopedias is called a _____.
2. The _____ lists all the subjects in an encyclopedia.
3. A different article in which you can find more information on an encyclopedia subject is called a _____.
4. Goods transported across the country by ship, train, or other means are called _____.
5. The _____ is a system for sending messages in code by wire.
6. A _____ is a small title in dark print that will help you find the information you want in an encyclopedia.
7. The _____ at the top of an encyclopedia page will help you find an article.
8. Land routes across the nation used by the Butterfield Stage were known as _____ routes.

Reviewing Main Ideas

Write "true" for the sentences that are true. Write "false" for the sentences that are false.

1. Communication and transportation linked East and West.
2. The Pony Express could carry mail faster than a stagecoach.
3. Stagecoaches and steamboats were not important to business.
4. The telegraph replaced the Pony Express for carrying messages.

Thinking Things Over

The speed of communication by telegraph changed people's lives. What inventions since the telegraph have changed people's lives? How?

Practicing Skills

Below are three encyclopedia subheadings. Beside each question number, write the subheading under which you would find information to answer that question.

Types of Maps
Map Language
History of Maps

1. What is the oldest known map?
2. What kinds of information are shown on a map by color?
3. In what ways are maps and globes different?

Theodore Judah

The Railroad Changes California

With the telegraph, California now had good communication with the East. But transportation was still a problem. Stagecoaches could hold very few people and packages. This means of travel was still difficult and expensive. And shipping freight from one side of the continent to the other was even slower and more expensive—whether the goods were shipped by ocean or by land, in wagons pulled by oxen. Another way to transport people and freight was needed.

Lesson 1 Building the Transcontinental Railroad

Theodore Judah had an idea of how to transport people across the country. His idea was to build a railroad across the whole continent.

At this time, there were no railroads west of the Mississippi. Many people thought it would be impossible to lay railroad track across the Sierra Nevada and the Rocky Mountains. Judah didn't agree. He made maps of a possible route for a **transcontinental** railroad. He even went to Washington, D.C., to try to get money for building the railroad. But Congress couldn't agree on a route. Judah came back to California empty-handed.

Theodore Judah didn't give up. He tried to persuade Californians to put money in the railroad. Finally, some people decided to **invest** in Judah's dream. Among them were Collis P. Huntington and Mark Hopkins, who owned a hardware store; Leland Stanford, who had a grocery store; and Charles Crocker, who owned a dry-goods store.

transcontinental, crossing a continent.

invest, to put money in a thing or idea in order to make more money.

The Big Four

On June 28, 1861, Judah and his four new backers set up the Central Pacific Railroad Company. The next year, they got some help from the government. Congress agreed to lend any company building a transcontinental railroad $16,000 to build each mile of track on flat ground and $48,000 to build each mile in the mountains. Also, Congress promised to give the railroad company much of the land that the tracks passed through. The railroad companies could expect to make money by selling this land to settlers. Soon the Central Pacific began laying track east from Sacramento, California. Meanwhile, another railroad company, the Union Pacific, began laying track west from Omaha, Nebraska.

The Central Pacific made money quickly from the government and from land sales. Soon the four investors became rich. Now known as the Big Four, these men were not always honest. To get more money from the government, the Big Four claimed that some flat land was in the mountains. They even began to talk about stopping the tracks at the Nevada state line. Then they could just take their quick profits.

Theodore Judah did not like this at all. He wanted to work honestly. And his dream was of a railroad stretching across the entire nation. Angry at the Big Four, Judah left for the East Coast to try to get other backers. He wanted to buy out the Big Four. Unluckily for Judah, there was no railroad to take him back east. He had to travel by ship to Panama, where he caught yellow fever. Theodore Judah died. But the Big Four continued to build the railroad.

Central Pacific tracks laid east from Sacramento, California, met Union Pacific tracks laid west from Omaha, Nebraska, at Promontory Point, Utah, to form the transcontinental railroad.

Working on the Transcontinental Railroad

It was difficult to find enough people to do the work of building the railroad. The work was very hard. People had to blast their way through mountains and use pick axes to carve paths around cliffs. They had to carry rocks away from the tracks. Workers had to hammer down the ties and bend metal rails for curved tracks. The work was also dangerous. Many people were hurt or killed while

Railroad workers laid track across rugged mountains and barren deserts.

building the railroad. Some workers died while blasting tunnels. Others fell off cliffs or were swept away by avalanches of snow and ice. Workers died of the cold and of diseases.

Thousands of Chinese were hired to build the Central Pacific. Other workers were from Ireland and Germany. These workers were paid very little money for all their hard work. Yet they did an amazing job. At one time, workers were let down a cliff in baskets to slowly chip away a ledge. In digging tunnels, the workers were often able to dig only a few inches each day. During the cold winters, the workers had to dig tunnels through the snow just to get to their work. They even built almost forty miles of wooden sheds to cover the tracks and keep them clear of snow.

The Transcontinental Railroad Is Finished

On May 10, 1869, eight years after the railroad was started, the Central Pacific and Union Pacific tracks were joined. They met at Promontory Point in Utah. The last spike used to hold the track was made of pure gold. The whole nation celebrated. Guns were fired, and church bells were rung. At last, California had been joined to the rest of the United States by the fastest, least expensive means of transportation available.

Checking Up

1. Which two railroad companies laid track for the transcontinental railroad?

2. How did the Big Four expect to make money from building the railroad?

3. Name at least two dangers involved in building the railroad.

4. What groups of people were hired as workers?

5. We say the transcontinental railroad joined the East and the West. Why was this important to California?

114

Lesson 2   The Power of the Railroad

The transcontinental railroad opened California to the East. Hundreds of people could ride in a train at one time, so the ride was less expensive. Also, trains were safer and more comfortable than stagecoaches. They weren't as likely to be stopped by bad weather or Indians. The ride was faster because trains don't have to stop for food or rest like horses.

The railroad was even more important in transporting freight. Californians could send food, leather, and wool back east more quickly and at less expense. They could also receive eastern products more easily. This was especially helpful to businesses and farmers.

The Big Four Get Bigger

Once the transcontinental railroad was built, Huntington, Hopkins, Crocker, and Stanford were rich. But the Big Four were not satisfied. They began to build new railroads inside California. They also began to buy other railroads, steamboat lines, and land. In the end, the Big Four controlled all of the railroads as far north as Portland, Oregon, and as far south and east as New Orleans, Louisiana. They also controlled every means of transportation in the state. They had a **monopoly** on transportation. They could charge whatever they liked. People who needed to travel or to ship goods had no choice but to pay their high prices!

monopoly, complete control of a product or service.

The railroad company had become so powerful that no one could stand up to it. Not even the government was safe from its control. The Big Four gave money and railroad tickets to state officials in return for helping the railroads. The Big Four also got their own workers to run for office. In these ways, the Big Four made sure that the laws favored the railroads.

The Story of Mussel Slough

The railroad planned to build a new line near Mussel Slough, in the San Joaquin Valley. As usual, the railroad was promised the land near the tracks. Meanwhile, settlers were told that they could farm this land and buy it from the railroad later. The price, settlers were told, would be $2.50 an acre and up. Everyone understood that the land was then worth between $2.50 and $5.00 an acre.

The settlers found the land in Mussel Slough terrible. It was too dry in some parts and too wet in others. They worked hard to build irrigation ditches, fences, and houses.

After a few years, Mussel Slough became good farming land. Then the railroad came to the settlers and said that they must pay between $17 and $40 an acre for the land. Otherwise they would have to leave. The settlers couldn't afford these high prices, and they were very angry. They pointed out that the land was worth so much money only because they had worked hard to improve it.

The settlers took their case to court. But the courts decided that the railroad could charge what it wanted.

People began to call the railroad "the Octopus" because its tentacles seemed to be strangling California.

116

Then two men named Crow and Hart bought some of the farmed land at the new high prices. The settlers, however, still considered the land theirs.

On May 11, 1880, Crow and Hart went with a United States marshal to claim the land they had bought. They were armed with guns. A group of armed settlers met the three men. At first, the settlers were polite. But they said that they would not allow their land to be taken. No one is quite sure what happened next. A horse reared and bumped into the marshal. Someone fired a shot. Then everyone seemed to be shooting. When the shooting stopped, seven men were dead.

The settlers gained nothing by fighting. Five were sent to jail, and most of them lost their land to the railroad. But this Battle of Mussel Slough made the railroad even more unpopular with the people of California.

Years later, in 1910, Californians finally elected a governor and lawmakers who were willing to stand up to the railroad. The new government changed the laws of California to take away some of the railroad's power. Today, both the state and the nation have laws to protect people's rights. No business can become as powerful as the railroad was in the 1800s. No business can use its power to control an entire state or the nation.

Checking Up

1. How did the railroad help to change life for Californians?

2. Why were the Big Four able to charge high prices for transportation?

3. Why were the settlers of Mussel Slough angry with the railroad?

4. What steps did the settlers of Mussel Slough take to protect their land? Did they succeed?

5. What, do you think, could happen today if there were no laws to control the power of business?

Be a Wise Consumer

If you walked to school today, you used up your shoes—a little. If you rode to school in a car or on a bus, you used up a little bit of the seat of your jeans—and some gasoline too. Using things up makes you a consumer. Spending money makes you a consumer too.

Consumers are important. Without them, there'd be no need for farms or factories or stores. Because consumers are so important, government and business want to protect them.

What is there to protect consumers *against*? Here are some examples.

- Your mom buys a new car. The design of the brakes makes them unsafe. Consumers need to be protected against unsafe products.
- You buy a hamburger. The meat has not been stored properly. It makes you sick. Consumers need to be protected against unhealthful products.
- Your family sees an ad for a very low-priced video cassette recorder. At the store, you find that the recorder has been sold. The salesperson tries to sell you an expensive recorder instead. Consumers need to be protected against false advertising.

A state service to protect consumers is the California Department of Consumer Affairs. In large cities, the department is listed in the telephone book under *Consumer Complaint and Protection*. Usually there are fifty or more subheadings to help consumers find the offices they need. Some examples are Auto Repair, Banks, Dentists, Foods, and TV Repair. If your family had a problem with an auto mechanic, you'd call the number listed for Auto Repair to get help.

Here are some tips to make you a wise consumer.

- Shop around. Compare prices and quality. If you have doubts, wait; think it over.
- Save the sales slip.
- If there's a problem with a product, take it back with the sales slip to the store. Explain the problem to the sales clerk.
- If the clerk can't help you, ask to talk to the manager. If the problem is still not solved, tell the manager that you plan to report the problem to the Department of Consumer Affairs.
- Call the department and ask for help in solving your problem.

Most adventures in Consumerland will be happy ones, but it's good to know how to get help if you need it.

Reviewing Chapter 10

Write your answers on paper. Do not write in the book.

Using Key Words

From the list below, choose the word that best completes each of the sentences. Write it on your paper.

invest
monopoly
transcontinental

1. The Big Four's control of all the railroads is an example of _____.
2. To put money into an idea is to _____ in it.
3. A railroad that crosses a continent is called a _____ line.

Reviewing Main Ideas

Choose the ending that makes each sentence true. Write its letter beside the question number on your paper.

1. It took a long time to build the transcontinental railroad because
   a. the Big Four ran out of money.
   b. no one knew how to build it.
   c. the work was difficult.
2. Because the Big Four controlled transportation in California
   a. travel and transporting freight cost less.
   b. travel and transporting freight cost more.
   c. travel and transporting freight were no longer a problem.

3. The building of the transcontinental railroad was important because it
   a. made the Big Four rich.
   b. ended the separation between the East and California.
   c. made transportation in California easier and faster.
4. Because the railroad became too powerful
   a. we now have laws to stop any business from having a monopoly.
   b. other kinds of transportation today are better.
   c. the railroad is no longer an important kind of transportation.

Thinking Things Over

The Big Four became very powerful and were able to influence people who made and carried out laws. How do rich people influence people in government today?

Practicing Skills

Write the letters of the events listed below in the correct order.
a. The settlers lost their case in court.
b. The government passed laws to protect people's rights.
c. The settlers were allowed to farm Mussel Slough.
d. The settlers were told the land would cost from $17 to $40 an acre.

Growing Up in California

In this chapter you will learn about children who grew up in California more than one hundred years ago. In many ways, their lives were very different from yours. As you read, think about the ways in which children's lives have changed.

Lesson 1   The San Francisco Newsboys

During the Gold Rush days, San Francisco became a big city almost overnight. And when the Gold Rush ended, people stayed in San Francisco because they liked the city. The gold from the mines had helped to build grand hotels, fine stores, and beautiful theaters. There were plays, operas, and dances for people to go to. San Francisco was a rich and busy city.

Many boys living in this rich city needed to earn money. Some were orphans. Their parents had died on the long journey to California. Other boys had to support their families because their parents could not work. Selling papers was one of the best jobs a boy could get. This was because San Franciscans would pay high prices for newspapers. Newsboys could make as much as twenty-five dollars a day. This was a lot of money then, and many newsboys became quite rich.

One newsboy wrote:

66 Never before in the history of the world were seen such a jolly, happy, well-dressed set of newsboys. As a rule, they were from twelve to twenty years of age; bright, sharp, good-looking, and enterprising. Nearly all wore fine clothes; many wore gold rings, elegant breast-pins and valuable diamonds.99

People

One newsboy, Joe Gates, made money by selling more than just newspapers. He also sold food such as oranges and peanuts. One day Joe had a chance to ride a hot-air balloon. He traveled fifty miles in the balloon and was the first person to see California from the air.

Joe used his balloon ride to make even more money. On stage and in print, he earned four thousand dollars telling about his ride.

120

Because of the Gold Rush, San Francisco became a big, rich, and busy city almost overnight.

Each day the newsboys raced to get the newspapers from a printer. Then they ran all over the city shouting, "Extra! Extra!" to let people know that they had the latest news.

When they were not working, the newsboys often hung around the streets in groups. Many visitors in San Francisco were surprised to see these groups of well-dressed boys. The newsboys played games and talked. Sometimes they went into expensive restaurants and ordered fine meals. Other times they raced their horses along the streets of San Francisco. This was against the law, for the city had speed limits even then—speed limits for horses!

One thing the newsboys did not do was go to school. Many children in those days didn't attend school. There weren't many free, public schools then. So getting a school education cost a lot of money. However, most of the newsboys saved enough money to go to school when they were older. Many became lawyers, judges, and businessmen. Some of the most successful men in San Francisco got their starts as newsboys.

Checking Up

1. Why was San Francisco a rich city in the late 1800s?

2. What made it possible for some San Francisco newsboys to become rich?

3. Name two ways in which your life is different from the lives of the San Francisco newsboys.

Before radio and television were invented, people had to read newspapers to find out what was going on. In San Francisco in the late 1800s, newspapers were not delivered to homes, and they were not sold at corner newsstands. People could buy papers only from the newsboys. As you might imagine, the newsboys were very important—and some of them became rich as well.

Lesson 2 A Little Girl of Old California

Sarah Bixby Smith was born on her father's sheep ranch in Northern California. But when she was seven years old, her family moved to Los Angeles. In the 1870s, Los Angeles was a small, sleepy town. It was nothing like the big, bustling city of San Francisco. The dirt streets were dusty in the summer and muddy when it rained. The houses were very far apart. They were so far apart that Sarah's family had enough land to keep chickens and a cow in the backyard. Sarah described Southern California as "a very empty land, empty of people and towns, of trees and cultivated fields."

Sarah went to a small private school in Los Angeles. There were ten students and one teacher. Later, when she was ten years old, she went to a public school.

When she wasn't in school, Sarah enjoyed visiting her cousins at their nearby sheep ranches. Sarah often went to a ranch in Los Cerritos. Her aunt, uncle, and cousins lived in a long, low adobe house. They owned more than thirty thousand sheep and grew oranges, lemons, figs, and grapes in the gardens. Each day, a sheep was killed to feed all of the workers on the ranch.

Sarah and her cousins liked to play in the barns and sheds of the ranch. They also enjoyed farm animals, especially the horses. Sarah's most favorite time of the year was the sheep shearing. This was when the wool was cut from the sheep. Skilled Mexican American sheep-shearers came to live on the ranch during this time.

Sarah described her life growing up in Los Angeles in two books. One was called *A Little Girl of Old California*. Sarah also wrote poems about her childhood. Here is one of her poems:

Los Angeles grew more slowly than San Francisco. In 1885, horses pulled carriages and wagons along still unpaved Spring Street in Los Angeles.

Watermelons
It is shearing time and summer,
And hot on the dusty floor.
There are fat round watermelons
Outside the wool-barn door,
Melons for sale for a nickel,

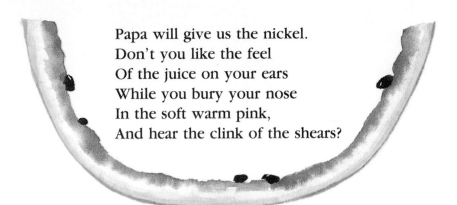

Papa will give us the nickel.
Don't you like the feel
Of the juice on your ears
While you bury your nose
In the soft warm pink,
And hear the clink of the shears?

During the 1880s, Los Angeles grew to be a big city. People **migrated**, or moved, there from the East Coast for many reasons. Some people came because the climate of Southern California was thought to make people healthier. Other people came to make money in business and farming. The railroads liked this migration. More people in California meant more people buying railroad tickets and land. The railroads kept cutting the price of the trip from the Midwest to California so more people would come. Finally, they made a special offer. For one day, the trip cost only one dollar! So many people came to California at this time that their migration started what was known as the **boom** of the 1880s.

Suddenly, the many people coming to Southern California needed houses. The ranch lands on which Sarah grew up were sold for housing. Southern California was no longer "empty of people and towns."

Sarah lived long enough to see another boom in the 1920s, when even more people came to live in Southern California. By the end of Sarah Bixby Smith's life, Los Angeles was a larger city than San Francisco.

Sarah Bixby Smith

boom, sudden fast growth in size or activity.

Checking Up

1. How did Southern California change in the 1880s?

2. How was Sarah's life different from yours? Tell at least two ways.

3. Why did railroads want people to come to California?

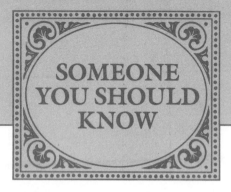
Don Cristobal Aguilar

Among the Spanish and Mexicans of early California, the title *don* [dôn] was a sign of respect and honor. As a community leader, Don Cristobal Aguilar [ä gē lär ′] earned the respect of Los Angeles voters for a quarter of a century.

As a boy growing up in the 1820s, Cristobal worked and played on his father's rancho. He went to school when he could. But at that time, Los Angeles had no regular schools. Sometimes retired soldiers would teach for a time and then move on. It must have been frustrating to want to learn and not be able to go to school.

It might have been that feeling that led Cristobal Aguilar to a career of working for the people of Los Angeles. He became a teacher and later was chosen to be a member of the board of education. This board set up regular schools in Los Angeles.

Then in 1850, Cristobal Aguilar became the first Hispanic elected to the Los Angeles City Council. He was reelected three times.

In 1866, Cristobal Aguilar was elected mayor of Los Angeles. While he was mayor, some interesting and important things happened. Los Angeles got its first fire engine. (It was called an "engine" because it used a steam engine to pump water for the fire hoses.) The city got its first bank. It also got its first ice factory.

Don Cristobal Aguilar served two terms as mayor of the city. But at that time in Los Angeles, there was a job that some people thought was even more important than that of the mayor. Somebody had to be responsible for seeing that water was brought from wells and nearby rivers to the city. The water was carried in aqueducts called *zanjas* [sän ′häs]. The person responsible was called a *zanjero* [sän her ′ ō]. Don Cristobal Aguilar was elected zanjero for two terms. He kept the water flowing to Los Angeles.

As a teacher, member of the board of education, city councilman, mayor, and zanjero, Don Cristobal Aguilar was a good leader and a good citizen of Los Angeles.

This waterwheel was used to raise water from a Los Angeles *zanja*.

Write your answers on paper. Do not write in the book.

Using Key Words

From the list below, choose the word that best completes each of the sentences. Write it on your paper.

boom
migrate

1. When many people move from one area to another, we say that they _____ to the new area.
2. A sudden growth in size or activity is called a _____.

Reviewing Main Ideas

Complete each sentence to make a true statement.

1. Newsboys made a lot of money selling papers because _____.
2. Many newsboys saved their money to _____.
3. San Francisco's beautiful theaters, grand hotels, and fine stores were built with money from _____.
4. The railroads' main reason for attracting people to California during the 1880s was to sell them _____ and _____.
5. Much of Southern California's ranch land was sold for housing because _____.
6. By the 1920s, _____ was a larger city than _____.

Thinking Things Over

The Gold Rush changed San Francisco almost overnight. Los Angeles grew more slowly. In which city would you rather have lived during the change? Why?

Practicing Skills

Use the map to match a latitude and longitude with each city listed below. Write the correct letter beside the city number on your paper.

1. San Francisco   a. 36° N, 119° W
2. Los Angeles   b. 37° N, 122° W
3. Fresno   c. 34° N, 118° W

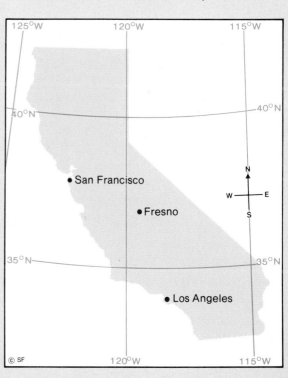

What Do You Know?

Write your answers on paper. Do not write in the book.

Words to Know

From the list below, choose the term that best completes each of the sentences. Write it on your paper.

ancestor	migrate
boom	monopoly
conflict	overland
deed	reservation
freight	subheading
index	telegraph
invest	transcontinental
key word	volume

1. A disagreement between people is called a _____.
2. Goods transported by train, truck, ship, or aircraft are called _____.
3. To move from one area of the country to another is to _____.
4. When the railroad had complete control of California transportation, it had a _____.
5. A highway that stretches from the west coast to the east coast is _____.
6. To put money into a business is to _____ in it.
7. A list of all the subjects in a book is called the _____.
8. One book in a series is called a _____.
9. You can find an article in an encyclopedia faster if you look at the top of the page for the _____.
10. To prove land ownership today, one must have a _____.
11. A _____ is a sudden growth in size or activity.
12. A very old member of your family tree is your _____.
13. A word that means *by land* or *across the land* is _____.
14. An area of land set aside for an Indian tribe is called a _____.
15. To find the exact information you want in an encyclopedia article, look for the right _____.
16. The _____ is a way of sending messages by wire.

Ideas to Know

Write "true" for the sentences that are true. Write "false" for the sentences that are false.

1. The American settlers, the Indians, and the Californios got along well together.
2. The Americans believed that whoever farmed the land should own it.
3. After California became a state, there were more Californios than Americans or Indians.
4. The Modocs enjoyed life on the Oregon reservation.

5. After the Pony Express began carrying messages, the telegraph was no longer necessary.
6. The telegraph and the railroad were important to California because they linked the state with the East.
7. The first four railroads built in California were known as the Big Four.
8. Theodore Judah's dream was to build a railroad that would connect California with the East.
9. The power of the railroad helped to make poor farmers and merchants wealthy.
10. Much of the work of laying the transcontinental railroad track was done by Chinese workers.
11. Tax money from the United States government was used to pay for improved transportation and communication between California and the East.
12. Modern laws prevent big companies from having as much power as the Big Four had.
13. The Land Act forced the Californios to prove that they owned their land.
14. Southern California's climate was one cause of a boom in the 1880s.
15. After the boom, California was "empty of people and towns."

Using What You Know

Use the volume list below to find the encyclopedia volume in which you would look for the answer to each of the following questions. Beside each question number on your paper, write the correct volume letter. Next to the letter, write the name of the topic you would look under.

Volume List

B	F	J	R
C	G	M	S
E	H	P	T

1. When was the first railroad built?
2. How long did the Gold Rush last?
3. Who was Collis P. Huntington?
4. Who invented the stagecoach? When was the first one built?
5. Who were the Big Four?
6. How long did the Pony Express run?
7. Is more than one code used on the telegraph?
8. What was the Modoc War?
9. To what industry besides railroads was the Huntington family important?
10. On what famous hill in San Francisco was the Mark Hopkins Hotel built?
11. When and where was Theodore Judah born?

Unit 4

Using California's Resources

Chapter 12
Using the Land

Chapter 13
Water

Chapter 14
The Booming Industries

California is a beautiful state. It is also a rich state. It has clean water and rich soil for growing crops. It has forests of trees that can be cut into lumber. Under the soil are oil and minerals that can be made into things people need and use.

People have always made choices about how to use these things. Choices made yesterday affect the way we are living now. The choices we make today will affect our lives tomorrow.

Chapter

12

Lesson 1 Growing Crops
Lesson 2 Mineral Resources

Using the Land

Land is a very valuable **resource** that is used in many ways. People farm the land for food and lumber. People dig up land for minerals and drill for oil. People also build homes, factories, and roads on the land. Some land is left in its natural state. It's important to make wise choices about using the land.

Today, California ranks first among the fifty states in the value of its agricultural products. Its most important farm products are milk, cream, and cattle. Its most important crops are cotton and grapes. Other foods grown in California include almonds, lettuce, oranges, peaches, rice, strawberries, sugar beets, tomatoes, walnuts, and wheat. On the map, each of these foods is pictured in an area where it is grown. Most of the foods are grown in other areas as well.

Foods Grown in California

Prunes
Apples
Rice
Tomatoes
Pears
Corn
Asparagus
Walnuts
Peaches
Apricots
Grapes
Almonds
Plums
Lettuce
Cantaloupes
Carrots
Broccoli
Potatoes
Olives
Lemons
Grapefruit
Sugar beets
Oranges
Tangerines
Strawberries
Wheat
Avocados

© SF

Lesson 1   Growing Crops

By the 1900s, farming was one of the most important activities in California. Many kinds of vegetables, fruits, nuts, grains, and dairy goods were produced here. Today, farming, or **agriculture**, is still important. In fact, more than one-tenth of the nation's crops are grown on California land. The map on page 130 shows some of the many different crops grown in California today.

Growing Oranges—A Case Study

Orange trees have always grown well in the mild California climate. The first California oranges were grown by the friars in mission gardens. These oranges were small, dry, and sour. Other people also planted orange trees, but the fruit they produced was little better than the mission oranges.

In the late 1800s, Luther and Eliza Tibbets helped to change the California orange. The Tibbetses grew oranges in Riverside, California. One day Eliza Tibbets heard about a kind of orange grown in Brazil. This type of orange, called a navel orange, was large, sweet, and had very few seeds. Eliza wrote to a friend who worked in the Department of Agriculture in Washington, D.C. She asked him where she could get some navel orange trees. Soon the Tibbetses received three trees from Brazil.

People loved the size and flavor of the oranges from the Tibbetses new trees. Many orange growers wanted to produce the better fruit. The Tibbetses sold thousands of cuttings from their trees to other growers. Soon the navel orange became the major orange crop in California.

Women worked in citrus packing plants. They put oranges and other fruits into boxes for shipment back east.

The boxes in which the fruit was packed carried labels such as this one. These colorful labels told what association the growers of the fruit belonged to.

Citrus crops are important to California today. This state is a major producer of the nation's oranges and grows more than three-fourths of its lemons.

History Update

Using one insect to control another is called biological pest control. Spraying plants with insect poisons is called chemical pest control. Biological control is often cheaper and does not pollute the air, soil, or water. Today, many farmers choose biological methods to control the pests that threaten their crops. But sometimes chemical pest control is still necessary.

People in the East were eager to buy the delicious California oranges. But transportation was a problem. Oranges had to be shipped quickly because they spoil. For this reason, California growers sent their oranges east by train. This cost a lot of money. So all of the California orange growers joined together. As a group, they hired whole trains to send their oranges east. In this way, they got better rates from the railroads.

Soon oranges became very important to California. Then the orange trees were attacked by tiny insects that caused cottony-cushion scale. These insects damaged or even killed the trees.

The orange growers tried everything they could think of to get rid of the scale. They tried to wash off the insects. They tried to kill them by spraying chemicals on the trees. But nothing worked. It looked like orange growing in California would have to stop.

Then a man who worked in the United States Department of Agriculture had an idea. He visited Australia, where there was very little cottony-cushion scale. There, he found a small ladybug that ate the insects and their eggs. He shipped these ladybugs to California. Within eighteen months, the cottony-cushion scale was under control. California orange growers grew healthy trees and produced delicious fruit once again.

Checking Up

1. Name five kinds of foods that are produced in California.

2. Why did oranges become an important crop in California?

3. Why was transportation a problem for orange growers in California? How did they solve the problem?

4. Do you think transporting food products could be a problem for other farmers too? Why or why not?

5. Explain how the scale was finally controlled.

Lesson 2 Mineral Resources

California is rich in mineral resources. A **mineral** is a nonliving material, such as gold, that is obtained from the ground. California's most important minerals are oil and natural gas. But many other minerals have also been found in the state. The map below shows these other important mineral resources.

Sometimes minerals are found beneath good farming land. Then, there is a choice between growing crops on the land and digging it up for the minerals. Other times minerals are found in beautiful, wild parts of the state. Then, people must choose between protecting the natural beauty and mining the minerals.

Today, Death Valley is a national monument because many people think that the desert landscape is beautiful.

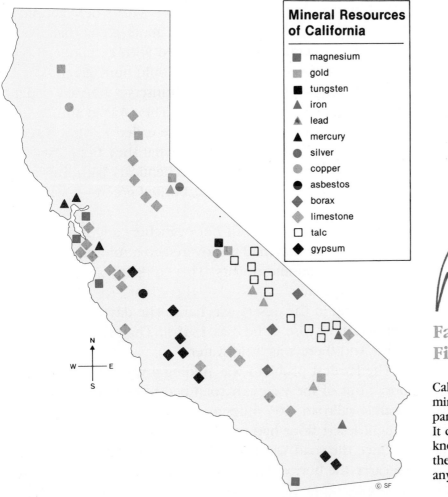

Mineral Resources of California

- ◼ magnesium
- ◻ gold
- ◼ tungsten
- ▲ iron
- ▲ lead
- ▲ mercury
- ● silver
- ● copper
- ● asbestos
- ◆ borax
- ◆ limestone
- ☐ talc
- ◆ gypsum

© SF

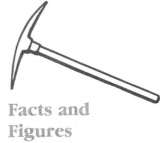

Facts and Figures

California is richer in minerals than any other part of the United States. It contains six hundred known kinds. Forty-five of them are not found anywhere else.

133

But in the late 1800s, when a mineral called borax was first found in Death Valley, few people thought of that place as beautiful. In fact, many thought it was as horrible as its name.

Borax Mining in Death Valley—A Case Study

Rosie and Aaron Winters lived in Ash Meadows on the edge of Death Valley. They were poor ranchers who led a lonely life two hundred miles from the nearest town. They made the few visitors who came their way feel very welcome.

One evening a **prospector** came by. He described the borax beds that he had seen in Nevada. He also told the Winterses that people could make a lot of money by mining borax. Borax was used to make washing powders, soaps, and other things.

Aaron Winters listened closely. He had seen beds in Death Valley that matched the prospector's description. The prospector told the Winterses about a test that would show if a mineral was borax. Mixed with certain chemicals and set on fire, borax would burn green.

When the prospector left, the Winterses hurried to get the chemicals needed for the test. Then Aaron and Rosie went across Death Valley to a place called Furnace Creek. There they collected a sample of what they hoped was borax. The Winterses mixed the chemicals with this sample and set a match to it. It burned green—it was borax!

The Winterses were not poor ranchers any more. They sold the borax they had discovered to a mining company for twenty thousand dollars. This company set to work to produce borax.

Working in the desert was hard. The daytime temperatures rose as high as 134° F. The nights were cold. And there was little water.

The hardest problem was finding a way to get the borax out of the valley. A road had to be built to the nearest railroad, 165 miles away. To build this road, the rough desert floor had to be smoothed out.

Once the road was finished, special wagons were built to carry the borax. The wagons were huge and heavy. It

prospector, person who explores an area looking for gold, silver, or other mineral resources.

By the Way

Borax is used in a wide variety of products. It is used in washing powders, water softeners, and soaps. It is used to make shiny glazes for stoves, sinks, and dishes. It is even used in making glass, tanning leather, and making paper.

took eighteen mules and two horses to pull them. Some people still remember these "twenty-mule" teams.

Borax is no longer mined in Death Valley. It has been found in other places in the West, places where it is easier for people to live and work.

Even though eighteen mules and two horses were used to pull borax wagons, they were called "twenty-mule" teams.

Checking Up

1. What is a mineral?

2. Name two minerals that are found in California.

3. What was borax used for?

4. How were Rosie and Aaron Winters able to tell that they had discovered borax?

5. What two things did the mining company have to do to take the borax out of Death Valley?

6. Did borax mining in Death Valley take away good farming land? Explain your answer.

EARTHQUAKES

Sometimes we humans are taught an important lesson: we can't always control the environment. On the morning of April 18, 1906, the people of San Francisco learned that lesson.

The lesson began shortly after five in the morning. For nearly a full minute, the earth trembled. The usually solid hills shook, tumbling houses, stores, and churches into the streets.

During that frightening minute, San Franciscans wondered if the world had come to an end. In some places, it was impossible to stand—impossible even to crawl. Inside buildings, cabinets and beds were thrown about like doll furniture. Outside, bricks rained down from tall buildings.

When the shaking stopped, there was silence. Frightened people wandered into the streets and saw piles of rubble.

Some people thought the earth had been struck by a huge meteor from space. But it was really an earthquake. An earthquake happens when masses of rock and soil suddenly move along great cracks in the earth. We call these cracks faults.

Once the earthquake stopped, fires started. Fallen electrical wires, broken

San Francisco after the 1906 earthquake

gas lines, and overturned stoves started the fires. Five hundred city blocks were burned, and twenty-eight thousand buildings were destroyed. It was hard to fight the fires because many water pipes had broken during the earthquake. Finally, soldiers stopped the fires by blowing up buildings in the path of the flames.

The earthquake and fires had killed more than four hundred people. Hundreds of thousands more had no homes. Thousands of businesses were gone. But San Francisco was rebuilt. In three years, twenty thousand new buildings were raised. These buildings were built to stand through the next earthquake.

Since the Great San Francisco Earthquake, Californians have tried to protect themselves from earthquakes. Scientists have studied why earthquakes happen. They have mapped earthquake faults. The state government has made laws so that buildings are built to stand through earthquakes. Students practice drills so that they know what to do during an earthquake. Do *you* know what to do in case of an earthquake?

> Today, how big an earthquake is can be measured. The system for this is called the Richter scale. This scale was developed by Charles F. Richter, a California scientist. Using this scale, scientists have figured that the Great San Francisco earthquake measured 8.3. The biggest earthquake ever measured was 8.9.

California's San Andreas [san an drā əs] Fault

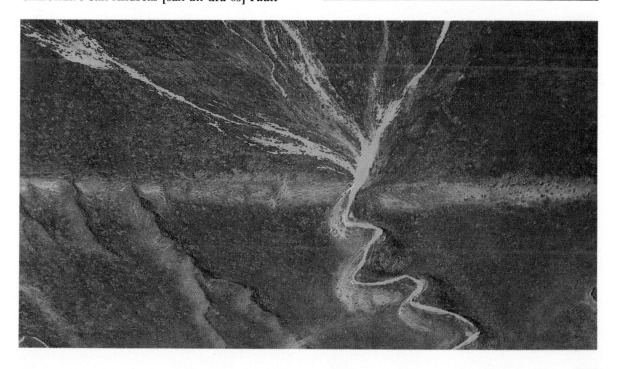

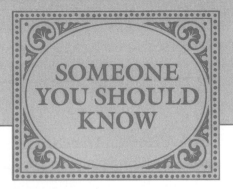
John Muir

John Muir [myür] loved wild places. When he stepped off a boat in San Francisco in 1868, a backpack on his back, he asked a stranger for the quickest way out of town. The stranger asked where he wanted to go. Muir said, "Anywhere that is wild."

John Muir then walked across the San Joaquin Valley toward the Sierra Nevada. He came to Yosemite [yō sem ′ ə tē] Valley, which he loved.

El Capitan, Yosemite National Park

For six years, John Muir explored Yosemite. He found that lumbering and sheep grazing were ruining the beauty of the area. John thought it was important to **conserve** land, to save it in its natural state for all to enjoy. He wanted Yosemite Valley to become a national park. Then laws would protect this land. The trees would not be cut down for lumber. The animals would not be hunted. And the ground would not be mined.

John Muir worked to make his dream happen. He wrote to magazines and newspapers. He wrote to the United States Congress and met with the President. In 1890, Congress created Yosemite and Sequoia [si kwoi ′ ə] national parks. John Muir's dream came true!

138

Reviewing Chapter 12

Write your answers on paper. Do not write in the book.

Using Key Words

From the list below, choose the word that best completes each of the sentences. Write it on your paper.

agriculture   prospector
conserve   resource
mineral

1. If people keep land in its natural state, they _____ the land.
2. A _____ is a nonliving material people dig from the ground.
3. Another word for *miner* is _____.
4. Minerals are a useful _____.
5. Another word for *farming* is _____.

Reviewing Main Ideas

Write "true" for the sentences that are true. Write "false" for the sentences that are false.

1. Foods grown in California are eaten all over the country.
2. Minerals are never found beneath land that is already being used.
3. Minerals must be mined wherever they are found.
4. One reason for conserving our resources is so that people can always benefit from them.
5. Biological pest control was used on cottony-cushion scale because chemicals didn't work.

Thinking Things Over

Redwood National Park has a huge forest of redwood trees. People prize lumber from redwoods for building and decoration. List one good and one bad result of allowing people to cut down trees in a national park.

Practicing Skills

Use this map to answer the questions.
1. What does ● stand for?
2. Name a national recreation area.
3. Which national park is on the coast of California?
4. Name the two national historic sites in California.

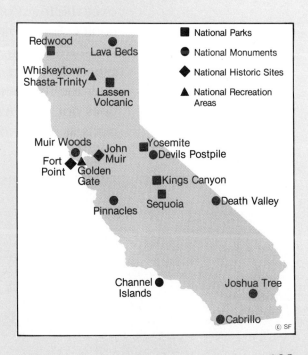

■ National Parks
● National Monuments
◆ National Historic Sites
▲ National Recreation Areas

Redwood
Lava Beds
Whiskeytown-Shasta-Trinity
Lassen Volcanic
Muir Woods
John Muir
Fort Point
Golden Gate
Yosemite
Devils Postpile
Kings Canyon
Pinnacles
Sequoia
Death Valley
Channel Islands
Joshua Tree
Cabrillo
© SF

Water

Many parts of California have little rainfall, but the people all over the state need a lot of water. People in cities need water for factories. In other areas, people need water for farming. And everybody needs water for drinking and cooking and cleaning. How can the state get enough water? Who should get more water, city people or farmers? In this chapter, you will read about some of the choices people have made about using water in California.

Lesson 1   The Geography of Water

The geography of California affects where rain and snow fall in the state. As air moves eastward across the Pacific Ocean, it picks up moisture. This moist air climbs over the low Coast Ranges. As it climbs, the air becomes cooler. Sometimes it is cooled enough to release some moisture as rain. This is why coastal California—especially the north coast—gets so much rain. Passing over the flat Central Valley, the air does not climb, and it does not cool much. So this area gets less rain. But the air cools as it rises over the tall Sierra Nevada. The cool air

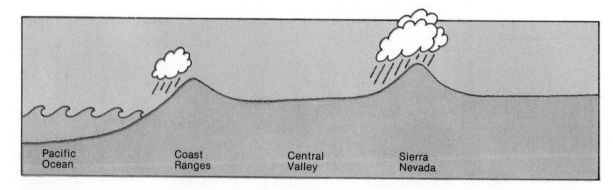

Pacific
Ocean

Coast
Ranges

Central
Valley

Sierra
Nevada

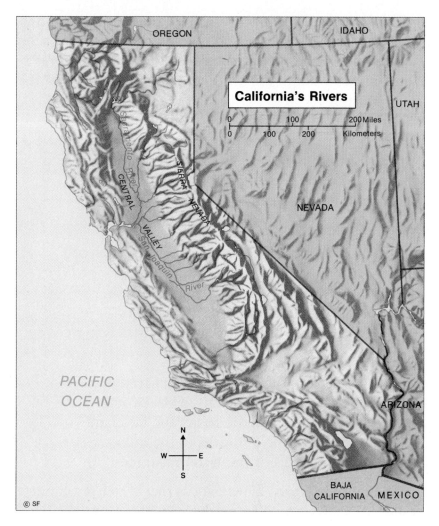

California's Rivers

| 0 | 100 | 200 Miles |
| 0 | 100 | 200 | Kilometers |

As you can see from this map, there are more rivers in Northern California than there are in Southern California. Find the Sacramento River. Each year, this river carries one-third of the runoff from all of California's streams. It has the largest flow of any river in the state.

dumps almost all of its moisture as rain or snow on the Sierra Nevada. Moving east to Nevada, the air is dry. Very little rain falls just east of the mountains.

Some of the rainwater and melting snow is stored in lakes. Some water soaks into the earth, where it is stored underground. But much of the water runs back to the ocean in streams and rivers. Study the map above. You can see that many streams carry water from the Sierra Nevada into the Central Valley. Many of these streams join to make California's major rivers, the Sacramento and San Joaquin rivers. These rivers empty into the Pacific Ocean. In this way, water is cycled through the environment over and over again. It goes from the ocean to the land, where it feeds plants and animals, and then back again to the ocean.

But there are a few problems for Californians. For one thing, most of the rain falls in the winter, and most of the water is needed in the summer. Also, most of California's rain and snow fall in the northern and eastern parts of the state. Most of the water is needed in the southern and western parts. This means that Californians have a problem with **distribution** of water. That is, they have a problem getting the water from where it is to where it's needed. Here are some figures that will help you to understand the problem.

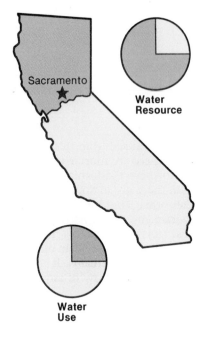

Water Resource

Water Use

The areas north of Sacramento
- have three-fourths of the state's water resources;
- have less than one-fourth of the people;
- have less than one-fourth of the farmland;
- have less than one-fourth of the industry;
- need only about one-fourth of the water resources.

The areas south of Sacramento
- have one-fourth of the state's water resources;
- have more than three-fourths of the people;
- have more than three-fourths of the farmland;
- have more than three-fourths of the industry;
- need three-fourths of the water resources.

Another problem for Californians is that water is a limited resource. There is only so much fresh water available in the state. Yet people need water for many uses, and our need for water keeps growing. How can people decide which uses of water are most important?

Checking Up

1. Does more rain fall in the Sierra Nevada or the Central Valley?

2. Where is most of California's water supply found?

3. What two problems does California have with water?

4. Think of a way to help solve one of California's water problems. Tell about your idea.

Today, date palm trees grow beside the American Canal in the rich soil of California's Imperial Valley.

Lesson 2 The Imperial Valley Flood

Where would you rather live, in the Imperial Valley or the Colorado Desert? The Imperial Valley sounds a lot better, doesn't it? In fact, they are the same place. The Colorado Desert is the old name for the Imperial Valley. When the area was called the Colorado Desert, few people lived there. Once the name was changed to the Imperial Valley, thousands of people flocked there. The name change helped to bring settlers, but more important was the arrival of water.

The man who thought of the name "Imperial Valley" was George Chaffey [chāf′ ē]. He was an **engineer** who knew how to transport water through **canals**. As California grew, so grew the need for water. Chaffey was hired to bring water to the Colorado Desert by building a canal from the Colorado River. Once water was brought to the Imperial Valley, farmers hurried to buy land there. The climate was good for growing fruit and vegetables. By 1905, fourteen thousand people were living in the Imperial Valley.

To bring even more water to the Imperial Valley, another group of engineers was hired to build a new channel from the Colorado River into the canal. Unfortunately, the new channel soon led to problems. Every summer, the Colorado River rises with water from melting snows and spring rains. The summer after the new channel was built, this extra water burst through the

143

Between 1905 and 1907, much of the Imperial Valley was under water. It took many workers and more than six thousand railroad cars full of rock to force the Colorado River back into its channel.

walls of the channel and flooded the Imperial Valley. Many farms and forty miles of railroad track were suddenly under water. The farmers moved out as fast as they had moved in.

It took two years to force the river back into its old channel. Enough rock to fill six thousand railroad cars was used to strengthen the channel. Eventually, farmers moved back into the valley.

One result of the flood is still easy to see. A low area of land had filled with water during the flood, forming the Salton Sea. The new sea was fifty miles long, fifteen miles wide, and seventy-five feet deep. The only way it gets more water is from rain and from water that drains off the nearby farmlands. No streams or rivers feed this "sea."

Checking Up

1. What did the Imperial Valley used to be called?

2. What was the main reason farmers moved to the Imperial Valley?

3. What was the cause of the Imperial Valley Flood?

4. How was the Salton Sea formed?

USING WATER WISELY

How much water do you think the average American uses every day at home? A gallon? More than that. Ten gallons? Keep guessing. *Fifty* gallons? Even more than that. Would you believe that each and every American uses an average of seventy gallons of water every day?

Much of the water we use in our homes is wasted. But, as you know, water is a limited resource. Our need for water grows, but our supply does not. It's important that people conserve water instead of wasting it. You and your family can use water wisely by following these steps:

1

For a toilet to flush, the tank must be filled to the top with water. This takes about seven gallons of water. You can save much of this water, by taking up space in the tank so that less water is needed to fill it. Just fill two half-gallon plastic jugs with water. Screw their tops on tight.

Then put the jugs in the tank where they won't get caught in the works.

2

Never use the toilet as a wastebasket. Using gallons of water to get rid of a tissue is wasteful.

3

Take shorter showers. You can save up to twelve gallons per minute.

145

How We Use Water in Our Homes

showers and bath

cooking

kitchen

flushing toilets

laundry

4 A low-pressure shower head helps save even more water. You can also buy low-pressure kitchen faucets.

5 Turn faucets all the way off. If a faucet leaks, fix it.

A leaky faucet can waste from fifteen hundred to three thousand gallons of water every month.

6 Wash only full loads in the clothes washer. Most machines use twenty to fifty gallons per load.

7 Don't let water run unnecessarily. When brushing your teeth, washing your face, or rinsing the dishes, take the time to turn the water off when it's not needed.

146

Lesson 3   Water for the Cities

By 1900, San Francisco and Los Angeles were both large cities. The people living in these cities needed more and more water. Each city faced a different problem in getting that water, and each city found a different solution. Not everyone was happy with the decisions that were made.

Water for San Francisco

San Francisco was a growing city. Although it had more rain than Los Angeles, it still needed to find more water. Near Yosemite National Park was a place called Hetch Hetchy Valley. San Francisco officials decided to build a dam there. The dam would flood the valley and create a **reservoir**. A reservoir is a lake made by a dam to store water for future use. This new reservoir would store water for the city. The officials also planned to build a pipeline, called an **aqueduct**, that would bring the water from the lake to the city.

In 1901, San Francisco began to put this plan into action. Some people, including John Muir, protested. They said that Hetch Hetchy was an area of beauty. They felt it should be saved in its natural state. For a while, these protestors were able to stop the building of the dam. But by 1931, both the dam and the aqueduct had been built.

Water for Los Angeles

Since the days of the pueblo, Los Angeles had struggled to get enough water. Nearby farmers had dug ditches so that they could use the water from the Los Angeles River to irrigate their crops. Every few years, Southern California would have a long dry spell called a **drought**. During these droughts, the people of Los Angeles would dig wells and save water until rain finally came again.

In 1904, after many years of drought, Los Angeles was desperate for water. The city officials decided to bring water down from the Owens River in the Owens Valley. In 1913, they built an aqueduct that carried water from the river to the city. The people of Los Angeles were delighted.

Pipes carry water from the reservoir created by the dam in Hetch Hetchy Valley to homes and businesses in San Francisco.

The Owens Valley aqueduct brings Owens River water to Los Angeles.

The people of Owens Valley were not so pleased. They were left with almost no water. With less water, it would be difficult to make a living by farming or ranching. Some people tried to destroy the aqueduct, but they could not change what had happened. The Owens Valley never became the rich agricultural area that it might have been.

The Hoover Dam

Another Southern California water project came about in the 1930s. Hoover Dam was built on the Colorado River. Besides collecting water, this dam controlled flooding and produced electric power. An aqueduct was built to carry Colorado River water to Los Angeles. Building it was difficult because the aqueduct had to go through six mountain ranges. But it brought much-needed water to Los Angeles.

People in California were pleased, but people in nearby Arizona were not. They did not want California to take so much of the river water. They asked the United States Supreme Court to decide how the water should be shared.

The Court decided, and Congress passed a law. Meanwhile, Arizona began to build a system of pipes and tanks to carry and store the water. The purpose of this system is to provide Arizona with more water—leaving less for California. People who live in Los Angeles still have to make difficult choices about getting and using water.

Dedicated in 1935, Hoover Dam formed the world's largest reservoir at that time. Lake Mead, as this reservoir was called, held nearly ten trillion gallons of water!

Checking Up

1. What were the results of building the Hetch Hetchy Dam? Explain why these results are good or bad.

2. Who was hurt by the decision to bring water from the Owens River to Los Angeles?

3. Name two things Hoover Dam did for Californians.

4. Why is water important for cities? For farm areas?

Building Social Studies Skills

Using a Decision Tree and a Flow Chart

A California town has a tough decision to make about water. The townspeople are using more and more water each year. If the need for water continues to rise, there won't be enough water to supply that need. The town needs more water.

Or does it? A committee set up to study the problem has shown that much water is wasted. Their report shows that if all the townspeople used water wisely, the town would have enough water for years to come.

The Water Committee has to do two things. First, it has to decide what to do about the water problem. Then, it has to come up with a plan for carrying out its decision.

The committee members have drawn a **decision tree** to help them decide what to do. Look at the model drawing on this page to see how to use the decision tree.

1. Look at the tree trunk. That's where the committee has described the water problem.
2. Now look at the tree branches. The committee used the lowest branches to list possible solutions to the problem.
3. Above each solution they wrote some bad and good results of that solution.
4. At the top of the tree, the committee members listed two goals.

The decision tree is a useful tool in making a decision. The committee members can choose the best solution by comparing the good and bad results of each. Or they can first decide on the best goal and then choose a solution that leads to that goal.

Now study the committee's decision tree on the next page. Which goal do you think is best? Which solution would you vote for?

The Water Committee decided to start a program to teach conservation. See if you agree with that solution.

149

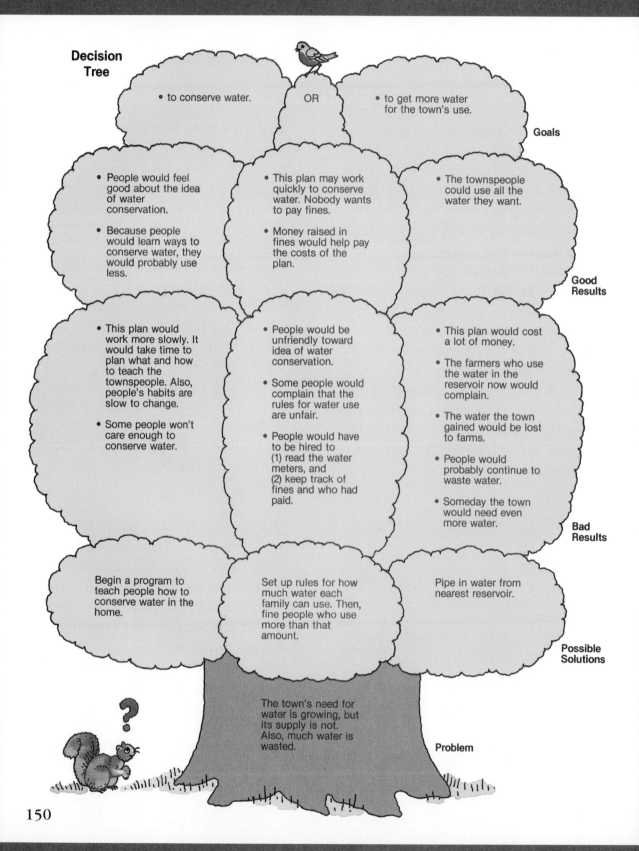

Decision Tree

Goals

- to conserve water.   OR   - to get more water for the town's use.

Good Results

- People would feel good about the idea of water conservation.
- Because people would learn ways to conserve water, they would probably use less.

- This plan may work quickly to conserve water. Nobody wants to pay fines.
- Money raised in fines would help pay the costs of the plan.

- The townspeople could use all the water they want.

Bad Results

- This plan would work more slowly. It would take time to plan what and how to teach the townspeople. Also, people's habits are slow to change.
- Some people won't care enough to conserve water.

- People would be unfriendly toward idea of water conservation.
- Some people would complain that the rules for water use are unfair.
- People would have to be hired to (1) read the water meters, and (2) keep track of fines and who had paid.

- This plan would cost a lot of money.
- The farmers who use the water in the reservoir now would complain.
- The water the town gained would be lost to farms.
- People would probably continue to waste water.
- Someday the town would need even more water.

Possible Solutions

Begin a program to teach people how to conserve water in the home.

Set up rules for how much water each family can use. Then, fine people who use more than that amount.

Pipe in water from nearest reservoir.

Problem

The town's need for water is growing, but its supply is not. Also, much water is wasted.

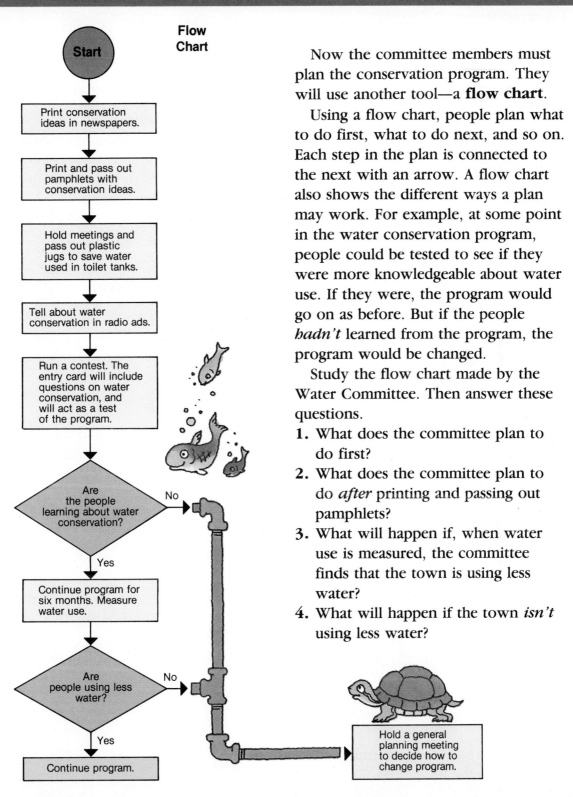

Flow Chart

Start

Print conservation ideas in newspapers.

Print and pass out pamphlets with conservation ideas.

Hold meetings and pass out plastic jugs to save water used in toilet tanks.

Tell about water conservation in radio ads.

Run a contest. The entry card will include questions on water conservation, and will act as a test of the program.

Are the people learning about water conservation? — No

Yes

Continue program for six months. Measure water use.

Are people using less water? — No

Yes

Continue program.

Hold a general planning meeting to decide how to change program.

Now the committee members must plan the conservation program. They will use another tool—a **flow chart**.

Using a flow chart, people plan what to do first, what to do next, and so on. Each step in the plan is connected to the next with an arrow. A flow chart also shows the different ways a plan may work. For example, at some point in the water conservation program, people could be tested to see if they were more knowledgeable about water use. If they were, the program would go on as before. But if the people *hadn't* learned from the program, the program would be changed.

Study the flow chart made by the Water Committee. Then answer these questions.

1. What does the committee plan to do first?
2. What does the committee plan to do *after* printing and passing out pamphlets?
3. What will happen if, when water use is measured, the committee finds that the town is using less water?
4. What will happen if the town *isn't* using less water?

151

Write your answers on paper. Do not write in the book.

Using Key Words

From the list below, choose the term that best completes each of the sentences. Write it on your paper.

aqueduct   drought
canal   engineer
decision tree   flow chart
distribution   reservoir

1. A diagram that shows the steps of a plan is a _____.
2. A _____ stores water for future use.
3. An _____ is a pipeline that carries water from one place to another.
4. A person who knows how to plan, design, and build waterways is an _____.
5. A river-like waterway built by people is called a _____.
6. A long dry period without rain is called a _____.
7. Moving a resource to places where it is needed is called _____.
8. A _____ is a useful tool for finding the best solution to a problem.

Reviewing Main Ideas

Write "true" for the sentences that are true. Write "false" for the sentences that are false.

1. Rain is a result of air warming as it rises over the mountains.
2. Water is a problem in California because it must be transported from one part of the state to another.
3. Bringing water to the cities caused suffering to the farmers.
4. Crops grow well in the Imperial Valley because its name was changed.

Thinking Things Over

San Francisco solved its water problem by building the Hetch Hetchy Dam. Can you think of other possible solutions? List at least two.

Practicing Skills

Copy this flow chart. Then fill it in to show how your family could conserve water.

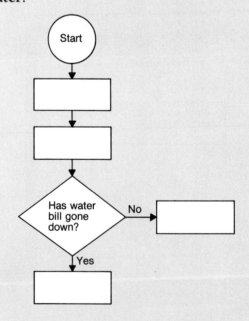

The Booming Industries

People are one of California's most important resources. Without the work of its people, the material resources of the state would lie unused. By the twentieth century, California had a large and growing population. This meant not only more mouths to feed but more hands to work. As human resources grew, businesses grew into new and booming industries for California.

Lesson 1   Labor and Management

When you read that George Chaffey built a canal in the Imperial Valley, you probably figured out that he didn't do it alone. After all, how could one man, even a very good engineer, do so much work by himself? Of course, Chaffey had many people to help him. We say that Chaffey built the canal because he planned and directed the project. In other words, Chaffey managed the building of the canal.

Chaffey probably never did any of the physical work of canal building. Instead, he and the other managers of the

Labor and management work together. Managers make plans, decide how the work should be done, and hire the workers to do it.

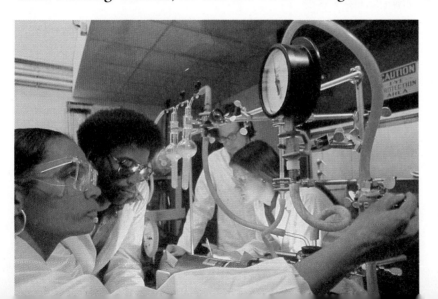

Labor and management are needed to get any job done. Careful workers are needed to get the job done right.

153

Machining is one job done by labor. If it's not done right, parts won't fit and tools won't work. Here, a woman carefully machines a custom part.

project made this work possible. They drew plans, found materials, bought machines, got the materials and machines to the right place at the right time, hired people to do the work, and explained how the work should be done. We use the word **management** to describe George Chaffey and the other managers.

The managers would not have been able to build the canal without the workers they hired. We call these workers **labor**. Management must make careful decisions about how money will be spent to get a job done. Labor must work hard to get the job done carefully, well, and on time. To get any job done, labor and management must work together.

Checking Up

1. List four things that management did in the Imperial Valley canal project.

2. Was labor important in the Imperial Valley canal project? Explain your answer.

3. How do labor and management work together to get a job done?

4. Why do we think of people as one of the state's most important resources?

Lesson 2 Automobiles and Oil

In Detroit, Michigan, in 1908, the Ford Motor Company built a car that would change California and all of America. It was called the Model T.

The first cars were made one at a time. Each car was put together separately. This took a long time and a lot of money. Cars cost so much money that only rich people could buy them. But by 1913, Henry Ford's factories were using an **assembly line** to make the Model T automobile. The workers stood in a long line. Car parts traveled on a moving belt from one worker to the next. Each worker did only one job over and over again as the parts moved by.

In this way, many more cars could be made at one time. Producing cars was faster and less expensive. For this reason, a car made on an assembly line could be sold cheaper. At first, the Model T cost $500. At its cheapest, it cost only $280. At that price, millions of American families could afford to buy a car.

Californians really took to the car. In California's mild climate, it was easy to drive all year long. By 1929, there were nearly two million cars in California. In Los Angeles, one person in three owned a car. The widespread use of cars in California affected the way people lived. Californians had more choices about where to live. Many people built their homes in the valleys and hills instead of

California has about 166,000 miles of city streets, county roads, and highways. Among these highways are broad freeways like this one in Oakland. Do you have freeways where you live?

On December 27, 1924, Mulholland Drive was opened in Los Angeles. A banner welcomed drivers to "fifty-five miles of scenic splendor."

155

Spaniards and Mexicans called the thick oil that oozed from the ground *brea* [brā′ ä]. They collected it and used it to roof their adobe houses. You can still see brea coming up from the ground at the La Brea tar pits in Los Angeles. The elephant shown is not real. It is a replica that was created to show how large animals became trapped in tar pits in prehistoric times.

in city centers. They could easily drive several miles to jobs or stores. Californians also had wider choices in places to visit, like mountains and beaches.

The automobile industry's growth helped another industry to develop in California. This was the oil industry.

Before the 1920s, Californians had more oil than they needed. In some places, thick, black oil oozed from the ground. In other places, engineers dug deep wells and pumped the oil up through pipes. People began to look for more uses for oil so more people would want to buy it. They made kerosene for heating and lighting and used oil to drive train engines. Still, oil companies had more oil than they could sell.

At last, in the 1920s, there was a demand for oil. The Model T and other cars ran on gasoline. And gasoline was made from oil. All of the new auto owners were eagerly buying the new oil product.

Suddenly, oil companies had to look for more oil to meet the demand. New wells were dug in Huntington Beach, Santa Fe Springs, and Signal Hill in Long Beach. Soon, the oil industry was the largest industry in the state.

The 1920s was a great boom period for California, especially for Southern California. Thousands of people moved here. Oil was just one part of a boom that looked as though it would never end.

Checking Up

1. Why did millions of Americans buy the Model Ts that were made on the assembly line?

2. Describe what happened on the assembly line.

3. Why did the oil industry grow in the 1920s?

4. Name two ways in which the automobile gave more choices to Californians.

5. How would California be different today if very few people owned cars?

Oil is found in pockets between rocks deep in the earth. Geologists drill through the rocks, put a long pipe down to the oil, and pump it out. Sometimes, there is so much pressure on the oil that it comes up the pipe without being pumped. When an oil well has a heavy natural flow of oil, it is called a gusher. Above is a Union Oil Company gusher on Signal Hill in 1925.

Lesson 3   The Movies

Movies were another part of the California boom. In the first years of the twentieth century, many movie makers came to Southern California.

One reason movie makers came was the good weather. The film they used in their cameras was not as good as the film used today. Almost all filming had to be done outside in bright sunlight. Movie makers needed to work in a place where there were many days of sunshine each year.

Another reason movie makers came west was to escape controls on movie making. Thomas Edison had invented the best kinds of movie cameras and projectors. He and other inventors had **patents** to protect their inventions. This meant that their designs were registered with an office of the United States government. No one was allowed to copy these designs, and the patent holders were supposed to get money when machines based on their ideas were sold.

But many movie makers saved money by making their own equipment. They copied patented designs without paying fees. The eastern patent holders hired lawyers to get their money. The movie makers came to California to be as far away as possible from these lawyers.

By the 1920s, the movies were big business in California. All across the United States, each and every

Many people besides actors and actresses are needed to make a movie—set designers, carpenters, scene painters, costume designers, makeup artists, writers, film editors, directors, and camera men and women. Here, actress Cicely Tyson learns how to be a director.

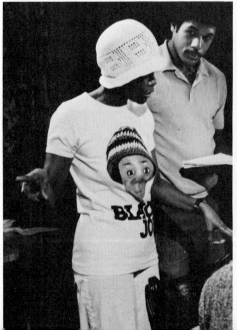

California movie maker George Lucas entertained millions of moviegoers with *Star Wars*. In this scene from that famous science fiction film, Han Solo and Princess Leia are boarding the *Millennium Falcon* on the Death Star.

week, millions of people went to see movies made in this state. Movies only cost a dime then. But movie makers earned millions of dollars on a single film. At a time when thirty dollars a week was considered a good wage, some movie stars like Charlie Chaplin were earning ten thousand dollars a week.

Newspapers and magazines told stories about the movie stars. Hollywood, the town in which the stars lived and worked, became famous thoughout the world. Many young fans dreamed of being as rich and famous as the actors and actresses they saw on the screen. Some of these fans came to Hollywood to try to become stars. Many who came ended up working for the movie industry in other jobs. Most ended up working in other industries. As you can see, growth of the movie industry was important to our state. It meant more work for people. It meant growth for California.

As a child star, Shirley Temple charmed film fans all over the world with her blonde curls, her blue eyes, and her appealing personality. As an adult and the wife of San Francisco businessman Charles A. Black, she has held several important government jobs. She has worked in the United Nations and has served as an ambassador.

Checking Up

1. Give two reasons the movie industry came to California.

2. Name at least five different workers needed to make a movie.

3. Why was the movie industry important to California?

Write your answers on paper. Do not write in the book.

Using Key Words

From the list below, choose the term that best completes each of the sentences. Write it on your paper.

assembly line   management
labor   patent

1. The people who did the physical work of building the Imperial Valley canal were _____.
2. _____ plans jobs and hires workers.
3. A government record that protects a new invention from being copied is called a _____.
4. On an _____, parts of a machine pass in front of workers on a slowly moving belt.

Reviewing Main Ideas

Read each item below. Decide which industry or industries the item describes. Write the letter or letters of the correct industries on your paper.

A = automobile industry
O = oil industry
M = movie industry

1. Included both labor and management.
2. Brought money and people to California.
3. Helped the oil industry in California to grow.
4. Had the most effect on where Californians lived and how they worked and played.
5. Made Hollywood famous all over the world.
6. First used the assembly line.
7. Used human resources.
8. Were part of a great boom in California industry.

Thinking Things Over

Tell about labor and management in the automobile industry. What does labor do? What does management do? Which is more important?

Practicing Skills

1. List these six words in alphabetical order:

    marigold
    mammal
    management
    material
    maple
    malt

2. Write each word below that would appear on the dictionary page with the guide words *koala* and *ladder*.

    lag
    labor
    knock
    lace
    lack
    kind

What Do You Know?

Write your answers on paper. Do not write in the book.

Words to Know

From the list below, choose the word that best completes each of the sentences. Write it on your paper.

agriculture   management
aqueduct   mineral
drought   reservoir
labor   resource

1. A nonliving substance that is dug from the ground is called a _____.
2. A lake made by people to store water for future use is a _____.
3. Workers who are paid to work for other people are called _____.
4. A pipeline built to carry water from one place to another is called an _____.
5. Another word for something a country or state has and can use is _____.
6. People who hire others to do work for them are called _____.
7. Farming is also called _____.
8. A _____ is a long period without rain.

Ideas to Know

Write "true" for the sentences that are true. Write "false" for the sentences that are false.

1. California has many natural resources.
2. Farming has never been an important activity in California.
3. Ladybugs from Australia once saved California's orange industry from cottony-cushion scale.
4. A mineral called borax was mined in Death Valley.
5. John Muir failed in his attempt to make Yosemite a national park.
6. People are an important resource in California.
7. Most of California's rain falls in the southern half of the state.
8. California has solved some of its water problems with reservoirs and aqueducts.
9. The Imperial Valley was once named the Colorado Desert.
10. The Salton Sea was formed from water left by the Imperial Valley flood.
11. Californians have so much water that they do not need to practice water conservation.
12. Both San Francisco and Los Angeles must transport water from far away.
13. Both labor and management are needed to get a job done.
14. The growth of the oil industry had nothing to do with the automobile industry.

161

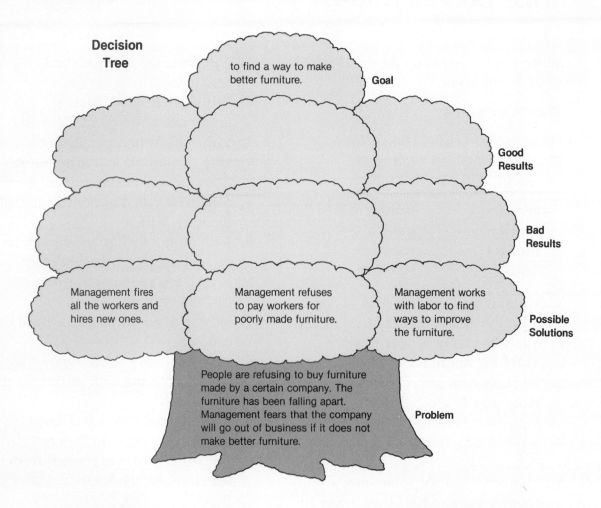

Decision Tree

to find a way to make better furniture. — **Goal**

Good Results

Bad Results

Management fires all the workers and hires new ones.

Management refuses to pay workers for poorly made furniture.

Management works with labor to find ways to improve the furniture. — **Possible Solutions**

People are refusing to buy furniture made by a certain company. The furniture has been falling apart. Management fears that the company will go out of business if it does not make better furniture. — **Problem**

15. The movie industry has been very important to the economy of California.

16. Better transportation did not help California farmers.

Using What You Know

1. On your paper, draw a flow chart that shows how borax was looked for and mined in Death Valley.

2. Study the decision tree pictured above. Read the Problem and Possible Solutions. Look at the Goal. Now, on your paper, complete the decision tree. Write each Possible Solution. For each solution, list the Good Results and Bad Results. Then tell which solution you would choose to reach the Goal and why you would choose it.

TIME OUT for Taking Tests

Part of going to school is taking tests. From time to time, you will take special tests designed to find out what whole classes or groups of students have learned.

These tests are usually printed in booklets from which you work. Separate answer sheets are used for marking your answers. Often you are given a time limit. It is important that you do your very best on these tests. They are sometimes used to make decisions about your studies in school.

Don't let tests scare you. They are not so bad if you learn to become a wise test taker.

First, make up your mind that you can do a good job on the test. Most tests are made so that you can answer the questions by carefully reading or studying what is given and by using skills and information you already know.

Above all, don't panic. The tests are made to be hard. You are not expected to get all of the questions right. You are expected to use your head and do the best you can!

Here are some more tips to help make you a wise test taker.

How should you go about taking the test?

Use time wisely.

- Make good use of the time. Plan to use all the time allowed. Leave time to check your answers and see that they are marked correctly.
- Don't waste time. Work as quickly as you can and still be careful. Skip very difficult questions; come back to them later.

Work carefully.

- Directions for taking the test as a whole are usually read to you. More directions are given to you to read as you go along. Listen to and read all directions carefully. Repeat to yourself what you are to do.
- Quickly look at the questions before you read a story or look at a picture. Find out what you are reading or looking for.
- Read the story or look at the picture before you try to answer the questions. Just looking for answers could take longer, and you are more likely to choose a wrong answer.
- Look at all the answer choices before choosing one. More than one choice may *seem* right. If you don't read them all, you might not choose the *best* answer.
- Carefully match the question number and answer choice in the test booklet to the question number and answer choice on the answer sheet.
- Mark your answers clearly and neatly, being careful to keep your marks inside the circles or other

spaces given. Erase any wrong answers or extra marks completely.

- When you finish the test, be sure your name and any other important information are on the answer sheet.

What kinds of questions should you look for?

- Some questions ask for exact answers. These are answers that you can find in the same words, or almost the same words, by reading the story or looking at the picture.
- Some questions ask you to "put two and two together." For these questions, you cannot find the exact answer, but you can figure out the answer from other information given.
- Some questions have no answer. For these questions, there is not enough information given to answer the question asked, and one of the answer choices will be something like, "can't tell." Be careful. That answer choice is sometimes put there to fool you. Be very sure the question cannot be answered before choosing that answer choice.
- Some questions ask you to identify a fact or an opinion. Facts can be proved. Opinions cannot be proved. The word *should* often appears in answer choices that are opinions.

What if you don't know an answer for sure?

Use what you do know to figure out what you don't know.

- Consider all answer choices. Decide against any you know don't make sense or can't be correct.
- Look at the choices left. Try to prove or disprove them. Think about everything you read or looked at. Also think about any clues given. Use these things to figure out the best answer choice.
- Stay away from choices that use ideas such as *all*, *none*, *never*, and *always*. Few things are always true or never true.
- If you still don't know, guess. Your best hunch may be right. And on most tests, a guess is better than no answer.

On the next few pages are some sample test questions for you to try. Pretend they are a real test. Think about what you just read when you do them. Remember to work carefully and to make good use of your time. Above all, make up your mind you will do a good job.

Mark your answers on the special answer sheet on page 36 of the workbook or on a separate piece of paper provided by your teacher. Do not write in the book.

TEST 9 SOCIAL STUDIES

DIRECTIONS

This test will show you how well you use social studies skills.

Choose the best answer for each item. Then fill in the space that goes with the answer you choose.

SAMPLE ITEM: Read the story.

Many gold miners could not afford enough food. Bread that was five cents a loaf in the East cost fifty to seventy-five cents in the mining camps. Eggs were fifty dollars a dozen. With prices like these, it was mostly storekeepers, not miners, who got rich.

WAIT

A Which of these sentences is true?
1 All merchants got rich.
2 Miners never had enough to eat.
3 Eggs were not expensive.
4 Food cost more in the mining camps than in the East.

Read the story and do items 1–4.

California has tall, jagged mountains. Few people live in the mountain areas because it is hard to build factories, homes, and roads there. It is also hard to grow food and raise animals on mountain land.

California also has several smooth, wide valleys through which rivers flow. Many people live in the valleys. It is easy to build homes and roads on the smooth land. Often the soil is good for farming or for raising cattle. Water from the rivers can be used on farms and in factories. The rivers are also used for travel and for shipping goods.

1 Which of the following is true about the mountains?
1 More people should live in the mountains.
2 Mountains have rough, high cliffs.
3 Many crops grow there.
4 Most people raise animals.

2 Which of the following is true about the valleys?
5 Products can be both grown and shipped.
6 There are no factories.
7 The roads are steep and winding.
8 There are very few homes.

3 Which one of the following people would most likely live in the mountains?
1 farmer
2 factory worker
3 doctor
4 cattle rancher

4 Which is an example of something produced in a factory?
5 beans
6 peanut butter
7 beef
8 corn

165

TIME OUT for Taking Tests

Test 9 Social Studies

Sample A

California's early trailblazers were trappers who found new trails in unknown and unmaped lands. Today's trailblazers would be

    A travelers to Europe
    B space explorers
    C truck drivers
    D railroad builders

Stop

Use this map to do numbers 1 through 4.

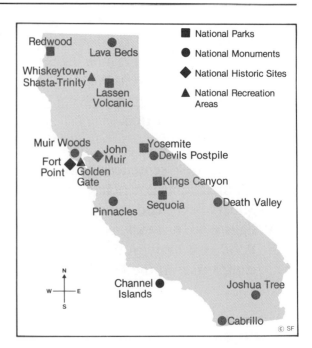

1 In California there are more
    A national parks
    B national monuments
    C national historic sites
    D national recreation areas

2 To get from Pinnacles to Lassen, you would go
    F north   **H** east
    G south   **J** west

3 Muir Woods is a
    A national park
    B national monument
    C national historic site
    D national recreation area

4 You would be most likely to have a picnic at
    F Redwood   **H** Joshua Tree
    G Pinnacles   **J** Cabrillo

Use this graph to do numbers 5 through 7.

Rainy Days in Los Angeles

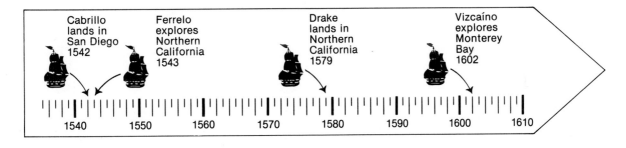

 = 2 Days of Rain

Winter	☔☔☔☔☔☔☔☔☔
Spring	☔☔☔☔☔☔
Summer	☔
Fall	☔☔☔☔

5 How many rainy days were there in fall?

A 18   C 8

B 12   D 7

6 Which season had more than half as much rain as winter?

F spring H fall

G summer J can't tell

7 According to the graph, which sentence is true?

A Two seasons had about the same amount of rain.

B One season had a half day of rain.

C All seasons had more than one day of rain.

D Two seasons had more than twelve days of rain.

Use this time line to answer questions 8 through 11.

| Cabrillo lands in San Diego 1542 | Ferrelo explores Northern California 1543 | Drake lands in Northern California 1579 | Vizcaíno explores Monterey Bay 1602 |

1540 1550 1560 1570 1580 1590 1600 1610

8 Which explorer was the first to land in California?

F Cabrillo H Drake

G Columbus J Vizcaíno

9 Which explorer landed sixty years after Cabrillo?

A Ferrelo C Vizcaíno

B Drake D Columbus

10 In what year did Ferrelo explore Northern California?

F 1542 H 1550

G 1543 J 1579

11 Which explorer came closest to the place Vizcaíno explored?

A Cabrillo C Drake

B Ferrelo D can't tell

167

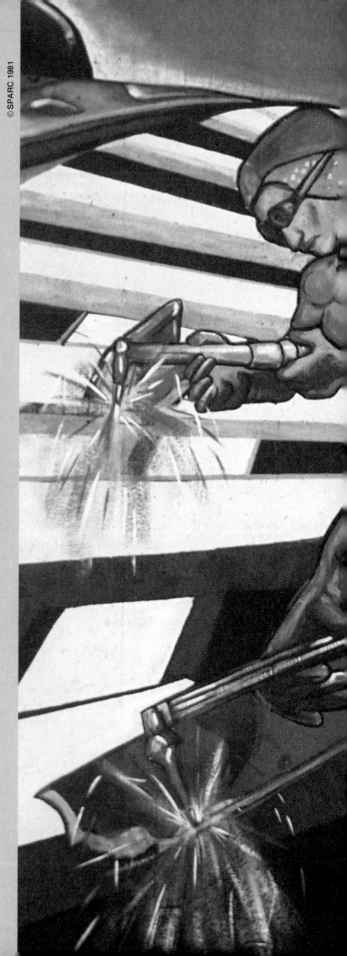

Unit 5

California Grows Up

As you know, the 1920s were a time of growth and wealth for California. But in 1929, the boom came to an end. People lost their jobs. Times became hard. Many people began to see themselves and the world differently.

Then came World War II. Between that time and the present, many important changes and events took place. These affected California and Californians in two ways. First, California went through a second boom that caused it to grow again in wealth and population. Second, Californians continued to question who they were. They searched for new and better places in their world. In these exciting years, California grew up.

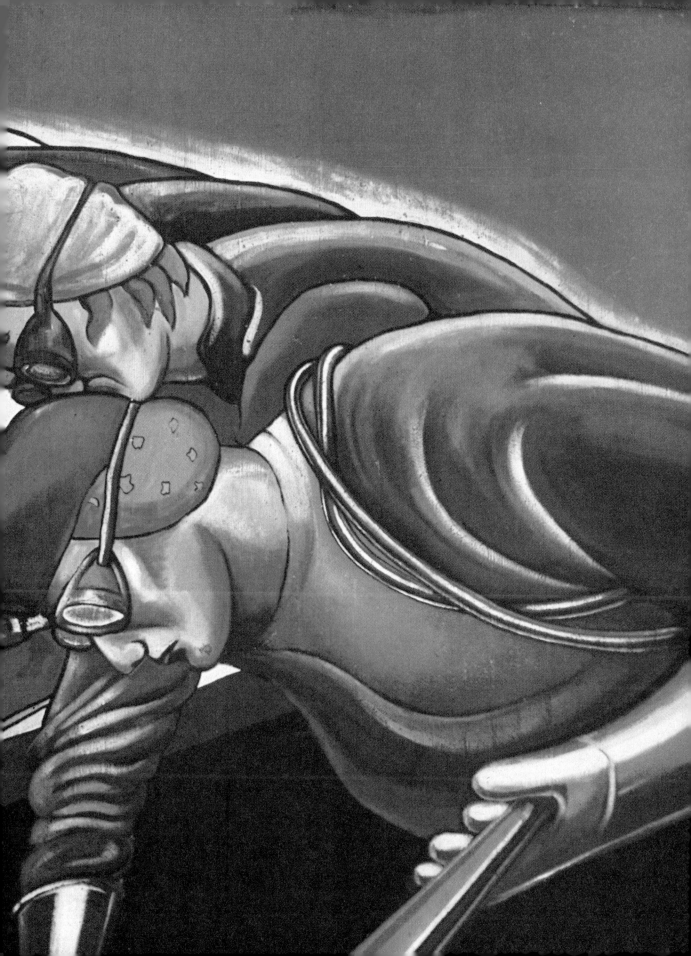

15

Lesson 1 Looking for Work
Lesson 2 The Dust Bowlers

The Depression

In 1929, millions of Americans lost their jobs. Suddenly, they had no money to buy food or clothes or housing. Many people went hungry. They wore rags and lived in tents or shacks. America was in a **depression**.

depression, a time when people are out of work, prices are falling, businesses cannot sell goods, and people have little money to spend or save.

Lesson 1 Looking for Work

To raise money, owners of companies sometimes sell small parts of their businesses. These parts, or shares, are called **stocks**. People who buy the shares are called **stockholders**. When businesses make money, they divide it among the stockholders.

During the boom of the 1920s, many Americans had money to spend on stocks. Businesses grew. People could buy stocks and sell them quickly for more than they paid. They became so eager to buy stocks that they paid more for them than they were worth. Suddenly, stock prices began to fall. Stockholders tried to sell their stocks before prices went down too far. But with everyone trying to sell, prices fell more and more rapidly. People lost money. Stocks became worthless. In October 1929, the stock market crash ended the boom of the 1920s.

Other problems also led to the Depression. During the boom, people had money to spend on the many wonderful, new products made by businesses. Businesses made more and more of these products. Soon, however, they made more of these things than people could buy. With the sudden need for fewer products, businesses had to stop making goods and lay off workers. Without paychecks, these workers had little money to buy things.

Another problem was credit buying. Many people bought on a ''buy now, pay later'' system. Few paid later.

Banks lost money because they had given loans to people who were unable to pay them back. Banks also lost money in the stock market. Many had to close.

Too many goods, people out of work, credit buying, and banks closing were all problems that weakened the country. These things combined with the stock market crash to plunge the nation into the Depression.

Janet Austin was a young girl at the time of the Depression. She still remembers the changes it made in her family's way of life.

Janet Austin and her family were living in California at the time of the crash. She remembers how it affected them. During the 1920s, the Austin family had lived well. They rented a nice house in Santa Monica. Janet's father was a geologist. His job was to look for oil.

Janet still remembers the newspaper headlines on the morning of the crash. She didn't think much about it then, but soon she could think of little else. Gasoline prices fell to eight cents a gallon. The low price made it no longer worthwhile to look for oil and make gasoline. Janet's father lost his job and had to look for other work.

Soon Janet's family couldn't pay their rent. Her mother explained to their landlady that they couldn't afford seventy-five dollars a month. Thirty-five dollars was the most they could pay. The landlady accepted the low rent. She was glad to get any money at all.

Janet remembers that many people who could not pay rent had to move out of their homes. Some lived in tents. Others lived in shacks made of scraps of metal, wood, or cardboard. Tent cities grew up everywhere—on the beach and on empty lots.

Later on, Janet's family had to move, but they didn't live in a tent city. They were lucky enough to be able to

The Dorothea Lange Collection, The Oakland Museum

This picture was taken by photographer Dorothea Lange during the Depression. What does it tell you about the way people felt at that time?

live rent free in Beaumont, California. In return for housing, the Austins took care of a cherry orchard.

During the Depression, some people began to have bad feelings about themselves. Parents felt bad that they couldn't feed and clothe their children. People who had no jobs felt that nobody needed them and their work. Of all the results of the Depression, the feelings of worthlessness were the worst.

Perhaps your grandparents or other people you know remember the Depression. You might ask them how it affected their families. What were their feelings during this time?

Checking Up

1. What were some causes of the Depression?

2. What were some things that happened because of the Depression? Name at least three.

3. Why did people have feelings of worthlessness?

4. Explain how you think you would have felt if your family had been out of work during the Depression.

172

Lesson 2   The Dust Bowlers

The Depression hit hard all over America, but it hit hardest in a large area of the United States that included parts of Oklahoma, Arkansas, and Texas. The farmers there had too few buyers for their crops. Then came several years of drought that left farmlands dry and dusty. Winds blew away the rich **topsoil**, leaving the soil underneath, which was not good for growing crops. This area became known as the **dust bowl**.

topsoil, the rich upper layer of soil that is good for growing crops.

The people who lived in the dust bowl were called dust bowlers. When the drought and winds ruined their lands, they could no longer farm at all. They had no choice but to move. Many thought that cities would be the best places to find new work. They had heard that the weather was good in California and that there were plenty of jobs. So many dust bowlers packed everything they owned in their cars and trucks and headed west.

Altogether, about 350,000 dust bowlers came to California. They were looking for work and a better life. But because of the Depression, there were not enough

Because of a long drought, the topsoil on farms in Oklahoma, Arkansas, and Texas became dry and loose. On November 11, 1933—"Black Sunday"— the wind picked up this dusty soil and began blowing it away. For three years, the winds blew. The dust was blown as far north as Chicago, Illinois, and as far east as Albany, New York. For a while, farmers in the dust bowl fought the drying ground and blowing dust. Finally, they piled all of their belongings on top of their cars and came west looking for work.

173

Photographs taken by Dorothea Lange have become famous for showing people's feelings of helplessness and hopelessness.

jobs in California for the people already here. The arrival of the dust bowlers just made things worse.

Many Californians didn't want the dust bowlers here and discriminated against them. They made fun of their torn clothes and their different way of talking. They said they were dirty and too lazy to work. Californians called the dust bowlers "Okies" because many of them had come from Oklahoma.

Actually, the dust bowlers were willing to take any work they could find. The work they could find most often was farm work. But wages were so low that every member of the family had to work. They worked long and hard for little pay.

Living conditions were terrible for the dust bowlers. Like others during this time, they lived in tents and shacks. Often there were no toilets and no running water. Many died from diseases.

Each year the Depression got worse. Then, in 1932, Franklin D. Roosevelt was elected President. Roosevelt made many changes during his first hundred days in office. The most important change was to make people *believe* that things would get better. Also, the government started programs to create jobs. By the end of the 1930s, things were better. But the Depression did not really end until America entered World War II in 1941.

Checking Up

1. Who were the dust bowlers?

2. Why did the dust bowlers come to California?

3. How did Californians treat the dust bowlers?

4. How do you think the dust bowlers felt about the way they had to live and about the way they were treated? Explain your answer.

5. Name two things that happened while Roosevelt was President that helped to end the Depression. How did these things help?

Reviewing Chapter 15

Write your answers on paper. Do not write in the book.

Using Key Words

From the list below, choose the term that best completes each of the sentences. Write it on your paper.

depression   stock   topsoil
dust bowl   stockholder

1. When someone sells a part of a business to raise money, that part, or share, is called a _____.
2. The parts of Texas, Oklahoma, and Arkansas that suffered from drought in the 1930s were called the _____.
3. A _____ is a time when people lose their jobs, prices fall, and many businesses close.
4. A person who owns one or more shares or small parts of a business is called a _____.
5. The _____ is the rich upper layer of earth that is good for growing crops.

Reviewing Main Ideas

Choose the ending that makes each sentence true. Write its letter beside the question number on your paper.

1. The Depression was mainly a result of the
   a. events leading to the stock market crash of 1929.
   b. election of President Roosevelt.
   c. coming of the dust bowlers.

2. One reason the dust bowlers were discriminated against was that
   a. they were dirty and lazy.
   b. they were not from California.
   c. Californians feared they would take away jobs.
3. During the Depression, people felt
   a. things would get better.
   b. worthless.
   c. sorry for the dust bowlers.
4. During the Depression, businesses were hurt because no one
   a. wanted to buy their goods.
   b. needed their goods.
   c. had money to buy their goods.

Thinking Things Over

Many Californians felt that the arrival of the dust bowlers made things worse. Why did they feel this way? Do you think the dust bowlers would have been treated differently if there had been no depression? Explain.

Practicing Skills

Choose the letter of the best answer. Write it on your paper.

Which reference source is the best to use to find out more about the Depression?

    a. dictionary
    b. atlas
    c. encyclopedia

Chapter

16

World War II

In 1939, the world went to war. Germany, led by Adolf Hitler, attacked and took over several countries in Europe. England and the Soviet Union were fighting Hitler. Italy joined the fight—on Germany's side. Meanwhile, Japan was fighting a war in Asia. The United States kept out of these wars for two years. But this uneasy peace didn't last. Americans had to join together to face new enemies.

Lesson 1   America Goes to War

At dawn on Sunday, December 7, 1941, the American Pacific fleet was in Pearl Harbor, Hawaii. All was quiet as the sun rose. Only a few American sailors were awake, watching over the ships. Then, out of the sky came Japanese bomber airplanes. The Japanese were attacking Pearl Harbor! They were attacking the United States!

The attack on Pearl Harbor was a total surprise. Before the Americans could fight back, the Japanese had badly damaged the fleet. Nineteen American ships were sunk, and twenty-three hundred people were killed.

After this attack, America had no choice but to enter World War II. Under President Roosevelt, the United States Congress declared war on Japan, Italy, and Germany. These three countries were known as the Axis powers. The United States became an **ally** of England and the Soviet Union. Together, these three countries were known as the Allied powers.

ally, person, group, or nation united with another for some special purpose.

Americans went to Europe and Africa to fight Italy and Germany. They fought Japan in the Pacific. The war in the Pacific was especially important to California. By looking at the map on page 177, can you see why?

On December 7, 1941, Japanese airplanes bombed Pearl Harbor.

As you can see from this map, California was much closer to Japan and to the war in the Pacific than were most other parts of the United States. For example, California is about 3,000 miles from Hawaii and 6,750 miles from Japan. On the other hand, New York is about 6,100 miles from Hawaii and 9,400 miles from Japan. And because California is on the Pacific coast, it was able to provide bases for the United States war effort in the Pacific.

**World War II
and California**

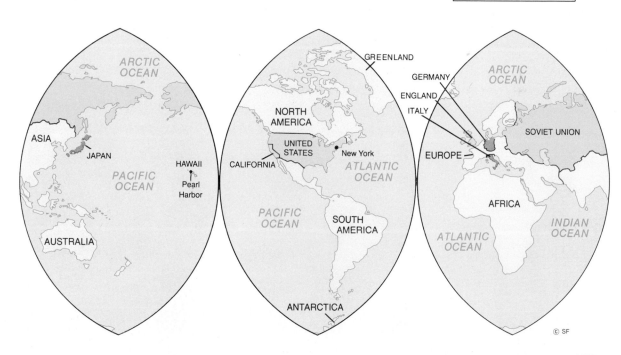

military base, a camp or location for housing soldiers or other armed forces.

California served as a **military base** for the United States. Thousands of pilots, soldiers, and sailors came to California before going on to battles in the Pacific. California provided supplies of all kinds for the armed forces. Damaged ships and planes were repaired here as well. The population of the state grew greatly.

After Japan's attack on Pearl Harbor, San Diego became an important naval base for ships being used to fuel and fight the war in the Pacific.

Walter Sanders, LIFE Magazine, © 1940 Time Inc.

World War II changed the mood of America and California. No longer were people out of work. Young men and women went into the armed forces. Other people worked in factories to produce the things needed to fight the war. And almost everybody felt very **patriotic**. Americans wanted to pull together and win the war.

During World War II, posters like the one on the left praised American men and women who helped to win the war, and America's patriotic feelings caused the biggest flag boom in more than twenty years. On the right, a factory worker stacks rolls of newly printed flags.

Checking Up

---

1. What event caused the United States to enter World War II?

2. Which countries were known as the Axis powers?

3. Which countries were our major allies?

4. Why was California important in World War II?

5. How did the mood of America and California change during the war? Why did this happen?

patriotic, having love and loyalty for one's country.

179

Lesson 2 The Japanese Americans

In the early 1900s, many Japanese men came to California to become farm workers. California farm workers did not like this. They thought that the Japanese workers were taking their jobs. And some of them became angry when Japanese farmers bought land and were able to grow new crops such as rice and potatoes. Californians in cities also feared that the Japanese would take their jobs. Other Californians discriminated against the Japanese because of their customs and appearance. They called the Japanese ''Japs'' and said things like, ''Japs must go.''

Because of this, the United States took steps to stop Japanese workers from coming to America. And California passed a law saying that people who were not American citizens could not own land. The Japanese workers were not American citizens. Even those who had worked hard and saved enough money could not buy land to farm.

Most of the Japanese men were not married when they came to California. Many wished to marry women from Japan. They wanted wives who spoke their language and shared their customs. It was very hard for them to go back to Japan to find brides. Instead, they often asked their relatives in Japan to choose wives for them.

The weddings were held in Japan, even though the men were in California. A new bride and groom would trade pictures so each could see what the other looked like. For this reason, the Japanese wives were called ''picture brides.'' After the weddings, these women left their homeland to come to America and meet their husbands.

Life in a new land with a strange language was difficult for the ''picture brides.'' Also, discrimination against the Japanese continued. But as the Japanese worked hard and had families, they slowly came to be accepted. Even though the parents were not American citizens, their children, who were born in the United States, were citizens. By the time World War II came, several **generations** of these Japanese American families had lived in California. Many, who were now citizens, owned

generation, all the people born about the same time; one step or level on a family tree.

homes and businesses. Japanese Americans voted and paid taxes like all other Americans.

After Japan attacked Hawaii at Pearl Harbor, discrimination against Japanese Americans took a turn for the worse. Most Americans feared that Japan would attack the Pacific coast of the United States. They also thought that the Japanese Americans would help the enemy army when it came. The United States government decided to move all of the Japanese Americans away from the coast.

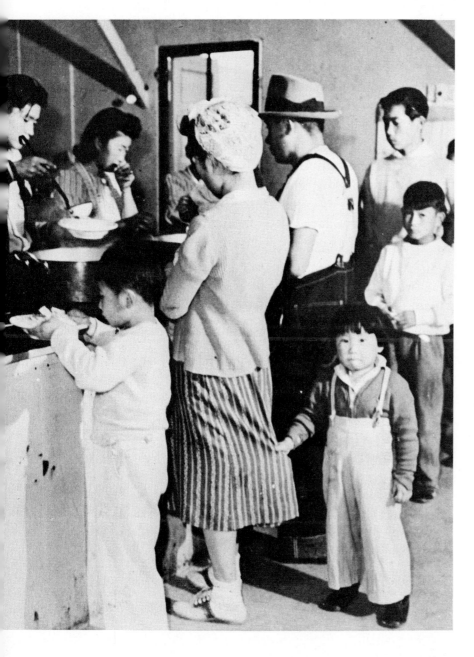

At relocation camps, meals were cooked and served in a separate building called a mess hall. This picture, taken in 1943, shows Japanese Americans from California lined up for a meal in the mess hall of an inland relocation camp in Denver, Colorado.

relocation camp, a place where Japanese Americans who were taken from their homes were sent to live during World War II.

During World War II, Japanese Americans fought bravely to defend their country. Here, two Japanese American soldiers move together along the road to Rome, Italy.

From April to August 1941, about 112,000 Japanese Americans were taken to inland **relocation camps**. They had to leave their homes, their jobs, and their schools. Many who owned land or businesses had to sell them quickly for much less money than they were worth. Even more Japanese Americans lost their property and businesses during the war.

Imagine how it felt to be an American citizen who was treated in this way. The Japanese Americans were sad to leave their homes. They felt angry to be living in crowded, dirty camps. Most were also angry that other Americans did not trust them. Even so, many Japanese Americans joined the United States Army. They fought bravely to defend America, their country. These soldiers proved their loyalty and won the admiration of their fellow Americans.

During the war, some Americans felt that it was wrong to put Japanese Americans into camps. They tried to get Japanese Americans released from the camps. And they worked to make conditions in the camps better.

Today it is generally realized that moving Japanese Americans to relocation camps was a mistake. On July 31, 1980, a special government commission, or committee, was organized. Its job was to study wrongs done to Japanese Americans and others during the war and to suggest remedies for these wrongs.

Checking Up

1. Why did Californians discriminate against Japanese Americans before the war?

2. Why were children of the "picture brides" and the Japanese farm workers American citizens?

3. Why were many Japanese Americans sent to relocation camps? How did they feel about this?

4. What did many Japanese Americans do to prove they were loyal to the United States?

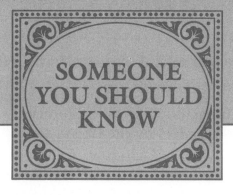
Jeanne Wakatsuki Houston

Jeanne Wakatsuki [wä kä tsü ′ kē] was seven years old when the Japanese attacked Pearl Harbor. She lived with her family of nine brothers and sisters in Ocean Park, California.

The Wakatsukis were Japanese Americans. In the minds of some people, this made them enemies. Along with ten thousand other Japanese Americans, they were taken to a relocation camp—Camp Manzanar.

Camp Manzanar [man ′ zə när] was a windy desert camp. It was at the foot of the eastern Sierra Nevada, in the shadow of Mount Whitney. This is how Jeanne describes her experience there.

66 Manzanar was surrounded by high barbed-wire fences. Soldiers with guns guarded the gates. Camp Manzanar was like a prison.

We lived in rough wooden buildings covered with tarpaper. The buildings were divided into small rooms. Each room was about half the size of a classroom. Six of us had to live together in a room. Toilets and showers were in another building. Meals were cooked and served in still another building. Normal family life was impossible at Manzanar. And family life was—and is—very important to Japanese Americans.

We were angry that our country didn't trust us. We were frustrated at having to live in such a crowded, dirty place. But we were determined to turn the desert camp into a community. We tried to keep our dignity. We wanted to show that we were loyal Americans. 99

Jeanne Wakatsuki was eleven years old when the war ended and her family left Manzanar. Once away from the camp, her family rarely spoke of their experiences there. But when Jeanne grew up, she realized that the story should be told.

Nearly thirty years after she left Manzanar, Jeanne Wakatsuki Houston and her husband, writer James D. Houston, wrote a book called *Farewell to Manzanar*. It tells how Jeanne and other Japanese Americans felt at Manzanar and how Manzanar influenced their lives. Jeanne Wakatsuki Houston hopes that the book will keep America from making another mistake like the one it made with 112,000 Japanese Americans during World War II.

Growth of Shipyard and Airplane Factory Workers

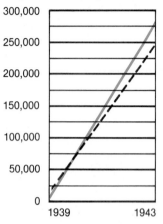

Shipyard Workers ————
Airplane Factory Workers — —·

The war brought the search for jobs to an end. Many workers were needed to do jobs in the shipyards and airplane factories. Which of the two industries grew the most and had the largest number of workers?

Lesson 3   Shipyards and Airplane Factories

World War II brought more than soldiers, sailors, and pilots to California. It brought money to California's industries. Between 1940 and 1946, the United States government spent $35 billion in California. This money was spent on the ships and airplanes needed to fight the war. The shipyards and airplane factories of California suddenly grew much larger and more profitable.

Other California industries grew because of the war too. The steel industry developed in order to supply the materials used to make ships and planes. The oil industry provided fuel for the Pacific fleets. Even the agricultural industry grew. California took a major part in feeding the armed forces.

Thousands of people moved to California during the war because there were so many jobs in the state. Many black Americans came to California at this time. Before the war, black people faced discrimination in jobs. During the war, employers were glad to get good workers.

Many women were able to find jobs during the war. When men left the factories to fight, women often took their places. Women were hired for jobs like welding and riveting that, until then, had been open mostly to men.

Between 1942 and 1946, California shipyards like this one near San Francisco busily built the ships America needed to carry soldiers and supplies and win the war.

184

With government money and many good workers, California produced large numbers of ships and airplanes in a very short time. By 1943, the Kaiser shipbuilding factories in California could build a large ship in twenty-five days. This meant that, up and down the state, one ship was finished every ten hours.

The airplane factories were also working hard. During the war, one California company, Lockheed, built twenty thousand airplanes. To do this, it employed ninety thousand workers.

All of these workers had to live somewhere. Many California cities more than doubled in size during the war. One city, Vallejo, had a population of 20,000 in 1941. By 1943, there were 100,000 people living in Vallejo.

California needed more houses, roads, schools, and stores. The war had started another boom. The Depression was over at last, and no longer were people begging for work. Instead, California was begging for workers.

These women are building bombers. Can you tell what part of the airplanes they are working on?

Checking Up

1. Which two kinds of factories grew fastest in California during World War II? Which of the two grew the most?

2. Why did the agricultural industry grow during the war?

3. Which two groups of people were able to get jobs in California during the war although they might not have been hired before?

4. Where did the money come from to pay for the boom in California?

5. What happened to California's population during the war? Why?

6. Why did the war cause the boom in California?

Write your answers on paper. Do not write in the book.

Using Key Words

From the list below, choose the term that best completes each of the sentences. Write it on your paper.

ally patriotic
generation relocation camp
military base

1. Parents are one _____ of a family.
2. A country that supports another during a war is its _____.
3. Feelings of love and loyalty toward one's country are _____ feelings.
4. A camp for the armed forces is called a _____.
5. During the war, Japanese Americans were taken from their homes and sent to a _____.

Reviewing Main Ideas

Write "true" for the sentences that are true. Write "false" for the sentences that are false.

1. California was an important base during World War II.
2. Japanese Americans fought on the side of Japan during World War II.
3. California could not build ships and planes because so many men had gone to war.
4. World War II brought an end to the Depression.
5. During the war, women and black people were hired in factories because many good workers were needed.

Thinking Things Over

World War II had both good and bad results. What were some of the good results? What were some of the bad results? Do you think the good results made the war worth it? Explain your answers.

Practicing Skills

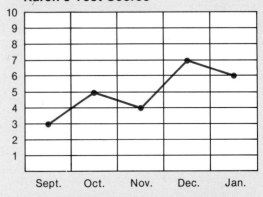

Karen's Test Scores

Study this graph of Karen's test scores to answer the questions. Write "true" for the sentences that are true. Write "false" for the sentences that are false.

1. For the most part Karen has made progress on her tests.
2. Karen studied best for her December test.
3. Karen's scores show large growth.

Changing Roles for People

Most Americans believe that all people should be treated fairly. Sometimes, though, different groups of people have had to struggle for fair treatment. People of various races have faced discrimination. Women, old people, young people, and handicapped people have all had problems getting equal and fair treatment. Many of these groups have **organized** themselves to work for the rights they deserve.

organize, form a group for the purpose of working toward a common goal.

Lesson 1   The Farm Workers

During World War II, thousands of people joined the armed forces and went to work in the factories. California farmers had trouble finding enough workers to plant and harvest their crops. So they hired many Mexican workers who came north looking for work in California's fields.

Later, the United States government started the bracero [brä ser ′ ō] program. *Bracero* is a Spanish word meaning worker. Under this program, Mexican workers were allowed to come into the United States to do seasonal

Grapes are one of California's most important crops. Picking grapes is hard work. In the early 1960s, farm workers who picked grapes were paid only $1.10 per hour and $.10 a box.

187

Cesar Chavez

work on farms. When the work was done, they had to return to Mexico.

Many American farm workers were against the bracero program. They said that the Mexican workers took their jobs and were willing to work for less money. American farm workers thought that growers would pay higher wages if the bracero program was stopped. Finally, in 1964, the program did end.

The California farm workers were largely Filipinos and Mexican Americans. Their working and living conditions were bad. Their pay was very low. For example, in the early 1960s, farm workers were paid $1.10 per hour and $.10 a box for picking grapes. And the work was very hard. Farm workers were not given sick leave, and most could not afford medical help.

A **migrant** is someone who moves often from one place to another. Because the farm workers had to move from farm to farm around the state to pick different crops, they were called migrant workers. They were unable to have homes because they had to move so often. Instead, they lived in shacks provided by the growers. These shacks had no running water or electricity. And because the workers' children moved from school to school, they had little chance to get a good education.

Farm workers joined together to change these conditions. Two groups of farm workers formed. A group of Mexican American farm workers was led by Cesar Chavez [shä ′ ves]. Larry Itliong [it ′ lē ong] organized a group of Filipino farm workers.

Cesar Chavez was the son of migrant farm workers and had been a farm worker himself. He had gone to so many schools as a child that he never got further than the seventh grade. He educated himself after he grew up. Chavez lived in Delano in the San Joaquin Valley. In 1962, he used money he had saved to start a farm workers' **union**. Within two years, fifty thousand workers had joined. Together, they got one farmer to pay higher wages and another to provide better houses.

In 1965, Itliong's group of Filipino farm workers came to Delano to pick grapes. They became angry because the growers paid them so little. Led by Itliong, the group of six hundred farm workers went on **strike** for better wages. They refused to pick grapes for such low pay. Within a few days, Chavez and his union joined the strike.

strike, a stopping of work by workers to get higher pay or better working conditions.

At first, the strike was not successful. After all, the growers had more money and power. They were sure they could break the strike. Then Chavez had an idea. He asked people all over the country to **boycott** grapes. Thousands of people supported the farm workers by boycotting, or not buying, grapes. Grape sales fell, and the growers made less money. Worried about losing their profits, the growers finally agreed to pay farm workers better wages for picking grapes.

Some people did not support the boycott. They did not want the farm workers to have poor working conditions. But they also understood the problems faced by the growers. If wages became too high, the price of the crops to the buyer might also be too high. And if the crops were poor or spoiled by bad weather, high wages and other costs could cause the growers to lose much money.

Farm workers have continued to work for higher pay and better working conditions. These conditions have improved, and some of the problems between growers and farm workers have been solved. Still the life of a migrant farm worker is very hard.

Checking Up

1. Describe the living and working conditions of migrant farm workers.

2. What did the farm workers do to improve their conditions?

3. Who were the leaders of California's migrant farm workers?

4. What were the good results of the farm workers' actions? Were there any bad results? Explain your answers.

Lesson 2   The Fight Against Discrimination

Imagine that you want to buy a banana split. You take your money to the ice cream parlor. When you get there, the owner stops you at the door.

"We don't serve children here," the owner says.

"But I just want to buy a banana split. I have enough money," you might say.

"I don't care," says the owner. "We don't want your kind in here. Go away!"

How would you feel if this happened to you? You would probably be very angry at this discrimination.

Blacks, Indians, Hispanics, Asian Americans, and members of other groups have all been discriminated against. We sometimes use the words **minority groups** to describe these people. It used to be that employers could refuse to hire members of minority groups. People who owned homes could refuse to rent or sell to them. Storekeepers and restaurant owners could refuse to serve them.

During World War II, this began to change. You read about the black people who came to California to work during the war. Employers gave them jobs because they needed workers. After the war was over, blacks and members of other minority groups wanted to continue to gain new rights. They wanted to be served by any store or restaurant. They wanted to live in any neighborhood they liked and to take any job they were able to do. The rights to be treated equally in all these ways are called **civil rights**. They are the rights guaranteed by government to all American citizens regardless of their sex, age, race, religion, or place of birth.

Various groups formed to gain these rights. Members of these groups told other Americans what their lives were like. Some groups marched with signs. Leaders gave speeches. People wrote books and articles. The groups took part in politics. They voted for lawmakers who would help them. Many minority group members began to run for office. As they worked together to gain rights, the groups also gained more pride in their backgrounds and more faith in their abilities.

Members of minority groups have worked hard to gain equal treatment in getting jobs. What does this picture tell you about the results of their efforts?

Gradually, the laws in America changed. The state laws of California also changed. No longer could people discriminate against blacks and members of other minority groups in jobs, housing, or schools. But life did not get better overnight. Many minority group members could not find jobs or could not afford to move into good housing.

In 1965 there was a **riot** in Watts, a black neighborhood in Los Angeles. There were many reasons for the riot. One reason was frustration. Even though the laws had changed, many of the people of Watts felt that their lives had not changed.

riot, a wild, noisy, and often violent disturbance made by a large number of people.

The Watts rioting became so violent so quickly that the National Guard was sent in to control it. Before most of the people in Watts knew what was happening, much of the area had been burned or otherwise damaged and looted. This guardsman's act of kindness—helping a woman safely across the street—is a sharp contrast to the anger and fighting that caused the ruin pictured in the background.

California Indians were also angry. In 1969, some Indians took over Alcatraz Island in San Francisco Bay. They said they would buy the island from the federal government for a few dollars. They wanted to show how unfair the government had been to Indians in the past. Many times it had bought Indian lands for very little money.

Once, members of minority groups could not live where they wanted. Some people who owned homes refused to rent or sell to them. Today, children from many different groups work together in neighborhood schools and play together in neighborhood parks, pools, and playgrounds.

Today, the struggle continues. Members of some minority groups still face discrimination. All Californians need to work together to make sure everyone gets fair and equal treatment.

Checking Up

1. In what ways have members of minority groups been discriminated against?

2. Name at least three things minority groups have done to gain rights.

3. Why did some minority groups become angry even though new laws had been passed?

4. What are civil rights?

5. How has gaining civil rights affected the way minority group members feel about themselves?

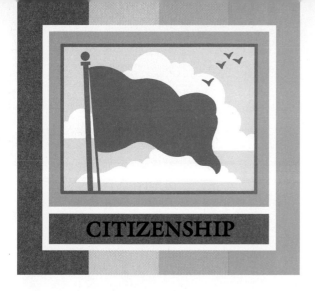

CITIZENSHIP

Rights for the Handicapped

Some Californians have been almost prisoners in their own homes. Why? Simply because they are physically handicapped. Until recently, much of the world of stores and theaters, churches and schools, offices and factories was closed to handicapped people.

One problem for the handicapped was barriers. To someone in a wheelchair, stairs, sidewalk curbs, and narrow doors are barriers. To a blind person with a guide dog, no-dogs-allowed signs on buses and in restaurants are barriers. Another problem was getting a job. Most employers wouldn't hire handicapped workers. Yet another problem was finding a place to live. Landlords sometimes refused to rent apartments or houses to the handicapped.

In the past, Americans believed that the handicapped should be "taken care of." Today, most handicapped persons want to take care of themselves. They feel they have the right to be independent. But they can't become independent without jobs, housing, and ways to get around.

To gain rights and independence, groups of handicapped persons organized. The groups included the blind, the deaf, and many other handicapped people. Together, they persuaded lawmakers to pass laws to help the handicapped become independent.

Some of the new laws say that handicapped people must be able to get into and around public buildings. Buildings with stairs must have ramps for wheelchairs. Doors have to be wide enough for wheelchairs to pass through. Drinking fountains, restrooms, and phone booths must be built low enough and wide enough for handicapped people to use.

Today, many buses have lifts so that passengers in wheelchairs can get on and off safely and easily.

Other new laws make it easier for handicapped people to travel. Special parking places are set aside for handicapped people near the doors of stores and buildings. Many buses have lifts, or moving platforms, to raise and lower wheelchairs. Sidewalks often have sloping curbs at each corner.

New laws also give the handicapped equal educational opportunity. In the past, handicapped children often went to special schools. They were "taken care of," but they were separated from other childen. Today, handicapped students can join regular classes.

Like most Americans, the handicapped want to earn their own way. New laws allow the handicapped to have equal opportunities for jobs. Jobs free handicapped people from their "prisons." Jobs make it possible for the handicapped to take care of themselves.

In many parking lots, spaces are reserved for handicapped people.

Handicapped people can now enjoy the freedom that equal job opportunities give them.

Lesson 3 Rights for Women

You read that many women worked in factories during World War II. After the war, when thousands of men returned from fighting, most of these women had to give up their jobs. Some of them were pleased to stop working, but others were not. They wanted to keep their jobs. They had enjoyed the work, and they liked being paid for the work they did.

Once the war was over, it was hard for women to get good jobs. Some people thought that all women should stay home. They also thought that women were unable to do most of the jobs that men could do.

Women had problems gaining other opportunities too. It was harder for women to get bank loans and credit cards. It was harder for women to get elected to political offices. After all, women had only been allowed to vote in state elections since 1911, and in national elections since 1920.

Some women organized to improve their lives. Women gave speeches and held marches to tell about their special problems. They joined together to elect lawmakers who would favor equal treatment of women. In 1966, the

Women serve alongside men in the police departments of Santa Ana and many other California cities.

In movies and television, women work both in front of and behind the camera.

195

Not long ago, few women practiced law. Many law schools would not let women in, and it was hard for them to get the education they needed. Today, women lawyers argue cases and women judges hear and decide cases in courts throughout the nation.

Network broadcasting was once a man's world. Today, women like Anna Chavez of Channel 7 in Los Angeles gather and report the news on radio and television.

National Organization of Women (NOW) was formed. Its goal is to work for equality in all areas of life.

Today, there are laws against refusing to hire a woman just because she is a woman. Laws also state that employers cannot pay a woman less than a man for doing the same job.

Some women have been helped by these laws. They have been able to get jobs in businesses and in fields that were once closed to them. But most women hold jobs that pay less than the jobs held by men. In 1980, for example, women as a group still earned only about two-thirds as much as men earned.

Checking Up

1. What happened to working women when World War II was over?

2. Name three problems women had at that time.

3. What organization was formed to help women?

4. Name two ways in which the law protects the rights of women today.

Building Social Studies Skills

Learning from a Survey

People who make toothpaste know that consumers will buy blue or green toothpaste, but not yellow. One Hollywood film producer makes films that appeal to people in their twenties; she know that's the average age of movie goers. American car makers know that people want cars with good gas mileage.

How do business people know these things? They take **surveys** to find out what people think. A survey is a set of questions about opinions. In taking a survey, the same questions are asked of many people, and the answers are counted. In this way, business people can learn what consumers think about their products or services.

A survey is a useful tool for getting people's opinions on a subject. It's a tool you can learn to use. For your first survey, find out what people think about the rights of the elderly. Here are the steps to use in making your survey.

Step 1. Decide on a topic for your survey. Your topic is the rights of the elderly.

Step 2. Write a list of questions about the topic. These questions should ask for people's opinions.

There are two main kinds of questions. One kind gives answer choices. In answering this kind of question, people must circle or mark one answer. The other kind of question gives no choices. It can be answered in any way.

Look at the survey below for some ideas for questions.

1. Should the elderly have the right to work as long as they want to?
   Yes ☐   No ☐
2. If you answered *No*, at what age should people be required to stop working? _____
3. Do the elderly have the right to medical care whether they can pay for it or not? Yes ☐   No ☐
4. Should the elderly pay lower bus fares and lower prices for movie tickets? Yes ☐   No ☐

Step 3. Include some questions that ask for facts about the people answering the survey. For your survey, it would be helpful to ask each person's age and sex. It would also help to ask where people live, about their jobs, and about their education.

This kind of information is important because it can tell you whose opinions you have gathered. Also, you can use this information to find out if, say, young people and older people have different opinions about the topic.

Step 4. Make copies of your survey and pass out the copies to people who will answer the questions. Or, ask the questions and write down people's answers.

How many people should you survey? The more people, the better. Imagine that a toothpaste company took a survey. The first ten people surveyed said that they *would buy* yellow toothpaste. If the survey stopped there, the company would never know that ninety out of one hundred people *hate* yellow toothpaste and would never, ever buy it. The more people you ask, the more accurate your survey will be.

Step 5. Organize and count the answers. Another word for this step is **tabulate**. Be sure to tabulate the answers of males separately from those of females. Also, tabulate separately the answers of people in each age group.

Step 6. Report the results of the survey. Here's a sample report:

1. Should the elderly have the right to work as long as they want to?

	Yes	No
Male	58	42
Female	63	37
Age 18–20	28	22
Age 21–40	18	32
Age 41–60	33	17
Age 61–above	41	9
Total	121	79

Total People Surveyed = 200

Now, study the report. How can you sum up the information tabulated? How do most people surveyed feel about the question? How do members of different age groups feel about it?

Step 7. Remember that your survey speaks for only a few people. A good survey tells the truth—as far as it goes. Be sure to keep in mind how far your survey goes.

Write your answers on paper. Do not write in the book.

Using Key Words

From the list below, choose the term that best completes each of the sentences. Write it on your paper.

boycott   riot
civil right   strike
migrant   survey
minority group tabulate
organize   union

1. A group of workers who have joined together is called a _____.
2. When workers refuse to work until they win better wages or working conditions, they are on _____.
3. When people _____ a product, they refuse to buy or use it.
4. You _____ the results of a survey by organizing and counting the answers.
5. Someone who moves often from place to place is called a _____.
6. Black people are members of one _____.
7. A right that is guaranteed by government to all citizens is called a _____.
8. A set of questions about opinions is called a _____.
9. To form a group for the purpose of working toward a common goal is to _____.

10. A _____ is a wild, noisy disturbance made by a large number of people.

Reviewing Main Ideas

Complete each sentence.
1. Minority groups organized to overcome _____.
2. Farm workers formed unions to gain _____.
3. New laws give _____ equal educational opportunity.

Thinking Things Over

Different groups of people have worked to gain many of the same rights. What are some of these rights?

Practicing Skills

Study the sample report from a survey on page 198. Write the letter of the best answer for each question.
1. How many men felt that the elderly should have the right to work as long as they want to?
   a. 58 out of 200
   b. 63 out of 100
   c. 58 out of 100
2. Which answer shows how the people over 61 years of age felt about this question?
   a. YES, 41; NO, 9
   b. YES, 28; NO, 22
   c. YES, 18; NO, 32

What Do You Know?

Write your answers on paper. Do not write in the book.

Words to Know

From the list below, choose the word that best completes each of the sentences. Write it on your paper.

ally   patriotic
depression   stock
migrant   tabulate

1. A _____ person is one who loves his or her country.
2. When you _____ a survey, you organize and count the results.
3. A country is having a _____ when people are out of work, prices fall, and businesses close.
4. A small part of a business sold to raise money is called a _____.
5. A _____ is a person who moves often from place to place.
6. A country that supports and helps another country is said to be its _____.

Ideas to Know

Choose the ending that makes each sentence true. Write its letter beside the question number on your paper.

1. A main cause of the Depression was
   a. the stockmarket crash.
   b. World War II.
   c. the drought in the dust bowl.

2. During the Depression, people felt
   a. that things would get better.
   b. good about themselves.
   c. worthless.

3. Californians discriminated against the dust bowlers because they
   a. wouldn't work.
   b. couldn't farm.
   c. took Californians' jobs.

4. During World War II, Californians discriminated against Japanese Americans because
   a. they married Japanese women.
   b. it was feared they would fight on the side of Japan.
   c. it was feared they would attack Pearl Harbor.

5. One good result of World War II was that it
   a. made Californians too patriotic.
   b. created jobs and growth in California.
   c. caused good feelings between Californians and Japanese Americans.

6. During the war, blacks and women
   a. were able to find jobs they couldn't get before.
   b. faced more discrimination.
   c. worked to gain more rights.

7. World War II made people feel
   a. patriotic.
   b. worthless.
   c. careless.

Write "true" for the sentences that are true. Write "false" for the sentences that are false.

8. California became a military base for the armed forces going to war in the Pacific.
9. During the war, Japanese Americans living in California were moved to relocation camps.
10. Many Japanese Americans proved their loyalty to the United States by fighting in the armed forces.
11. Shipyards and airplane factories were big industries in California during the war.
12. The Depression continued long after the war started.
13. Forming a union helped migrant farm workers gain higher wages and better working conditions.
14. Minority groups lost their civil rights at the end of World War II.
15. Women have won many rights since World War II.
16. The best way to help handicapped people is to take care of them.

Using What You Know

Read the following sentences about surveys. Write "true" for the sentences that are true. Write "false" for the sentences that are false.

1. Surveys are taken to find out what people think.
2. It is not important to know facts about the people answering a survey.
3. It is important to keep your survey as small as possible and not interview too many people.
4. After you get answers to your survey, you must organize and count them.
5. The report of your survey should include conclusions you have drawn about people's opinions.

Use the line graph to answer the questions.

Women Working at Jelly Bean Factory

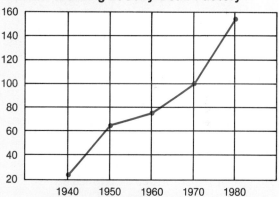

6. In which year did the most women work at the factory?
7. Between which years was the change in the number of women workers the least?
8. Between which years was the change in the number of women workers the most?

Unit 6

California's Government and Laws

When people live together in groups, they need rules to live in an orderly way. They need rules to protect people and the environment. You have rules in your home and in your school. These rules tell you what you must do and what you must *not* do. When rules are agreed to by many people, we call them laws. In our society, laws are made and carried out by the governments of our cities, counties, states and nation. People have the power to help shape the laws our governments make. Working together, people also have the power to change old laws and to make new ones. But to do these things, they need to know how our governments work.

18

Lesson 1 People Need Government
Lesson 2 City Government

Local Government

Why do people want rules and laws and government? Here are some reasons:

- People need order in their lives. Rules and laws help to give this order.
- People want to be protected from harm. They also want their property protected. Rules and laws help to protect people and property.
- People want services. Rules and laws tell governments what services to provide.
- People want good leaders. Good leaders are needed to make and act on rules and laws that protect and serve people.

Lesson 1   People Need Government

In a very small group or community, all of the people can get together at one time. They can meet to talk over problems. They can decide what rules or laws they want. Very small groups don't even have to write down their rules.

Let's say that you went on a camping trip with four other people. You would not need to make a written list of rules for the trip. With only five people, you could discuss any problem that came up.

What would happen if you went camping with one thousand people? All the people could not discuss every problem. If each person spoke for three minutes about a problem, the discussion would last fifty hours! Instead, it would be necessary for a smaller group to meet to discuss problems and decide what rules were needed. This governing group would write down the rules for everybody to read.

Today, most communities in California are large enough to need a special governing group made up of **representatives**. A representative is someone who is elected by the people of the community to help make laws for the community. He or she listens to the problems of the voters and suggests laws that will solve these problems. Then, all of the representatives vote on the suggested laws.

This kind of government is called a representative government. The people give power to their representatives by voting for them. But the people also have power. If a representative votes for or supports a law that people don't like, they will not vote for her or him again.

In America, we have three levels of government. Our national government in Washington, D.C., rules the whole country. The state governments rule the states. We also have **local governments**. These governments rule the **counties** and the cities.

Governments have two main jobs—to *protect* the people and to *serve* the people. A government does these jobs according to laws that say what the people want. There are many laws that tell government to protect people. For example, laws protect you from being served unclean food in restaurants. They protect you from being

county, one of the districts, or areas, a state is divided into.

One job of government is to serve people. A service usually provided by local government is garbage and trash collection.

Another job of government is to protect people. Local governments set up police departments and hire police officers to protect people in the communities they govern.

Governments build schools, buy desks and other furniture for them, and pay teachers to teach in them. Governments also set aside land to be used as parks for everyone to enjoy.

robbed. And they protect you from drinking water that has been poisoned by factories.

Laws also tell government how to serve people. Our cities and counties have paved streets and libraries and schools and parks because we have laws telling our local governments to provide them. We have fire departments and police departments because our laws tell the governments to provide these services also. You and your family probably could not afford to pave all the nearby streets. You probably could not afford to hire your own

Governments build libraries, buy books, and hire librarians to help people find the books and information they want or need.

As part of their job to protect, governments set up fire departments. Men and women are hired to fight fires and give first aid to people who are seriously ill or hurt.

fire fighters and police officers. That's why people have joined together to form governments.

Abraham Lincoln said that the purpose of government is to do for the people of a community whatever they need to have done—but cannot do for themselves as individuals. You'll want to keep that idea in mind as you read about city and state governments.

Checking Up

1. Name four reasons people want rules or laws.

2. Why do most California communities need a special governing group?

3. What do we call government made up of leaders elected by the people?

4. What are the two main jobs of government?

5. Name six services provided by local government.

6. In what way do people have power over representatives and government?

Lesson 2   City Government

The state of California is divided into fifty-eight counties. In each county, there are many cities. These cities are governed by **councils**. A council is a group of women and men chosen to make laws for and manage a city. As representatives of the voters, city councils have the power to decide how the city will be run.

In some cities, the voters also elect a **mayor**. A mayor is someone chosen to head the government of a city. He or she is the chief official of the city. In other cities, the council chooses the mayor or a city manager to head the city government.

What work does a city council do? It makes laws for the city. City laws are usually called **ordinances**. City councils pass ordinances about such things as traffic flow and parking. They pass ordinances for fire safety. They also pass ordinances about animal care and control. And they decide what businesses will be allowed to open and where.

Some of the city council's decisions are difficult to make. People in a city often have different ideas about how the city should be run. They cannot always agree on what would be best for the city.

To make these difficult decisions, council members study the facts. They also invite concerned citizens to come to their meetings. Council members listen to what these citizens have to say. After the council members have learned all they can by studying and listening, they vote.

Sometimes, the decisions council members make mean they must also decide how to spend money. For example, it costs money to provide parks and to buy and put in parking meters and traffic lights. It costs money to pay fire fighters, police officers, and garbage collectors. Where do the council members get the money?

City councils raise money by collecting taxes and by selling **licenses**. A license is a piece of paper showing that someone is allowed by law to do something. In some cities, the councils have licenses that allow people to build houses and schools, to run businesses, and to keep and care for animals.

Members of a city council have the power to make important decisions. But the citizens of a city have the power to make the most important decision of all. With their votes, they can decide who will represent them on the council.

At this council meeting for the city of Los Angeles, concerned citizens and council members discuss local problems.

Checking Up

1. What is the governing group of a city called?

2. What are the two names given to heads of city governments? In what two ways can they be chosen?

3. In what two ways do cities raise money?

4. What are two things a city council does before voting on difficult decisions?

5. What important decision do a city's people have the power to make? What else can they do to make sure their city government does what people want?

6. What are some kinds of ordinances city councils pass? What would happen if cities did not have ordinances?

209

Tom Bradley

Tom Bradley grew up in Los Angeles. He went to high school and college in that city. He was part of the community of Los Angeles. And he wanted to help his community.

Tom Bradley joined the Los Angeles Police Department. As a police officer, he helped youngsters in trouble. One way he helped was by forming athletic clubs. These clubs gave young people a chance to develop pride. They learned to respect themselves and others.

For twenty-one years, Tom Bradley was a police officer. But he wanted to serve Los Angeles in other ways too. Bradley had studied law and become a lawyer. Finally, he decided to run for the Los Angeles City Council. "I decided that, as a city councilman, I could truly have a good influence on the lives of the people in my district," he explains.

Tom Bradley was elected to the city council three times. He worked hard for the people, but he wanted to do more. In order to gain more power to help the people of Los Angeles, he decided to run for mayor. In 1973, Tom Bradley became the first black person to serve as mayor of Los Angeles.

As mayor, Tom Bradley continued to serve the people of his community. He

worked hard to help businesses. He knew that more business would mean more good jobs. Bradley also helped to create a water conservation program.

In 1982, Tom Bradley ran for governor of California. He says, "I have always looked for the job that would let me be of service to others."

Write your answers on paper. Do not write in the book.

Using Key Words

From the list below, choose the term that best completes each of the sentences. Write it on your paper.

council   mayor
county   ordinance
license   representative
local government

1. A person who is elected to help make laws for a community is a _____.
2. The government of a county or a city is called a _____.
3. The governing group of a city is called a _____.
4. The name for a city law is _____.
5. The chief official of a city is often a _____.
6. A piece of paper that says someone is allowed by law to do something is called a _____.
7. One district, or area, of a state is a _____.

Reviewing Main Ideas

Write "true" for the sentences that are true. Write "false" for the sentences that are false.

1. The jobs of government are to protect and provide services for people.
2. People give all their power to their elected representatives.
3. Rules and laws tell government what services to provide.
4. The mayor of a city makes all the important decisions.
5. Council members study facts, listen to people, and vote on issues.
6. The only way a city council can raise money is by collecting taxes.
7. Rules and laws help give order to people's lives.
8. Good leaders are needed to make and act on laws that protect and serve people.
9. City governments are always headed by mayors.

Thinking Things Over

Abraham Lincoln said that the purpose of government is to do for people of a community what they cannot do for themselves as individuals. How might your community be different if there was no government?

Practicing Skills

Your city council is studying police protection in your community. As a council representative, you have decided to take a survey on whether or not the city should have more police protection. Write three questions you would include on your survey.

Chapter

19

Lesson 1 The Legislature
Lesson 2 The Governor
Lesson 3 The Courts

The State Government

You have read that city governments protect and serve people by making laws. California's state government does these things too. Voters elect representatives to make state laws that will protect and serve the whole state. But making laws is only part of the job. The state government must also see that the laws are carried out. And it must decide when laws have been broken and how lawbreakers should be punished.

Do you remember that California's constitution divides the government into three parts? Each part does one of these important jobs:

- making and changing laws,
- putting laws into action,
- deciding if laws are fair, deciding if laws have been broken, and punishing lawbreakers.

Assemblywoman Teresa Hughes has served with Art Torres on the Health Committee. She has also given her energy to the Education, Housing Development, and Business and Professions Committees, as well as the Joint Committee on the State's Economy. Hughes has put her experience as a teacher and school administrator to work as chairwoman of the Post-Secondary Education Committee and by serving as legislative consultant to the State Commission for Teacher Preparation and Licensing.

Lesson 1   The Legislature

One part of California's government is made up of the state assembly and the senate. Together, the assembly and senate are called the **legislature**. It's the job of the legislature to make and change laws. The assembly and senate meet in Sacramento to suggest, discuss, and pass laws. A suggested law is called a **bill**. A bill cannot become a law unless both the assembly and the senate vote to pass it.

Art Torres began his service in the legislature in 1974 when he was elected to represent Los Angeles in the assembly. In 1982, he decided to run for state senator. We asked him how members of the senate and assembly represent the people. He noted that the two jobs are very similar and invited us to follow him around for a day of his life in the assembly. This is what that busy day was like.

Nine o'clock—Art Torres arrives at the capitol. The assembly begins its work with a prayer and the Pledge of Allegiance. Then Torres introduces a bill that will improve school meals. He tries to persuade the members of the assembly to vote for his bill. When the vote is taken, the bill is passed. This time, his ideas have won.

Twelve o'clock—Art Torres has lunch with his staff. They talk about problems in his **district**, or the part of Los Angeles that he represents.

One thirty—Art Torres goes to a Health Committee meeting. He is chairman. The thirteen members of this committee study every bill that has something to do with health. On this day, they listen while an assemblywoman explains a health bill she has suggested. Everyone on the committee asks questions. Citizens share their ideas about the bill. Then the Health Committee will decide what changes, if any, should be made to the bill before it is sent to the assembly for a vote. Or the committee may decide *not* to send the bill to the assembly.

Seven o'clock—Art Torres has dinner with a group of doctors. He tells them about several health bills that are before the legislature. They discuss what should be done now to improve the California health system in the future.

Torres explains that, from Monday through Thursday, this is the kind of life legislators lead. Late Thursday afternoon, most of them fly home to spend time with their families. Says Torres, "A good legislator takes time to meet with people in his or her district to find out what they want and need. Sometimes, people come by the office to describe their problems. Other times, the legislator goes out to meet people. Talking with and listening to people are the ways a legislator learns what new laws are needed."

Art Torres thinks everyone should take a turn in public office. He plans to teach people about politics. In this way, he will be able to help future members of the assembly and senate do a better job for the people they represent.

Like other legislators, Art Torres listens to the people in his district to learn what new laws are needed. He answers questions and tells these people how he plans to solve problems and meet their needs.

How Else Can Laws Be Made?

In California, most laws are made or changed by the legislature, which represents the people. But some laws are made or changed directly by the people.

The people of California can make or change laws by using a **petition**. A citizen, or group of citizens, writes an idea for a new law on a piece a paper. Then, the citizens try to get other voters to show that they support the law by signing this paper, or petition. If enough voters sign, the suggested law is voted on in the next election. Then, if a majority of the voters approve it, it becomes a new law.

Checking Up

1. What two groups make up California's legislature?

2. What is the job of the legislature?

3. What is a suggested law called?

4. What do you call the area represented by an assemblyman or assemblywoman?

5. How can the people of California make or change a law directly?

6. What is the most important part of a legislator's job? Explain your answer.

Lesson 2   The Governor

Every four years, California voters elect a **governor**.
To be elected governor of California, a person must be a
citizen of the United States. He or she must be at least
twenty-five years old and must have lived in California
for at least five years.

The governor is head of another part of the
government. It is his or her job to see that laws are put

Ronald Reagan was born in Illinois. After
graduating from college, he spent several
years as a sports announcer in Iowa. Later,
he moved to California and became an
actor in the movies. During World War II,
he served in the air force. In 1966 and
again in 1970, he was elected governor of
California. Then, in 1980, the American
voters elected him President of the United
States.

Earl Warren was born in Los Angeles in
1891. He went to the University of
California and graduated from its law
school. As state attorney general during the
1930s, he fought crime. He was elected
governor of California three times and held
that office longer than any other person.
In 1953, President Eisenhower appointed
Warren Chief Justice, or head, of the
United States Supreme Court.

215

into action. One person cannot do this job alone. The governor needs many people to help. The voters elect an attorney general, a secretary of state, and a treasurer to help the governor. The governor also hires a staff. Besides these workers, 130,000 people work for this part of California's government.

The governor has a lot of power. But he or she cannot make laws. The governor must work with the legislature to have an effect on our laws. The governor can suggest bills to the legislature. But the legislature decides whether or not to pass these and other bills. Bills passed by the legislature must be signed by the governor before they can become laws. The governor has the power to **veto**, or refuse to sign, a bill. However, if enough legislators want a bill to become a law, they can pass it even without the governor's signature.

The governor and the staff prepare the state's budget. The budget says how much money the state will spend on the different things it has decided to do. Once again, the governor must work with the legislature. The legislature may vote against any part of the governor's budget.

Because California is such a large and important state, a California governor who does the job well can be one of the most powerful people in the country.

Checking Up

---

1. What is the governor's job?

2. The governor cannot make laws. What can the governor do to have an effect on the laws that are made?

3. Why must the governor work with the legislature when the state's budget is being prepared?

4. What three things are necessary before a person can run for governor?

5. Why isn't the governor allowed to make laws?

Lesson 3 The Courts

The third part of California's government is made up of the courts and judges. Do you remember what job the courts do? They decide if laws passed by the legislature are fair. They decide if laws have been broken. If a person has broken a law, the courts also decide how to punish that person.

Courts also handle another kind of **case**, or problem. In these cases, no laws have been broken. Instead, two people or groups of people disagree about something. They can't settle their disagreement themselves. So they go to court and let a judge decide who is right and who is wrong. Read an imaginary court case that is very much like cases that have happened.

Mary lost her bike. She was upset but did not know what to do about the loss. Meanwhile, Selma found a bike. She took it to the police. After a few months, the police gave the bike to Selma because no one had claimed it.

Selma rode her new bike to the park. When Mary saw it, she exclaimed, "That's my bike!"

"No, it isn't," Selma answered. "The police gave it to me."

Who should get the bike?

The Modoc County courthouse is in Alturas. Where is the courthouse for the county you live in?

Selma and Mary could go to court to have a judge decide which one of them should keep the bike. First, the judge would ask questions to find out the facts in the case.

Judge: Can you prove that this is your bike, Mary?

Mary: It looks like my bike. I remember that long scratch under the seat.

Judge: Did you ever register your bike with the police?

Mary: No. I forgot.

Judge: Did you report the loss of your bike to the police?

Mary: No. I didn't think they could do anything about it.

Judge: Selma, what did you do when you found the bike?

Selma: I took it to the police.

Judge: How long did the police keep the bike?

Selma: Three months.

Judge: Have you any way to prove that this bike is yours now?

Selma: Yes. When the police gave the bike to me, I registered it in my name. Here is the registration slip.

The judge would take some time to decide who should keep the bike. Then she would announce her decision.

Judge: This is a difficult case. The bike probably was Mary's bike once, but she has no way to *prove* it. Every bike has a few scratches.

On the other hand, when Selma found the bike, she did the right thing. In this city, we have an ordinance saying that, when a person finds something valuable that does not belong to him or her, it must be turned in to the police. Then, if the owner does not claim it within a certain period of time, the police give the item to the person who found it.

When Selma found the bike, she followed all of these steps. Also, when the police gave the bike to her, she registered it in her name.

It's my decision that Selma should be allowed to keep the bike.

There are many kinds of courts in California. Some are city courts. Others are county courts or state courts. The California Supreme Court is the highest court in the state. When people disagree with a lower court's decision, they can take their case to a higher court. But the California Supreme Court has the last say in this state. The only higher court in the nation is the United States Supreme Court.

Checking Up

---

1. What are the jobs of California's courts and judges?

2. Describe two kinds of cases handled by the courts.

3. Name the four kinds of courts that we have in California.

4. Which court is the highest court in California? Which court is the highest court in the United States?

5. In the case of Mary and Selma, do you think the judge made a fair decision? Why or why not?

Write your answers on paper. Do not write in the book.

Using Key Words

From the list below, choose the word that best completes each of the sentences. Write it on your paper.

bill   legislature
case   petition
district   veto
governor

1. The governor can _____, or refuse to approve, a law.
2. The _____ makes new laws and changes old ones.
3. A suggested law is a _____.
4. The people of a _____ elect an assembly representative.
5. The people of California can make or change laws with a _____.
6. A problem to be solved in court is called a _____.
7. The _____ heads state government.

Reviewing Main Ideas

Write "true" for the sentences that are true. Write "false" for the sentences that are false.

1. California's constitution divides the government into three parts.
2. It is the job of the legislature to see that the laws are put into action.
3. The governor chooses representatives.
4. The governor has the power to make laws.
5. The legislature must approve the governor's budget.
6. The legislature cannot pass a law that the governor has vetoed.
7. Courts decide if the laws have been broken and how to punish those who break them.
8. There is only one kind of court in California.
9. Courts decide if laws are fair.
10. Courts sometimes handle cases in which no laws have been broken.

Thinking Things Over

People have the power to affect laws. If you and a group of people had an idea for a new state law, what are some things you could do to help get the law passed?

Practicing Skills

Two neighbors have gone to court to solve a problem. The roots of Neighbor A's tree are ruining Neighbor B's sidewalk. Neighbor B thinks Neighbor A should take out or move his tree. Neighbor A does not think he should have to move the tree. After all its in *his* yard. Draw a decision tree to show how the court might make a decision in this case. Remember to state the problem and list possible solutions.

20

Protecting the Environment

You have learned that the job of government is to provide services and protections people want but cannot provide for themselves. Many people want government to protect and conserve the **environment**. Some of these people have organized groups to influence the government and other people. They know that a group of people speaking together has more power than individuals speaking separately.

environment, all the surrounding things, conditions, and influences affecting growth of living things.

Lesson 1 Smog

What is **smog**? The word is a combination of *smoke* and *fog*. But the stuff in the air that looks brown and smells bad is more than just smoke and fog. It's dust from tires and bare fields. It's smoke from home fireplaces and factory chimneys. It's chemicals released by automobiles and airplanes. All of the things that make clean air dirty are called **pollutants**.

Pollutants from all these sources rise into the air. Sometimes, a breeze blows them away. At other times, however, they build up in the air. That's when you can see and feel smog.

On smoggy days, your eyes sting and your throat hurts. When you breathe deeply, your chest may hurt too. The pain is your body's way of telling you to protect yourself. When you feel this pain, you know it's time to stay indoors. It's time to take it easy. It is *not* the time to run fast and play hard. When you run, you breathe more rapidly. That means that more pollutants find their way into your lungs.

Smog is harmful to people. But it also harms other things. Smog dirties buildings, statues, and fountains. It

Smog is California's worst pollution problem. On a smoggy day, some of the buildings in Los Angeles and the mountains around it are almost completely hidden by the dirt in the air.

rots fabrics. It eats away paint and concrete. It harms trees and animals and farm crops.

Because smog damages all these things, smog costs money. Each year smog damage costs Americans $15 billion. That's about $65 for every man, woman, and child in the United States.

Smog is the state's number one pollution problem, but it used to be worse! Many Californians have worked hard to fight air pollution. Some have formed or joined groups such as the Sierra Club, the American Lung Association, or the Coalition for Clean Air. These groups have studied the effects of smog. They have worked to get laws passed making pollution a crime.

Today, there are laws that say people cannot burn their trash. In the past, many people burned trash and garbage every day. This caused bad-smelling smoke. Now trucks collect trash and garbage and haul it away.

Other air pollution laws control the amount of smoke factories can release into the air. Still other laws control pollution by cars, trucks, and buses. Because of these laws, cars sold in California must burn gasoline cleaner than cars sold in most other states.

Many people have joined together to fight smog and other kinds of pollution. On a clear day, the Los Angeles skyline is beautiful!

More can be done to fight air pollution. Environmental groups are still working to prevent it. But individuals can help too. People can drive less often. They can share rides and form carpools. What else can people do?

Checking Up

1. What is smog?

2. Why is it important to Californians to prevent smog?

3. How can you tell smog is affecting your body? What should you do about it?

4. Name at least five things that are affected by smog.

5. What do laws designed to prevent air pollution control?

6. Name two groups that have worked to stop air pollution.

7. What can individuals do to fight air pollution?

Building Social Studies Skills

Using a Road Map

The Garcia family is planning a trip. They want to visit Lassen Volcanic National Park and Shasta Lake. They will be traveling from their home in Sacramento. Can you find these three places on the road map?

- Lassen Volcanic National Park
- Shasta Lake
- Sacramento

1. What route should the Garcia family take?

Look at the map key. It shows several kinds of roads. The major highways, which have several lanes, are shown on the map with double red lines. Other roads are shown with single red lines.

The key also tells what the symbols on the map mean. Point to the symbol that means an interstate highway. Point to the one that means a state highway.

The Garcia family wants to travel on major highways as much as possible. Use your finger to trace the best route using major highways from Sacramento to Lassen Park. Then trace the route to Shasta Lake, and back to Sacramento. On a piece of paper, write down the kinds and numbers of the highways the Garcia family will use. Next to each highway number, write down the direction the Garcias will travel.

2. How many miles will the Garcias' trip be?

In addition to deciding which highways to use, the Garcias want to know how long their trip will be. They want to know how many miles they will have to drive. How can you find the distance, or mileage, of the Garcias' trip?

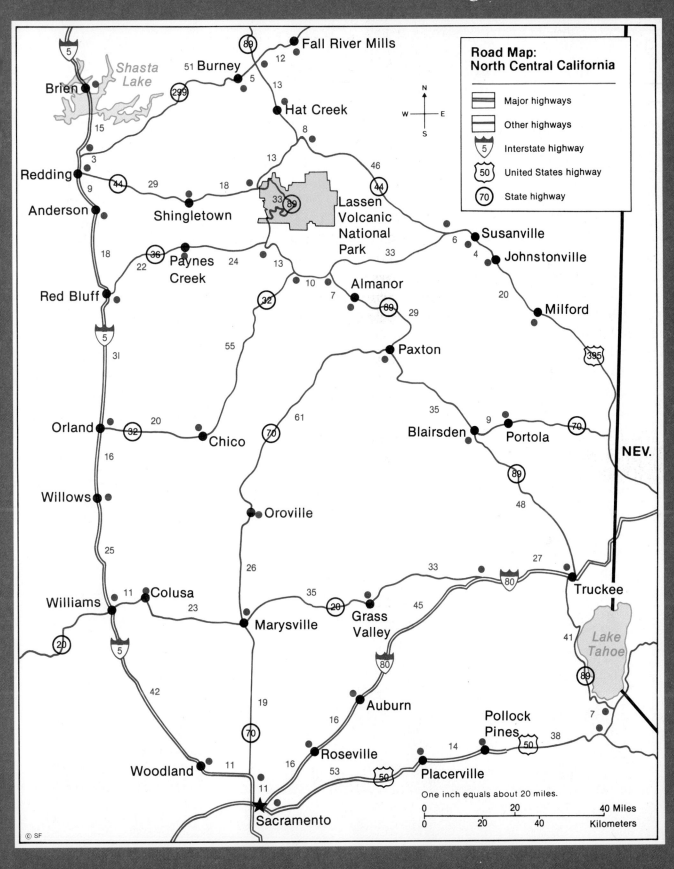

Road Map:
North Central California

Major highways

Other highways

5 Interstate highway

50 United States highway

70 State highway

One inch equals about 20 miles.

0   20   40 Miles
0   20   40   Kilometers

© SF

There are several ways of finding mileage on a road map. One way you probably already know about is using a bar scale. Find the bar scale at the bottom of the map. It shows how many miles one inch represents. The words above the scale also tell you how many miles are shown by one inch. Using the scale and a ruler, you could guess about how many miles the trip will be.

A more exact way of finding mileage is using the mileage dots on the road map. Each city or **junction**, which is a place where roads meet, is marked by a red dot called a mileage dot. Between any two dots is a number. That number tells how many miles of road are between the dots.

Look at the road between the star for Sacramento and the dot for Roseville. What number do you see there? There are 16 miles between those two cities.

You can figure out how many miles the Garcia family will travel by adding together all of the mileage numbers along their route. Figure out the mileage

numbers needed to answer these questions. Write them on your paper.

1. How many miles will the Garcias travel between Sacramento and Lassen Park?
2. How many miles will they travel to get through the park?
3. How many miles will they travel to get from the park to Shasta Lake?
4. How many miles must they travel to get home from the lake?
5. How many total miles will the Garcia family travel?

Check your mileage total by using your ruler and the map bar scale. Is the mileage the same when measured this way? Why or why not?

Lesson 2 Agriculture and Pollution

Smog is one kind of pollution in California. Another kind of pollution is caused by **pesticides**. Pesticides are chemicals used to kill pests. Pests are insects and other animals that harm crops. To get rid of pests, many farmers spray their fields and crops with pesticides.

Pesticides can be very useful. Without them, many California crops, which are important to the world's food supply, might be lost. And pesticides can help kill insects that carry diseases.

Pesticides can also cause problems. Sometimes they kill animals that are not pests. Sometimes rain washes pesticides from fields into nearby streams and lakes where they poison fish and plants. And sometimes people and animals get sick from eating foods sprayed with pesticides.

To prevent pollution, scientists have worked to find safer ways of controlling pests. One way is to attract pests into traps. Another way is called biological pest control. With this method, pests are kept from multiplying or are killed by insects or other animals brought into an area to eat them. Do you remember how this method was used to save the California orange crop in the 1890s? Ladybugs were brought to California from Australia to eat the insects that were causing cottony-cushion scale.

As with pesticides, biological control can also cause problems. Sometimes, insects brought in for biological control can't live in their new environment. Other times, insects used to fight a pest become so successful that they, too, become pests. And sometimes, biological efforts to keep a pest from multiplying are unsuccessful.

This was true in 1981 when the dreaded Mediterranean fruit fly nearly destroyed many of California's fruit crops. Despite biological efforts to control the Medfly, it spread quickly over much of Northern California and the San Joaquin Valley. It became necessary to spray pesticide over large areas of the state to stop this pest. The spraying was done at night. Much care was taken to make sure it was not harmful to people and animals.

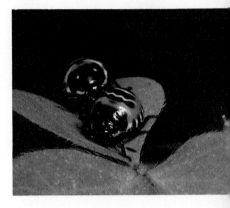

One kind of biological pest control is using insects to destroy other insects. Ladybugs are often used in this kind of pest control. They have very big appetites for their size. And they like to eat tiny insects called aphids. If not controlled in some way, aphids kill plants by sucking the juices from their leaves and stems.

227

Sometimes chemical pest control is necessary to protect California's valuable crops. Here, a field is being sprayed with pesticide.

Some people argue that use of pesticides is bad for the environment. They want laws to prevent pesticide use. Other people think pesticides are needed and, if used carefully, are harmless. Most people agree we must find ways to control the pests that harm California's valuable crops and, at the same time, keep pollution down. Scientists and farmers work together to find safe, effective methods of controlling pests and protecting crops. Their search goes on.

Checking Up

1. What are pesticides?

2. What problems are caused by pesticides?

3. What are some other methods of pest control?

4. What problems do these methods cause?

5. Do you think use of pesticides should be stopped even if it means crops might be destroyed? Why or why not?

Gil Chavez, Jr.
Professional Horseman

"How are my babies?" Gil Chavez asks.

The other man, who is an animal doctor, says, "Fine, Gil. They're doing fine."

"Well, take good care of them," Mr. Chavez says.

Mr. Chavez's "babies" are new Arabian foals, born only a few days before. These are lucky babies. They were born in one of the finest stables in California. And their trainer will be Gilbert Chavez, Jr. Mr. Chavez is, in his own words, a "professional horseman."

"Horsemen and horsewomen train horses. They also train their owners to ride or drive the horses," he says. "They breed horses. They may help owners buy and sell horses. They care for the horses. They see that they're well fed—and correctly fed. They see that the stables and the horses are kept

229

clean. The professional horseman or horsewoman not only cares *for* the horses, but really cares *about* them."

Gil Chavez has a brand new stable. It is clean and airy. A carpet of fresh wood shavings covers the floor. There are apartments in the stable for Mr. Chavez's workers. "The horses are never—but *never*—left alone," he says. "Someone is with them all the time."

For Gil Chavez and his workers, the day starts at 4:30 in the morning. "That first hour is a good time for thinking and planning," Mr. Chavez says. The horses are fed at 5:30 sharp. Why so early? "I might want to sleep in, but the horses' natural clocks tell them it's breakfast time. Besides, we need the whole day for exercising and training the horses."

Each horse is ridden or exercised every day. Most are also trained in show-ring manners. In training horses, Mr. Chavez treats each one as an individual. Each horse has a different training routine that will build on its strong points and overcome its weak points. "I'm like a coach," Mr. Chavez says. He wants each horse to look its best and perform its best.

Gil Chavez has known lots of horses. He owned his first horse when he was eleven. He first earned money for training a horse when he was fourteen. In college, he earned money by training horses and giving riding lessons. Soon he was known as a good trainer. Mr. Chavez got his first full-time job as a horseman on a ranch near San Diego.

After working for other people for several years, Gil Chavez went into business for himself, breeding and training horses. "I started here with one horse," Mr. Chavez says. "Now I have forty-two. The business has been good to me. And it *is* a business—a complicated business. I'm going to need a computer before the year is over. I studied business in college. From that training and from my experience, I've learned to *run* a business." He smiles and says, "I've also learned to be a plumber, an electrician, a veterinarian, and a truck driver. I've learned how to be a salesman. I've learned the social graces—good manners, proper dress, good language. My language and social skills are as important to my business as my abilities as a horseman."

How does Gil Chavez feel about his work? "I *love* the business. I have to get up at 4:30, seven days a week. I haven't had a vacation in ten years. And *still* I love the business. I like the animals. And I'm learning all the time. Whether I'm training horses or teaching owners or training my workers, *I'm* still learning too."

Is this a good business for kids to get into? "Yes. Anybody who is determined and patient and works hard can be successful. People like to see you work hard. You don't have to *be* the best, but you have to try to *do* your best."

230

Lesson 3 Gray Whales and Sea Otters

If you travel along the California coast during the winter months, you may see jets of water shooting up in the ocean. If you look more carefully, you may see large gray forms moving close to the surface of the water. These shapes are California gray whales.

During the late spring and summer, the gray whales feed in the cold waters off Alaska. Then they swim south for the winter. They travel from Alaska to Baja California and then back again. This trip is five thousand miles one way. The whales swim twenty hours each day. It takes them nearly three months to reach the warm waters of Baja California. There they give birth to their young. Then, soon after, they begin the long swim back to Alaska.

There was a time when you could *not* see gray whales along the California coast. Before people had figured out how to get oil out of the ground, they got oil out of whale fat. They burned the oil in lamps. They used the oil to make the wheels of wagons and machines turn more smoothly.

In the 1800s, whaling was an important industry in California. People went out in boats to find gray whales. They caught them and killed them for their oil.

By the early 1900s, no more gray whales could be found. Many people thought that they had all died, that is, that the gray whales had become **extinct**.

But there were a few whales left. By then people were pumping oil from the ground. They did not really need whale oil. Many people protested the killing of the whales. A group of people from many nations met to discuss the problem. Together, they wrote and signed an agreement saying that they would protect the gray whales. They would no longer kill them. Today, thanks to the agreement, the population of gray whales is high again.

Another sea mammal that almost became extinct is the sea otter. For years sea otters were caught and killed for their fur. Finally, after many years of hunting, sea otters could no longer be found. There were a few sea otters

Mammals are not the only animals that have become nearly extinct. Some birds are also in danger. The number of brown pelicans has been going down since the 1940s. Pesticides in the fish these birds eat have caused them to lay eggs with very thin shells. Many of these eggs have broken before the young birds in them could grow and hatch.

With buttons and bumper stickers, a group known as Greenpeace urges people to save the whales and seals.

left, however. In the 1930s, people began to spot otters again. Laws were passed to protect them. Today, there are many sea otters. They are out of danger.

Some animals have not been so lucky. For example, fur seals did become extinct. They were hunted and killed for their fur. Now there are no more fur seals.

Facts and Figures

In 1976, the California legislature made the gray whale the state's official marine mammal.

Checking Up

1. Why did the gray whale and the sea otter nearly become extinct?

2. How were the gray whales saved?

3. How were the sea otters saved?

4. What animal was hunted until it became extinct?

5. What might happen if groups of people and laws did not work to protect California's animals?

Reviewing Chapter 20

Write your answers on paper. Do not write in the book.

Using Key Words

From the list below, choose the word that best completes each of the sentences. Write it on your paper.

environment   pesticide
extinct   pollutant
junction   smog

1. The word _____ is a combination of *smoke* and *fog*.
2. Anything that makes clean air dirty is a _____.
3. The place where two roads meet is called a _____.
4. A chemical used to kill pests is called a _____.
5. When all the animals of a kind are dead, that animal is _____.
6. Our surroundings are part of our _____.

Reviewing Main Ideas

Write "true" for the sentences that are true. Write "false" for the sentences that are false.

1. Smog is made up of more than smoke and fog.
2. Smog is harmful only to people.
3. Biological pest control has never been used successfully in California.
4. Laws have been passed to protect endangered animals.

Thinking Things Over

Most people understand the bad effects of pollution. If this is true, why do we still have pollution? Why are laws sometimes necessary to protect our environment?

Practicing Skills

Use the map to answer the questions.

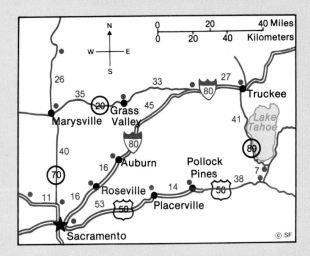

1. The Garcia family now plans to visit Lake Tahoe. In what two main directions will they be traveling as they go from Sacramento to Lake Tahoe?
2. Which major highways could the Garcias take?
3. If they go through Placerville, how many miles will they travel?
4. If they go through Auburn, how many miles will they travel?

What Do You Know?

Write your answers on paper. Do not write in the book.

Words to Know

From the list below, choose the word that best completes each of the sentences. Write it on your paper.

bill mayor
environment ordinance
extinct pollutant
governor smog
license representative

1. The _____ is the head of the part of state government that makes sure the laws are carried out.
2. A _____ is a person elected by voters to help make laws for a community.
3. A city law is called an _____.
4. A suggested state law is called a _____.
5. A city government is sometimes headed by a _____.
6. A _____ is something that makes the air dirty.
7. A _____ is permission by law to do something.
8. An animal that no longer exists is _____.
9. Dust, smoke, and other chemicals cause _____.
10. Surroundings and other conditions that affect the growth of living things make up the _____.

Ideas to Know

Write "true" for the sentences that are true. Write "false" for the sentences that are false.

1. When people live together in groups, they need rules to live in an orderly way.
2. Government gives people protection and services.
3. The people of California give all of their power to elected representatives.
4. Local government includes city and state government.
5. California cities are governed by councils.
6. City councils raise money by collecting taxes and selling licenses.
7. California's government is divided into two parts.
8. The state legislature is made up of the assembly and the senate.
9. It is the job of the legislature to decide if laws are fair or have been broken.
10. The people of California can make or change laws with a petition.
11. The governor makes our laws and puts them into action.
12. The governor can refuse to sign a bill passed by the legislature.
13. Courts do not handle cases unless laws have been broken.

14. City courts are the highest courts in the state of California.
15. Some people have formed groups to protect the environment.
16. Smog is harmful to buildings.
17. Today there are laws that make polluting the air a crime.
18. Pest control is not necessary.
19. Pesticides can be helpful.
20. The gray whale and the sea otter have been saved from extinction.

Using What You Know

1. Use this newspaper index to answer the questions.

INDEX	
SUBJECT	**PART**
Business	D
Classified	F
Editorial	B
Entertainment	E
Finance	D
Local News	B
Sports	C
Weather	A
World News	A

In which part of the newspaper would you find
    a. baseball scores?
    b. results of a city election?
    c. daily temperatures?
    d. movies playing today?
    e. your favorite TV show?
    f. today's news headlines?

2. Use the map and the bar scale to answer the following questions.

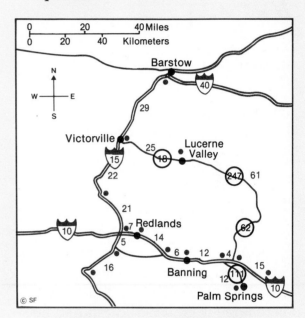

    a. What are the numbers of the highways you would travel from Redlands to Palm Springs?
    b. In which direction would you travel to go from Redlands to Palm Springs?
    c. About how many miles is it from Redlands to Palm Springs?
    d. Is Barstow north or south of Banning?
    e. Is Lucerne Valley east or west of Victorville?
    f. Is Banning north or south of Lucerne Valley?

235

Unit 7

California—The Golden State of Variety

Chapter 21
California's Regions

Chapter 22
California's People

Chapter 23
California's Role in the Nation and the World

California is a land of great variety. You can find huge sand dunes and snow-fields, green farmlands and rocky places were nothing grows. You can find huge cities with tall buildings and crowded freeways. You can also find large areas with only a few tiny towns or no towns at all. In California, you can see many crops growing—from wheat to grapes to oranges. You can see many different industries, from the oil industry to the movie industry. California also has a great variety of people. These people bring together cultures and customs from all parts of the world.

This variety makes California a rich and exciting place to live.

California's Regions

Historically, California has been thought of as two major regions: Northern California and Southern California. Today, some people think of the Central Valley as a separate region. There are differences among these regions. But in many ways, the regions are similar. Together, they make California a strong, rich state.

The map of California below shows how land is used in these regions. How is land used in Northern California? In

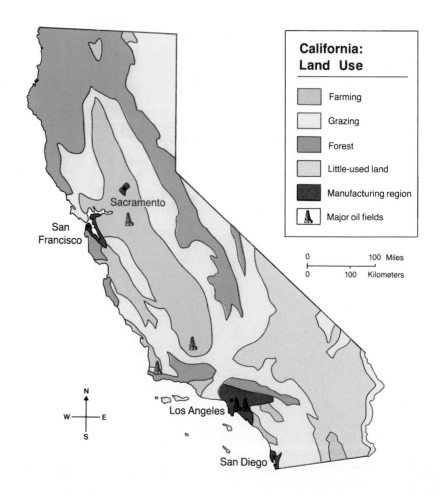

the Central Valley? How is land used in Southern California?

In this chapter, you will learn more about the northern and southern regions of California. You will discover how the climate and resources of each region affect the crops grown in that region and the variety of products made there.

Lesson 1   Northern California

If you like dark, green forests of tall pines and firs and redwoods, Northern California is the place for you. The cool, rainy climate of Northern California's coast has created hundreds of miles of forests. These forests are one of the region's most important natural resources. For years, the lumber needed to build California's homes has come from the sawmills of this region. Paper mills also depend on trees.

Farming is another important business in Northern California. There are farms along the rainy coast and in the drier upper Central Valley. Grapes, cotton, vegetables, hay, rice, chickens, dairy products, and beef are only a few of the farm goods produced in Northern California.

Once gold was Northern California's most important mineral resource. Today there are some active mines, but most of the gold is gone. Now sand and gravel are important resources. These materials are used to make cement for building. Natural gas, oil, and gasoline are also important products of this region.

Have you ever thought of beauty as a resource? The redwood forests draw thousands of visitors each year. Founders' Tree, which is thought to be the tallest tree in the world, grows in Redwood National Park. It is a favorite of **tourists**. Visitors to Lassen Volcanic National Park can climb a volcano and enjoy boiling, colorful pools and mud pots.

On the Monterey Peninsula, people can visit the popular seaside village of Carmel and take the famous seventeen-mile drive through Del Monte Forest. Or they can take a winding ride down Highway 1 overlooking steep cliffs and breathtaking ocean scenery.

California's Central Valley

By the Way

Many people think that the state should be thought of as three regions: Northern California, Southern California, and the Central Valley. The Central Valley is the large area outlined on the map above. It includes the Sacramento Valley in the north and the San Joaquin Valley in the south.

There are many ways in which the Central Valley is very different from both the northern and southern regions. And because most of the Central Valley is used for agriculture, the people and businesses there have many needs in common.

For these reasons, we sometimes take a separate look at the Central Valley when studying the regions of our state.

239

The beautiful Mammoth Lakes Recreation Area in Northern California is a four-seasons tourist spot. It covers about two hundred thousand acres, including parts of the Muir Trail and Devils Postpile National Monument. People go to Mammoth to fish, boat, and hike. Perhaps the biggest attraction is popular Mammoth Mountain, famous for its exciting and breathtaking ski runs.

Yosemite Valley and Lake Tahoe are two other beautiful and popular places. Cities such as Sacramento and San Francisco are also important tourist spots. Many people visit these cities during their vacations.

Sacramento is important for other reasons too. Since 1854, it has been the capital of California. It is also a center of agricultural industry.

Factories in Northern California make aircraft parts, missiles, computers, and electronic parts. As you can see, the region is rich in resources and full of varied activities.

Checking Up

1. Look at the land use map on page 238. Name one use of land in Northern California.

2. What products are made in Northern California? Name at least five.

3. Name three crops grown in this region.

4. Why are the Northern California sawmills along the coast?

5. What do Northern California's biggest industries produce?

6. Why is the beauty of an area considered a resource?

Lesson 2   Cities of Northern California

San Francisco

San Francisco is an important trade center. This is because it is built on the largest port on the west coast, San Francisco Bay. This bay is one of the most perfect natural harbors in the world. More than a million tons of cargo pass through this port each year.

By providing loans, San Francisco helped the mining industry grow in the West. The city is now the second largest **financial** center in the United States and the home of the nation's largest banks.

San Francisco is often remembered for its special features and landmarks. One of these is its cable cars. A man named Andrew Hallide, who made mining cables, decided that he could use his thick wire ropes to carry people up and down the city's steep hills. Hallide rigged some cables to passenger cars, and in 1873, the first cable car in history climbed Clay Street to the top of Nob Hill.

Cable cars, once very necessary to San Francisco transportation, are still an important part of San Francisco's charm. With clanging bells, they have carried thousands of people up and down the city streets. Today, though the real need for cable cars is gone, much money and effort have been spent to keep them running. They remain dear to the hearts of both San Franciscans and tourists.

Beautiful bridges bring people across San Francisco Bay to the city. One, the Golden Gate Bridge, is one of San

financial, having to do with money matters.

A popular spot in San Francisco is Fisherman's Wharf. There, visitors can enjoy eating foods from all over the world and shop for just about anything.

Cable cars like this one carry people up and down San Francisco's busy streets.

241

The Golden Gate Bridge, a beautiful part of the San Francisco skyline, also has a colorful history. When the bridge was finished, there was a rush to be the first to cross it. Some people crossed the bridge in unusual ways just to be the "first"—the first to push a baby carriage across, for example, or the first to walk across on stilts.

All of San Francisco helps celebrate the Chinese New Year.

Francisco's most famous landmarks. Built in 1937, it is considered a great engineering feat for its time. The builders of the bridge started in the middle and worked their way back to the land on either side.

Besides driving across bridges, many people travel to San Francisco on BART (Bay Area Rapid Transit). BART is a railway that moves underground and underwater along part of its route. It's a speedy way of getting many people who live in nearby towns to their jobs in the city.

One of the most interesting things about San Francisco is the great variety of people who live and work there. People of almost every race and culture live in San Francisco. The biggest group is Chinese Americans. As you know, one part of San Francisco is called Chinatown and features Chinese shops, restaurants, and newspapers. San Francisco has the largest Asian American population of any city in the United States.

Sacramento

Sacramento is located in the upper end of the Central Valley. Because it is the state capital, Sacramento is one of our most important cites. Many people live in or travel there to work in state government.

Sacramento is also an important industrial city. Its major industry is the canning and freezing of foods grown

The capitol, which was completed in 1874, is a beautiful sight for city dwellers and visitors alike. It has a gold-leafed dome that is topped by a ball plated with gold coins. The surrounding park is a showplace for more than eight hundred different trees and flowers from all over the world.

on rich Central Valley farmlands. Factories there also make sugar from sugar beets and flour from grain.

Goods are shipped to and from Sacramento along inland rivers and the many rail lines that come into the city. A forty-three-mile (sixty-nine-kilometer) channel from Sacramento to the San Francisco Bay area allows boats to travel between these two places and dock in Sacramento's port.

Many tourists come to Sacramento to visit the beautiful capitol and the city's historical sites. These include Sutter's Fort, where gold was first discovered, and old Sacramento, the original Gold Rush town, which has been restored.

Checking Up

1. Describe one thing San Francisco is famous for.

2. What is the largest cultural group of San Francisco?

3. Name two reasons Sacramento is important.

4. If you visited Northern California, what one thing would you most want to see? Why?

Dianne Feinstein

Dianne Feinstein's [fīn ′ stīn] first task as the mayor of San Francisco was a very sad one. She had to report to the people of her city that Mayor George Moscone [mos cōn ′ ē] had just been shot and killed in the city hall. The San Francisco Board of Supervisors—of which she was president—elected her to take George Moscone's place. A year later, she was elected to another term by city voters. In this way, Dianne Feinstein became the first woman to be elected mayor of San Francisco.

When she was a young girl, Dianne's uncle often took her to meetings of the Board of Supervisors. He was very interested in local government. He told Dianne she should get an education and become a supervisor. He was sure she would do a good job.

By the time she was a teen-ager, Dianne Feinstein knew she wanted to work in government. To prepare for this work, she studied history and government at Stanford University. Then she worked at several different government jobs. She served on the Mayor's Committee on Crime, as well as on other committees. Through her work, Feinstein became an expert on crime and on the treatment of lawbreakers.

In 1969, Dianne Feinstein was elected to the San Francisco Board of Supervisors. Just as her uncle predicted, she did a good job. She was elected to two more terms.

At the time that Dianne Feinstein became mayor in 1978, San Francisco was troubled. There was much crime. There were difficulties among people of different races. Many people wanted to make changes to improve the city. But they could not agree on what changes to make. As mayor, Feinstein worked to help different groups cooperate with one another. She also worked with the police and the community to reduce crime. She said she wanted to give San Francisco a government as good as its people.

Lesson 3   Southern California

Throughout history, sunshine and warm weather have drawn thousands of people to Southern California. Climate has always been one of California's most important resources. As you know, industries such as the aircraft and movie industries have located in Southern California because of its climate. Another important industry of this region is the tourist industry. People come to visit the warm, sunny beaches, to play golf and

Southern California is famous for its wide, sandy beaches and warm sun. Visiting the beach for a day of fun in the sun is one of the area's favorite recreations for local people and tourists. California has 840 miles (1,352 kilometers) of coastline. What parts of California's coast have you visited?

245

tennis, and to swim. Tourists also come to see Hollywood and Disneyland.

As in Northern California, agriculture is important in Southern California. Thanks to the water brought into the area, many crops can be grown in the rich soil of this region. Oranges, lemons, strawberries, and avocados are all grown in Southern California. Other important farm products include cotton, dairy products, vegetables, beef, and eggs.

Oil and natural gas are some of Southern California's most important resources. This region produces more than half of the state's oil. Gasoline, fuel oil, and many other chemicals are made from the oil.

Los Angeles and San Diego are the state's major fishing ports. From these ports, fishing fleets sail as far as South America. Their most valuable catch is tuna.

Because of its harbor, San Diego is also a center for shipbuilding and for the navy. And, like San Francisco, both Los Angeles and San Diego are trade centers.

Many of the industries and activities of Southern California depend on the high population of the area. All the people living in the region need food, clothing, housing, and services. Factories in this region make automobiles and clothing. Southern California, like Northern California, is rich in its variety of activities.

Checking Up

---

1. Name five industries that are important to Southern California.

2. Besides good climate, what makes it possible to grow many crops in Southern California?

3. Name five farm products produced in Southern California.

4. What industries depend on the high population of Southern California?

5. Why is climate considered an important resource?

Lesson 4   Cities of Southern California

The Los Angeles and San Diego areas are two of California's most populated areas. Many smaller cities surround the cities of Los Angeles and San Diego. When you travel between them, it's often hard to tell where one city ends and another begins.

Like big cities everywhere, the cities of Southern California have some problems. Among them are smog and crowded freeways. Despite these problems, Southern California cities are popular places to live.

Cities offer **opportunities** of all kinds. There are many different schools, churches, libraries, and hospitals. There are stores of all kinds. A great variety of jobs can be found in cities. And opportunities for fun, or **recreation**, are varied too. People can enjoy themselves at museums, zoos, movie theaters, restaurants, or amusement parks. In Southern California, city people can also drive to nearby beaches, forests, and mountains.

The San Diego Area

Some of the opportunities for fun offered by San Diego include Sea World, the San Diego Wild Animal Park, and the San Diego Zoo. The zoo began in 1915 as a collection of animals left over from the World's Fair. Today it boasts the largest collection of wild animals in the world!

opportunity, a good chance to do something.

recreation, play or amusement; something done for fun.

In a children's zoo—such as this one at the famous San Diego Zoo—it is possible to pet and sometimes feed the animals.

San Diego's environment includes water, sunshine, and hills. The recently built Coronado Bridge is San Diego's link to beautiful Coronado Island. For many years, the only way to travel between these two places was by ferryboat.

247

Our cities' museums offer many exciting opportunities to learn. The Experience Center science museum in Irvine provides hands-on activities for both children and adults. Pictured here is a film set from the movie, *Alien*. This display shows museum visitors a Hollywood designer's view of a computer in the future of space and a behind-the-scenes look at how Hollywood sets are built today.

People in San Diego can also visit the Aerospace Museum and the Reuben H. Fleet Space Theater. The space theater is the largest planetarium in the United States. Just north of San Diego is the two-hundred-inch telescope of the Mount Palomar Observatory. Also located near San Diego is the Scripps Institute of Oceanography. As you can see, San Diego is an important center for the study of both space and oceans.

The Los Angeles Area

Los Angeles is California's largest city. It has been called the Industrial Center of the West because many different products are made there. Los Angeles also has many interesting spots for city dwellers and tourists.

One of the oldest sections of Los Angeles, part of the original Spanish pueblo, was restored in 1930. Known as Olvera Street, this area was made into a Mexican marketplace. Visitors can buy anything from leather paintings to clay figures to silver jewelry—all brought from Mexico.

Los Angeles has a huge music center and many different museums. Nearby, in San Marino, is the Huntington Library and Art Gallery. There visitors can see famous paintings and rare books. They can walk through a rose garden, a Japanese garden, and the world's largest cactus garden.

The first highway in California was El Camino Real. It was built along the path used in the 1700s to travel between the Spanish missions. Today, Southern California's large freeway system ties together the area's many cities and towns. Is your home near a freeway? Which one?

The Los Angeles area is also important in the world of science. The Griffith Park and Mount Wilson observatories are in this area. In Pasadena is the California Institute of Technology, which is a university known and admired all over the world. Also in Pasadena is the Jet Propulsion Laboratory, which is important to America's space effort.

Nearby are two famous amusement parks, Disneyland in Anaheim and Knott's Berry Farm in Buena Park. The Knott family started a fruit stand on their berry farm in the 1920s. Today it has grown into a tourist attraction with rides, shows, and lots of history. In this park are recreations of a Gold Rush town and of Independence Hall in Philadelphia.

Beautiful floats in Pasadena's New Year's Day Rose Parade attract people from all over the world. Pictured to the left is Olvera Street. This red brick street with some seventy sidewalk shops and restaurants, features fiestas, foods, and handicrafts of Mexico.

Checking Up

1. Why do people like to live in cities?

2. Name one opportunity for fun offered in San Diego and one offered in Los Angeles.

3. Why is San Diego important to science? Los Angeles?

4. What is Olvera Street?

5. What one thing in Southern California would you most want to see? Why?

Sleeping Beauty Castle at DISNEYLAND Park.

Write your answers on paper. Do not write in the book.

Using Key Words

From the list below, choose the word that best completes each of the sentences. Write it on your paper.

financial   recreation
opportunity   tourist

1. A person who vacations in another place is called a _____.
2. Because San Francisco has many businesses that deal with money, it is called a _____ center.
3. Something we do for fun is called _____.
4. A good chance to do something is an _____.

Reviewing Main Ideas

Write "true" for the sentences that are true. Write "false" for the sentences that are false.

1. Lumber is an important product of Northern California.
2. Gold is an important resource of Southern California.
3. Both Northern California and Southern California cities offer people many opportunities.
4. San Franciscans only use buses to get around.
5. Climate draws many people and industries to Southern California.
6. An important land use in the Central Valley is agriculture.
7. An area's climate and resources often affect what products are made there.
8. Agriculture is important to the businesses of Sacramento.

Thinking Things Over

Northern California and Southern California are different in many ways. They are also alike in some ways. Tell how they are alike and how they are different.

Practicing Skills

Use the chart below to answer the questions.

Death Valley Temperatures

	Sunday	Monday	Tuesday	Wednesday	Thursday	Friday	Saturday
High	100	92	94	94	97	98	101
Low	77	80	73	72	65	69	68

1. Which day was hottest?
2. Which day had the greatest difference in temperatures?
3. Which day had the least difference in temperatures?

Lesson 1 People Who Have Made a
Difference
Lesson 2 Many Other Cultures

California's People

California not only has a variety of resources and cities,
our state also has a variety of people. You have read
about the many groups of people who have come to
California from all over the world. These different groups
have brought their own cultures and their own ideas to
California. People of every color and background have
made **contributions** to our state. The mix of people,
cultures, and ideas in California today makes it a rich,
exciting place to live.

contribution, something
given or added; something
that benefits others.

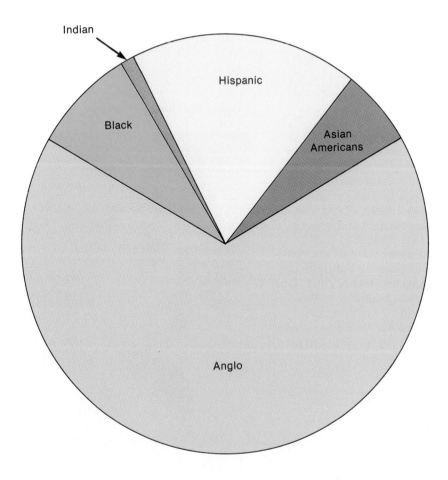

This circle graph shows
the five major groups of
people in California.
Which group is the
largest? The second
largest? Which group is
the smallest?
Each of the five major
groups is made up of a
variety of people with
different backgrounds. For
example, the group called
Asian Americans includes
Japanese, Chinese, Korean,
and Southeast Asian
Americans as well as other
groups!

Lesson 1   People Who Have Made a Difference

In this lesson you will read about just a few of the thousands of Californians who have made contributions to our world.

Californians in Public Service

Many Californians have made important contributions through public service. An example is Yvonne Braithwaite Burke. This Los Angeles woman served in the California state legislature. While there, she helped to pass several important bills. For example, she developed bills to provide child care to those who need it and aid to those who lose their homes because of governmental action.

In 1972, Burke became the first black woman elected to the United States House of Representatives from California. Yvonne Braithwaite Burke has been named a fellow in the Harvard University Institute of Politics, and KNX News Radio named her Woman of the Year. Burke also served as vice-chairman of the 1972 Democratic National Convention.

Yvonne Braithwaite Burke

Dorothy Chandler influenced the growth of a newspaper and a city. As the wife of Norman Chandler, owner of the *Los Angeles Times*, she encouraged that paper's commitment to public service. She also led the campaign to build the Los Angeles Music Center. One of the buildings in that center—the Dorothy Chandler Pavilion—stands as a special tribute to her efforts.

Vilma Martinez

Ralph Bunche

March Fong Eu has served the public in many ways. For example, she has been a school board member. She served on the White House Conference on Youth and was president of the Chinese Young Ladies Society. She is perhaps best known for her service as California's Secretary of State.

Shirley Hufsteadler is a Californian who served the entire nation. She practiced law in Los Angeles and later became a judge. Widely respected, Hufsteadler was chosen by President Jimmy Carter to be the first head of the new Department of Education.

Many Hispanic Californians are involved in helping their communities. Lawyer Vilma Martinez, for example, has served as president of the Mexican American Legal Defense and Education Fund (MALDEF). This organization is trying to improve job and educational opportunities for Mexican Americans. Martinez is thought by many to be the most respected Hispanic woman lawyer in the country. Another Hispanic who is involved in public service is the popular actor Ricardo Montalban. He works through church groups to help other Mexican Americans.

Ralph Bunche is a Californian who has made outstanding contributions to the entire world. In the 1920s, Bunche was at the top of his class, but he was not allowed to join the high school honor society—because he was black. Luckily for the world, Ralph Bunche overcame the discrimination he faced. As an adult, he taught at Harvard University. He also helped to form, and later worked for, the United Nations. In 1950, Bunche received the Nobel Peace Prize.

Walt Disney

Diana Ross has made outstanding contributions in entertainment. Her famous Supremes became the second-most popular singing group of the 1960s behind the Beatles. Later, she made her mark as an actress. Her role of Billie Holliday in *Lady Sings the Blues* won her an Academy Award nomination. She also won a special Tony award for a one-woman Broadway show.

Californians in the Arts

Many Californians have made contributions in the arts. For example, Paul R. Williams is an architect who has designed more than three thousand buildings. The Beverly Wilshire Hotel is one famous example. As a black architect, Williams faced discrimination early in his career. But today he is highly respected.

Norberto Reyes is a Filipino American artist from California. His works, which hang in the National Museum of Art, sell for ten thousand dollars or more. Another respected Californian artist is photographer Ansel Adams. Adams has displayed his work all over the world. He has also published more than thirty books. Some of his books are collections of photographs of California—books such as *Death Valley* and *Yosemite Valley*. Among other awards, Adams won the Muir Award from the Sierra Club.

California has produced many famous entertainers, producers, and screen writers. This is because the heart of the movie industry is in Southern California. Walt Disney was one of the most famous movie producers in history. He created many cartoon characters, including Mickey Mouse and Donald Duck. Later, he created the first full-length cartoon films ever made. Both his cartoon films and his movies starring real people and animals have been very popular. Disney also produced educational films and movies for television. His biggest success was opening Disneyland in 1955. Walt Disney's contributions are loved and enjoyed by children and adults throughout the entire world.

There are many famous Californian writers. Have you ever read a book by Dr. Seuss? This creator of entertaining stories in rhyme lives in the San Diego area. Ray Bradbury, in the Los Angeles area, has written many novels and short stories. His books are science fiction and fantasy, with settings as far out as Mars. Alice Walker, who lives in San Francisco, has won several awards for her writings. Walker writes poems, short stories, and novels about her experiences as a black woman in America.

Californians in Science

Californians have made scientific contributions in several fields. Linus Carl Pauling, a chemist, has won two Nobel prizes. His first Nobel prize was for his work in chemistry. Later, he won a Nobel Peace Prize for trying to stop atom bomb testing. David Blackwell, a black mathematician, was elected to the National Academy of Science. This is a great honor for a scientist. Another Californian, Roger W. Sperry, won the respected Lasker Award and later a Nobel prize for his discoveries about the human brain. This was among other contributions made as a professor at the California Institute of Technology.

Judith Baca, an artist, has organized the Great Wall of Los Angeles. This mural shows the history of the state in pictures. More than two hundred students have helped Baca paint the mural. Already more than one-third of a mile long, it is still growing!

255

Ron McNair is a Californian scientist who has become an astronaut.

By the Way

Jackie Robinson grew up in California. He became the first black American to play major league baseball. Can you imagine sports today without the contributions of black Americans?

Linda Morabito

Astronomer Linda Morabito, from the Jet Propulsion Laboratory, was the first person to discover an active volcano *not* on the earth. She found a volcano erupting on one of Jupiter's moons, Io. Another Californian astronomer is Eleanor Halin. She has discovered more asteroids than any other person in the country. Asteroids are chunks of rock and metal, smaller than planets, that move around the sun.

You may remember another famous Californian, Charles F. Richter, who developed a way to describe how strong an earthquake is. Today, scientists all over the world use the Richter scale to measure an earthquake's strength.

These are just a few of the Californians who have made a difference. Countless others have contributed in many ways.

Checking Up

1. Name two Californians who have contributed to science. What fields of science have they contributed to?

2. Name a California woman who has made a contribution to our world. Describe her contribution.

3. Who is Ralph Bunche? What problem did he overcome?

4. In what field would you most want to make a contribution? Explain why.

Lesson 2 Many Different Cultures

Where did your ancestors come from? Perhaps your ancestors came from Mexico or Europe. Perhaps, like many Americans, you have ancestors from many parts of the world.

There are Californians from many different groups and cultures. Many people still keep some parts of their culture alive. Today, all Californians can share in the state's rich mixture of cultures.

Throughout the state are many reminders of Hispanic influence. The names of many streets, cities, and natural features are Spanish. Hundreds of restaurants serve Mexican food. Families cook and eat Mexican food in their homes. And many of the homes themselves are built in the Spanish **style**. This style, or building design, is well suited to California's climate.

Some communities reflect Asian American cultures. You can find communities called Chinatown, Little Tokyo, and Koreantown. In these towns, the buildings look like those in China, Japan, and Korea. The stores sell goods brought

Santa Barbara's Hispanic roots run deep. Once a year, this city proudly celebrates its Hispanic heritage with a week-long fiesta.

At Los Angeles's Chinatown, visitors enjoy eating foods such as roasted duck and fried shrimp, chop suey and fried rice.

This is the Japanese garden at the Huntington Library and Art Gallery in San Marino. Many homes and institutions in California have Japanese-style gardens.

257

An important tradition of the Jewish community is the celebration of Hanukkah.

This is the Danish American town of Solvang. Here visitors enjoy eating pastries and other delicious Danish foods. They can shop for everything from wooden shoes to toys from Europe.

In recent years, many Southeast Asians have come to California from Vietnam, Cambodia, and Laos.

from these countries, and the signs are often written in their languages. All Californians can visit and enjoy these communities.

One of the largest Jewish communities in the world is in Los Angeles. Danish Americans have built a special community in the Santa Ynez Valley. And all over the state, restaurants, theaters, museums, and stores allow people to share parts of many different cultures.

Checking Up

1. Name two things in California that reflect our Hispanic roots.

2. Who built the town of Solvang?

3. In what ways do you and your family share in Asian cultures?

4. Name three cultures from which we enjoy foods in California.

5. From what group or groups do your family ancestors come? In what ways have you kept parts of their culture?

258

Write your answers on paper. Do not write in the book.

Using Key Words

From the list below, choose the word that best completes the sentence. Write it on your paper.

contribution

style

1. What a person gives or adds to something is his or her _____.
2. The special way in which something is designed is its _____.

Reviewing Main Ideas

Write "true" for the sentences that are true. Write "false" for the sentences that are false.

1. California has a variety of people who came here from all over the world.
2. Many black Californians have made important contributions to our state and our world.
3. Californians share in customs and celebrations from many cultures.
4. Hispanic culture is a big part of California's way of life.
5. Many Californians have recently come from Southeast Asia.
6. Asian Americans have not kept their cultures alive in California.
7. People in California enjoy eating foods from all over the world.

Thinking Things Over

There are many ways to learn about the contributions of people from other cultures. What are some of these ways? Describe some ways in which you have learned about the customs and cultures of other groups.

Practicing Skills

Look at the land use map below to answer the questions.

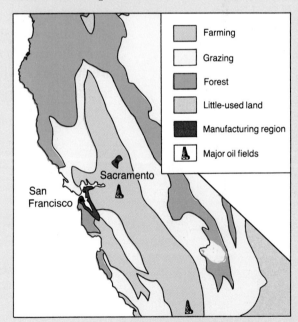

1. How is most of the land near the coast used?
2. Which land use takes up the smallest amount of land?
3. Which land use is represented by light green?

Chapter

23

Lesson 1 Products to Trade
Lesson 2 Computers and Spaceships

California's Role in the Nation and the World

California has more human and natural resources than many of the world's nations. With these resources, California has been able to make many contributions to the United States and to the world.

Lesson 1 Products to Trade

Every day, cargo ships leave and enter California's ports. Airplanes take off and land, and trucks cross the state line. The ships, planes, and trucks all carry products. The products coming into California from other nations are **imports**. The products leaving California for other nations are **exports**. Together, the imports and exports

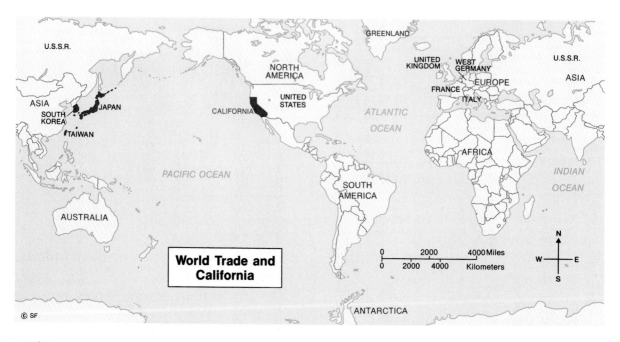

World Trade and California

260

make up California's trade—a trade worth tens of billions of dollars.

One way in which California contributes to the United States is as a trade center. Because it is on the Pacific Ocean, California can easily trade with Asian countries. Cars from Japan, radios from Taiwan, and clothes from South Korea are just a few examples of products Americans import from Asian countries. Look at the map on page 260. Can you find these countries? California's excellent harbors—San Francisco, San Diego, and Los Angeles—make the state even more important to trade with other countries.

California also contributes to the nation and the world by exporting products. California produces goods that people everywhere want to buy. Agricultural products are some of the state's major exports. Rice, cotton, fruit, and nuts from California can be bought all over the world. More than one-tenth of the agricultural products of the United States are grown in California. Other important California products include airplanes, engines, and other machines. Medical equipment made in California, such as X-ray machines, is used in clinics and hospitals all over the world.

Giant cranes load and unload ships in Los Angeles Harbor at San Pedro. The Saint Vincent Thomas Bridge connects San Pedro with Long Beach, another California port.

In Oakland, a boat is fixed and painted while in dry dock. A dry dock is made of watertight walls so that the water inside it can be pumped out or kept high. Dry docks are used to build and repair ships. Why would it be hard to paint or repair a large ship without a dry dock?

Trade is very important to California. California's trade business makes our state one of the richest places in the nation and the world. Trade also makes it possible for Californians to enjoy a wide variety of goods from all over the world.

Checking Up

1. What two kinds of products make up trade?

2. Describe the difference between imports and exports.

3. Name two things about California that make it an important trade center.

4. Name at least five of California's major exports.

5. In what ways is California helped by its trade business? How are other countries helped?

6. Why is it easy for California to trade with Asian countries. Why is it harder to trade with countries such as England, France, and Germany?

Lesson 2 Computers and Spaceships

Computers

The Santa Clara Valley, not far from San Jose, is called Silicon [sil ′ə kən] Valley. This is because many businesses there make silicon chips. These chips—about the size of a thumbnail—are actually tiny computers. They are used to make larger computers. They are also used in making calculators, radios, video games, televisions, cars, and spaceships. Every year new inventions are made in Silicon Valley. The computer chips get smaller and cheaper, and they are used in more and more ways.

Computers are becoming very important to modern life. Scientists, businesses, and industries are all using and depending on computers. Schools are beginning to teach with and about computers. And many families now have computers to keep track of money, to learn about things, and to play games. Californians are helping to make all this possible.

Spaceships

In Pasadena, a quiet city north of Los Angeles, stands the Jet Propulsion Laboratory. Known as JPL, this laboratory is involved in the excitement of space exploration.

In the 1960s, JPL sent four spacecraft to the moon to take television pictures of its surface. These pictures were the clearest ones ever taken at that time. They were used to help prepare for the Apollo program, when astronauts walked on the moon. The lab also sent spacecraft to take close-up photographs of Mercury, Venus, and Mars.

By the Way

The Santa Clara Valley became important to the computer industry partly because of Stanford University. Many people who knew about electronics and computers lived in the area because they went to school or taught at Stanford. Since the 1950s, the computer industry has helped the area to grow.

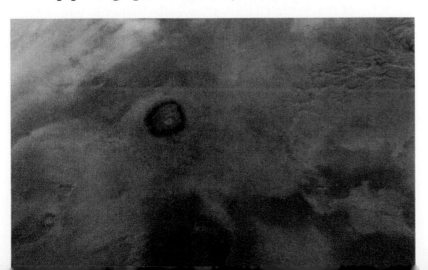

This picture, taken by JPL's Viking Orbiter 1, is a view of Tharsis Ridge, a large volcanic region on Mars. The total area of this scene is nearly two million square miles (five million square kilometers)!

263

Voyager 2 took this picture of Saturn and its beautiful, bright rings. The rings are probably made of chunks of ice.

By the Way

You may remember that the aircraft indrustry first came to California because of our state's clear weather. The space industry grew here for the same reason. Not only JPL, but also companies like Lockheed, Hughes Aircraft, and McDonnell Douglas contribute to the nation's space program.

Today, the scientists at JPL are working on the Voyager missions. Both the Voyager 1 and Voyager 2 spacecraft have flown past Jupiter and Saturn. They sent back clear, close-up pictures of the planets, their families of moons, and their beautiful rings. Voyager 1 is now on its way out of the solar system. Its mission is finished, and it will never return to the earth. The mission of Voyager 2 may not be over yet. It still may get pictures and information about Uranus and Neptune.

Thanks to JPL, California is making important contributions to space science. And people all over the world can share in the excitement of photographs and information from space!

Checking Up

1. Why is the Santa Clara Valley called Silicon Valley?

2. Why are businesses there important to modern life?

3. What are some things we have learned from work done at JPL?

4. Why is working with computers and spaceships important?

5. In what ways might computers and spaceships help us in the future?

A SPACE SCIENTIST:

DR. CHEN-WAN YEN

If you decide you want to visit one of the other planets in our solar system, call on Dr. Chen-wan Yen. Dr. Yen is a mission designer for Jet Propulsion Laboratory. She has worked on most of the United States space-exploration projects.

"You tell us where you want to go in space," Dr. Yen says with a smile. "We'll put together a spaceship for you that will do what you want it to do. We'll recommend a power source that will get you there fast—a rocket, or a sail that uses solar wind. We'll design the brain of the spacecraft so it will tell us what it finds out in its travels."

Born in Formosa, Chen-wan Yen was always curious about the world around her. In school, she studied science to satisfy that curiosity. Her friends often told her she would become a famous scientist. Today, she does not admit to being famous. But Dr. Yen certainly is a scientist.

After she moved to the United States in 1956, Dr. Yen worked in a branch of science that studies some of the smallest things in the world—atomic particles. She now works in a branch of science that studies larger things—planets, stars, and the universe itself.

Dr. Yen sees beauty in the study of the natural world. "Working in science, using math as a tool, is working with truth and beauty," she says. But to Dr. Yen, knowledge of science and math is only part of being good at the job.

265

"You must keep your mind flexible—open for new ideas."

What advice does she have for young people? "Be your own person. Understand that it's okay to be different."

Dr. Yen has two sons. She thinks that being both a mother and a scientist is natural—as natural as science itself. She likes her work. She likes putting science to work in practical ways. "Many of our ways of life have become better because of space exploration," Dr. Yen says. "We know more about weather and about the earth's resources. Communications have improved. I'm curious now about how we can put our space-exploring robots to work here on the earth."

Curiosity. Truth. Beauty. For Dr. Chen-wan Yen, they all work together in space science.

California's Jet Propulsion Laboratory

Building Social Studies Skills

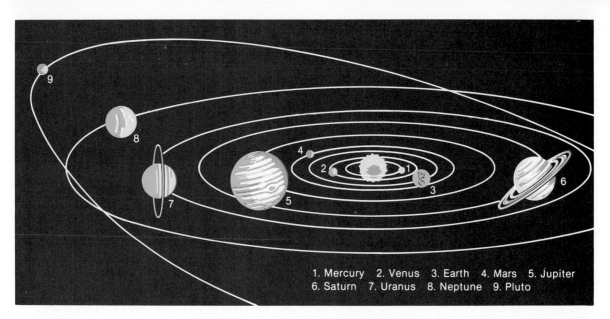

1. Mercury   2. Venus   3. Earth   4. Mars   5. Jupiter
6. Saturn   7. Uranus   8. Neptune   9. Pluto

Earth in the Solar System

On a clear night, we can see about three thousand stars. On a clear day, we can only see *one* star. It is so near and bright that its scattered light washes out the light of all the other stars. This nearby star is the sun.

Earth and eight other planets circle around the sun. Along with the nine planets are many smaller bodies—moons, asteroids, and comets. This collection of space travelers is our solar system.

All the planets **revolve** around the sun. That is, they travel around the sun in circular paths called **orbits**. Earth's revolution around the sun takes about 365 days. We call that period a year. The "year" for each planet is different. Mercury is the closest planet to the sun. Its orbit is the shortest, so its year, 88 days, is the shortest. Pluto, the farthest

planet from the sun, has much farther to travel around the sun. Pluto's year would equal 248 Earth years.

While the planets are revolving around the sun, they also **rotate**, or spin. Earth rotates once every 24 hours. We call that period a day. The "day" for each planet is different because each planet spins at a different speed. A day on Jupiter is only 10 hours. A day on Venus is *much* longer—5,832 hours! One day on Venus is longer than its own year and as long as 243 Earth days. If you were born on that strange planet, you'd be a year old before you were one day old!

Each of the planets has its own special features. Earth has air to breathe, huge oceans of water, and life. No other planet is like it. Mercury is small and rocky. Because its so close to the sun, Mercury gets very hot—hot enough to melt lead. Venus is covered with a thick, cloudy, poisonous **atmosphere**, or air. It is as hot as Mercury. Mars is cold. A world of reddish rocks and sand, Mars has thin air and icy patches at its poles.

Jupiter, the largest of the planets, is more than ten times the size of the earth. Jupiter is a giant ball of gas. Its upper atmosphere has colored belts, swirling clouds, and a giant Red Spot. Jupiter has thin rings and at least sixteen moons. Saturn is also made of gas. It has thousands of rings made of chunks of rock and ice. It also has as many as eighteen moons. Saturn is so light that, if it fell in a giant ocean in space, it would float.

We don't know much about Uranus, Neptune, and Pluto. They are very cold because they are far from the sun. Uranus and Neptune are large, frozen balls of gas. Pluto is a small world with at least one large moon.

By learning about the solar system, we also learn about the earth. For example, understanding the earth's yearly revolution around the sun helps us understand our seasons. Look at the diagram on this page. Find the Northern Hemisphere and the United States. Notice how the earth is tilted. Can you figure out how this makes our seasons? In summer, the Northern Hemisphere tilts toward the sun, and we get more direct sunlight. In winter, we get less

sunlight. At this time, the Northern Hemisphere is tilted away from the sun.

There is much more to learn about our solar system. Each time a spaceship flies by or lands on a planet, we learn more about our neighbors. By comparing it to the other planets, we also learn more about the earth.

To see what you've learned, answer these questions. Use the diagram on page 267 to help you.

1. Which planet is coldest, Mercury or Uranus? Why?
2. Which planet has the longest year, Jupiter or Mars? How do you know?
3. Is there likely to be life on Mercury? Why?
4. Why do the earth's seasons change?

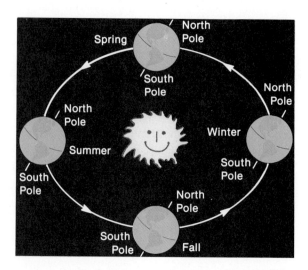

The seasons change because places on the earth receive different amounts of sunlight during the year. The tilt of the earth's axis causes the amount of sunlight striking the earth to vary.

Write your answers on paper. Do not write in the book.

Using Key Words

From the list below, choose the word that best completes each of the sentences. Write it on your paper.

atmosphere	orbit
export	revolve
import	rotate

1. A product that is brought into a country from somewhere else is called an _____.
2. A product that is sent out of a country is called an _____.
3. All planets in our solar system _____ around the sun.
4. Each planet has its own path or _____.
5. All planets also _____, or spin.
6. The earth's air is its _____.

Reviewing Main Ideas

Write "true" for the sentences that are true. Write "false" for the sentences that are false.

1. California has more resources than many of the world's nations.
2. California contributes to the United States as a trade center.
3. Because it is on the Atlantic Ocean, California can trade easily with Europe.
4. Silicon chips are found in many things we use today.
5. Industries, schools, and families all use computers.
6. The work of JPL helps us understand the earth and the other planets in our solar system.
7. The sun is one of the planets in our solar system.
8. It takes the earth 24 hours to revolve around the sun.

Thinking Things Over

How have computers from Silicon Valley made our lives different? What are some ways in which computers are used in school? How are they used at home? How are they used at work? How do you think they will be used in the future?

Practicing Skills

Use the following diagram to answer the questions.

1. Which picture, A or B, shows summer in the Northern Hemisphere?
2. In picture B, which hemisphere is getting the least light from the sun?

What Do You Know?

Write your answers on paper. Do not write in the book.

Words to Know

From the list below, choose the word that best completes each of the sentences. Write it on your paper.

atmosphere   opportunity
contribution   recreation
export   rotate
import   style
orbit   tourist

1. Shirley Hufsteadler has made a _____ to the nation by serving as Secretary of Education.
2. Another word for *chance* is _____.
3. A product brought into California is an _____.
4. People use weekends and vacations for _____.
5. The planets _____, or spin, while they are moving around the sun.
6. The design of a building can be called its _____.
7. A product sent out of California is an _____.
8. The air or gas around a planet is its _____.
9. A _____ is a person who is traveling for pleasure.
10. A planet's path around the sun is its _____.

Ideas to Know

Choose the ending that makes each sentence true. Write its letter beside the question number on your paper.

1. The main difference between Northern California and Southern California is the
   a. variety of people and customs.
   b. groups that have organized.
   c. climate and resources.
2. People have wider choices and opportunities in
   a. farms areas.
   b. cities.
   c. forest or mountain areas.
3. Northern California is known for
   a. Disneyland.
   b. computers.
   c. space exploration.
4. Southern California is known for
   a. redwoods.
   b. the Golden Gate Bridge.
   c. space exploration.
5. A Californian who has contributed to the arts is
   a. Vilma Martinez.
   b. Norberto Reyes.
   c. Ron McNair.
6. The names of many Californian cities and streets reflect
   a. Hispanic influence.
   b. Asian American influence.
   c. Danish American influence.

7. One of the largest Jewish communities in the world is in the city of
   a. San Diego.
   b. San Francisco.
   c. Los Angeles.
8. A main cause of California's seasons is the earth's
   a. tilt.
   b. rotation.
   c. climate.

Write "true" for the sentences that are true. Write "false" for the sentences that are false.

9. California is a land of great variety.
10. Gold is still Northern California's most important resource.
11. The tourist industry is important to Southern California.
12. People from many cultures have made contributions to California.
13. California is an important trade center.
14. California has no great sea ports.
15. Space exploration and computer development are important contributions of California.
16. The solar system is made up of the sun and seven planets.
17. The Northern Hemisphere has winter when it gets less sunlight.
18. The earth is always moving in two ways.

Using What You Know

Use the chart below to answer questions 1–3.

High Temperatures					
	M	T	W	TH	F
Los Angeles	70	80	90	85	75
San Francisco	70	85	65	60	60

1. Which city had the coolest temperatures?
2. Which city had the highest temperatures?
3. On which day did both cities have the same high temperature?

Use the diagram below to answer questions 4 and 5.

4. Which planet, A, B, or C, probably has the hottest temperatures?
5. Which planet probably has the longest year?

271

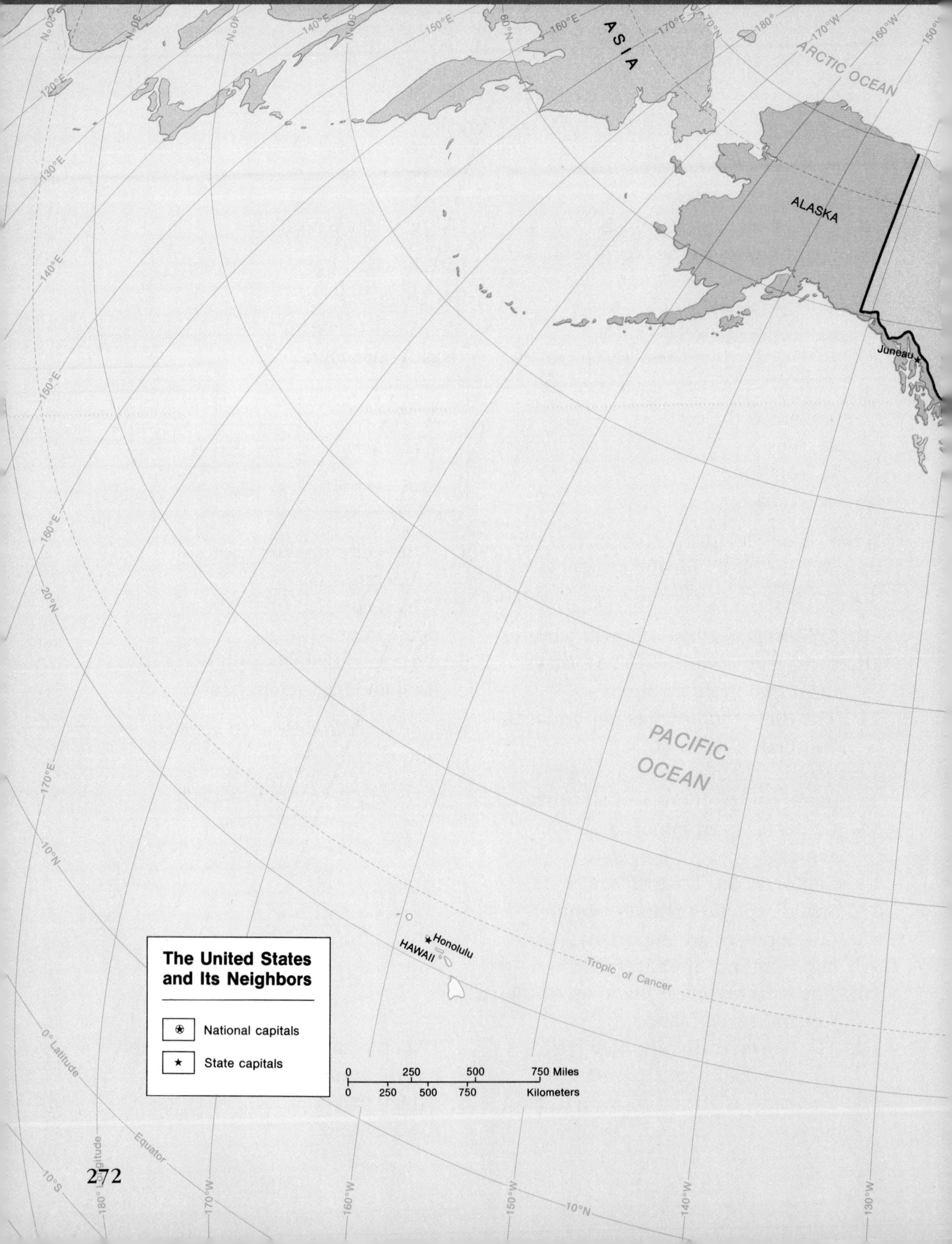

The United States and Its Neighbors
National capitals
State capitals
0 250 500 750 Miles
0 250 500 750 Kilometers
ASIA
ARCTIC OCEAN
ALASKA
Juneau
PACIFIC OCEAN
Honolulu
HAWAII
Tropic of Cancer
Equator
0° Latitude
180° Longitude
60°N
70°N
30°N
40°N
50°N
20°N
10°N
10°S
120°E
130°E
140°E
150°E
160°E
170°E
180°
170°W
160°W
150°W
140°W
130°W

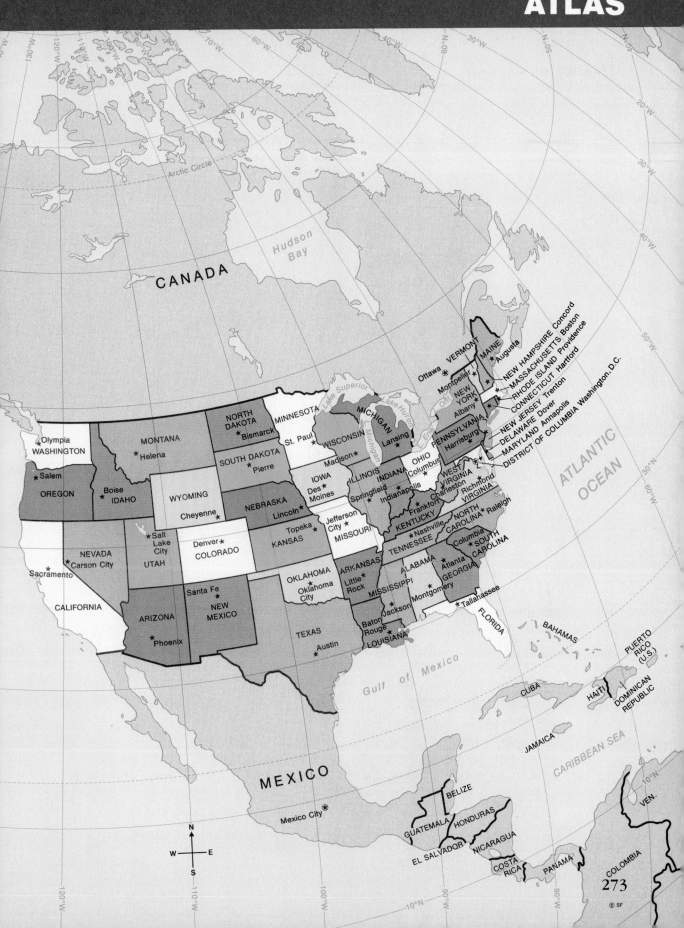

CANADA

Hudson
Bay

Arctic Circle

Lake Superior

Lake Michigan

Lake Huron

Lake Erie

NORTH
DAKOTA
★ Bismarck

MINNESOTA

St. Paul ★

MICHIGAN

Lansing ★

VERMONT

MAINE
★ Augusta

Ottawa ✦

Montpelier ★

NEW HAMPSHIRE Concord
MASSACHUSETTS Boston
RHODE ISLAND Providence
CONNECTICUT Hartford

NEW
YORK

Albany ★

NEW JERSEY Trenton
DELAWARE Dover
MARYLAND Annapolis
DISTRICT OF COLUMBIA Washington, D.C.

★ Olympia
WASHINGTON

MONTANA

★ Helena

SOUTH DAKOTA
★ Pierre

WISCONSIN

Madison ★

ILLINOIS

OHIO
Columbus ★

PENNSYLVANIA
Harrisburg ★

WEST
VIRGINIA
Charleston ★

Richmond
★

★ Salem

OREGON

Boise
★ IDAHO

WYOMING

Cheyenne ★

IOWA
Des ★
Moines

NEBRASKA

Lincoln ★

INDIANA

Indianapolis ★

Springfield ★

Frankfort
★

VIRGINIA

NORTH
CAROLINA ★ Raleigh

★ Salt
Lake
City

Denver ★
COLORADO

Topeka
★

KANSAS

Jefferson
City ★
MISSOURI

KENTUCKY

Nashville ★

TENNESSEE

Columbia
★ SOUTH
CAROLINA

Sacramento
★

NEVADA
★ Carson City

UTAH

OKLAHOMA

Oklahoma
City ★

ARKANSAS
Little ★
Rock

ALABAMA

Atlanta
★
GEORGIA

CALIFORNIA

Santa Fe
★

ARIZONA

★ Phoenix

NEW
MEXICO

TEXAS

Austin
★

MISSISSIPPI

Jackson ★

Montgomery
★

Tallahassee ★

Baton
Rouge ★

LOUISIANA

FLORIDA

ATLANTIC

OCEAN

BAHAMAS

PUERTO
RICO
(U.S.)

Gulf of Mexico

CUBA

HAITI

DOMINICAN
REPUBLIC

JAMAICA

CARIBBEAN SEA

VEN.

MEXICO

Mexico City ✦

BELIZE

GUATEMALA

HONDURAS

EL SALVADOR

NICARAGUA

COSTA
RICA

PANAMA

COLOMBIA

N
W ✦ E
S

273

© SF

The World: Political

ARCTIC OCEAN

Greenland
(DENMARK)

Alaska
(U.S.)

Arctic Circle

CANADA

NORTH AMERICA

ATLANTIC OCEAN

Aleutian Islands

40°North Latitude

UNITED STATES

Azores
(PORT.)

Bermuda
(U.K.)

PACIFIC OCEAN

Midway Islands
(U.S.)

Tropic of Cancer

Hawaii (U.S.)

MEXICO

CUBA

BAHAMAS

DOMINICAN REPUBLIC

Puerto Rico (U.S.)

CAPE VERDE

ANTIGUA-BARBUDA
DOMINICA

JAMAICA

HAITI

BELIZE

Virgin Is.(U.S.-U.K.)

ST. VINCENT AND
THE GRENADINES

GUATEMALA

HONDURAS

ST. LUCIA

BARBADOS

EL SALVADOR

NICARAGUA

GRENADA

TRINIDAD AND TOBAGO

COSTA RICA

VENEZUELA

GUYANA

PANAMA

SURINAME

COLOMBIA

FR. GUIANA
(FRANCE)

P O L Y N E S I A

KIRIBATI

Galapagos
Islands
(ECUADOR)

ECUADOR

SOUTH AMERICA

0° Equator

PERU

BRAZIL

WESTERN SAMOA

American
Samoa (U.S.)

TONGA

French

BOLIVIA

20°S

Polynesia
(FRANCE)

Tropic of Capricorn

PARAGUAY

Easter Island
(CHILE)

CHILE

PACIFIC OCEAN

URUGUAY

ARGENTINA

40°S

Falkland Islands
(U.K.)

South Georgia
(Falkland Is.)

60°S

Antarctic Circle

80°S

ANTARCTICA

EUROPE

NORWAY

SWEDEN

IRELAND

UNITED KINGDOM

DENMARK

NETHERLANDS

EAST GERMANY

POLAND

U.S.S.R.

BELGIUM

WEST GERMANY

CZECHOSLOVAKIA

LUX.

FRANCE

AUSTRIA

HUNGARY

ROMANIA

ATLANTIC OCEAN

SWITZERLAND

YUGOSLAVIA

PORTUGAL

ITALY

BULGARIA

SPAIN

ALBANIA

GREECE

MALTA

CYPRUS

| 0 | 500 Miles |
| 0 | 500 Kilometers |

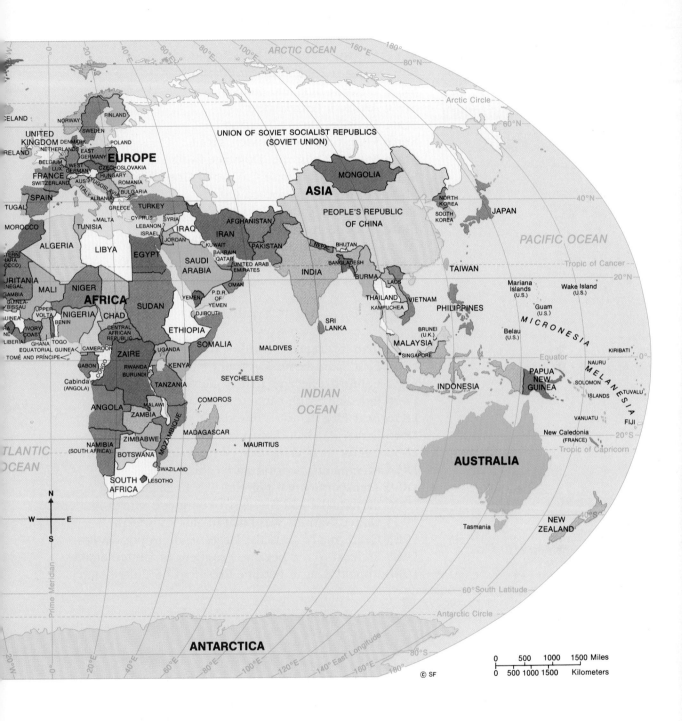

ARCTIC OCEAN

Arctic Circle

CELAND

NORWAY FINLAND

SWEDEN

60°N

UNITED
KINGDOM

POLAND

UNION OF SOVIET SOCIALIST REPUBLICS
(SOVIET UNION)

IRELAND

NETHERLANDS
DENMARK

EAST
GERMANY

BELGIUM
WEST
LUX. GERMANY

EUROPE

CZECHOSLOVAKIA

MONGOLIA

FRANCE
SWITZERLAND

HUNGARY

AUS.

ASIA

NORTH
KOREA

JAPAN

40°N

YUGOSLAVIA

ROMANIA

SPAIN

ITALY

BULGARIA

SOUTH
KOREA

ALBANIA

PEOPLE'S REPUBLIC

TUGAL

GREECE

TURKEY

CYPRUS

SYRIA

AFGHANISTAN

OF CHINA

PACIFIC OCEAN

MALTA

MOROCCO

TUNISIA

LEBANON
ISRAEL

IRAQ

JORDAN

IRAN

PAKISTAN

Tropic of Cancer

20°N

ALGERIA

LIBYA

EGYPT

KUWAIT
BAHRAIN
QATAR

NEPAL

BHUTAN

TAIWAN

Mariana
Islands
(U.S.)

Wake Island
(U.S.)

URITANIA

SAUDI
ARABIA

UNITED ARAB
EMIRATES

INDIA

BANGLADESH

BURMA

ENEGAL

MALI

NIGER

OMAN

P.D.R.
OF
YEMEN

LAOS

THAILAND

VIETNAM

Guam
(U.S.)

MICRONESIA

GAMBIA

AFRICA

YEMEN

GUINEA
BISSAU

UPPER
VOLTA

SUDAN

CHAD

DJIBOUTI

KAMPUCHEA

PHILIPPINES

NIGERIA

Belau
(U.S.)

GUINEA

IVORY
COAST

BENIN

CENTRAL
AFRICAN
REPUBLIC

ETHIOPIA

SRI
LANKA

BRUNEI
(U.K.)

KIRIBATI

NE
LIBERIA

GHANA TOGO

SOMALIA

MALDIVES

MALAYSIA

MELANESIA

EQUATORIAL GUINEA

CAMEROON

TOMÉ AND PRÍNCIPE

GABON

CONGO

ZAIRE

UGANDA

KENYA

SINGAPORE

Equator

NAURU

0°

RWANDA

INDONESIA

SOLOMON

TUVALU

Cabinda
(ANGOLA)

BURUNDI

TANZANIA

SEYCHELLES

PAPUA
NEW
GUINEA

ISLANDS

COMOROS

INDIAN

ANGOLA

MALAWI

ZAMBIA

MOZAMBIQUE

OCEAN

VANUATU

FIJI

MADAGASCAR

ZIMBABWE

New Caledonia
(FRANCE)

20°S

NAMIBIA
(SOUTH AFRICA)

BOTSWANA

MAURITIUS

Tropic of Capricorn

SWAZILAND

AUSTRALIA

TLANTIC

OCEAN

SOUTH
AFRICA

LESOTHO

N

W E

S

Tasmania

NEW
ZEALAND

40°S

60°South Latitude

Prime Meridian

Antarctic Circle

ANTARCTICA

80°S

0°
20°E
60°E
80°E
100°E
120°E
140° East Longitude
160°E
180°

© SF

| 0 | 500 | 1000 | 1500 Miles |
| 0 | 500 1000 1500 | | Kilometers |

AUS.—AUSTRIA
LUX.—LUXEMBOURG
P.D.R. OF YEMEN—PEOPLE'S DEMOCRATIC REPUBLIC OF YEMEN
PORT.—PORTUGAL
U.K.—UNITED KINGDOM
U.S.—UNITED STATES
U.S.S.R.—UNION OF SOVIET SOCIALIST REPUBLICS

Facts About California

California Factfinder

Nickname: The Golden State
Capital: Sacramento
State Motto: Eureka ("I have found it!")
State Song: *I Love You, California*
State Colors: Blue and Gold
State Animal: Grizzly Bear
State Reptile: Desert Tortoise
State Fish: California Golden Trout
State Insect: California Dog-face Butterfly
State Marine Mammal: California Gray Whale
State Fossil: Saber-toothed Cat
State Mineral: Native Gold
State Rock: Serpentine
Area: 158,693 square miles (411,013 square kilometers)
Greatest Length: 770 miles (1,239 kilometers)
Greatest Width: 360 miles (579 kilometers)

California Dateline

1542 Juan Rodríguez Cabrillo explored San Diego Bay.
1769 First Spanish mission founded in San Diego.
1822 California became part of Mexico.
1826 Jedediah Smith came to California by land.
1846 Bear Flag Revolt resulted in California Republic.
1848 James Marshall discovered gold.
1850 California became thirty-first state of the Union.
1854 Sacramento became state capital.
1869 Transcontinental railroad was finished.
1906 Earthquake and fire destroyed much of San Francisco.
1945 United Nations was born in San Francisco.
1963 California became the largest state in population.
1968 Richard Nixon became President of United States.
1980 Ronald Reagan became President of United States.

State Flower:
California Golden Poppy

State Flag

California Record Book

World Records

Oldest living thing: bristlecone pine tree—almost 5,000 years old

Tallest living thing: coast redwood tree—366.2 feet (109.4 meters) tall

Largest living thing: giant sequoia tree—36.5 feet (11.2 meters) in diameter

Great Seal of the State of California

National Records

First state park: Yosemite—1864

Lowest point: Badwater, Death Valley—282 feet (86 meters) below sea level

Highest peak (outside of Alaska): Mt. Whitney—14,494 feet (4,418 meters) above sea level

Highest waterfall: Ribbon Falls, Yosemite—1,612 feet (491 meters) high

Highest dam: Oroville Dam—770 feet (235 meters) high

Highest recorded temperature: Death Valley—135° F (47° C)

California Calendar

A few interesting events

January   Tournament of Roses: Pasadena—January 1
New Year Regatta: San Diego—January 1

February   Chinese New Year Celebration: San Francisco

March   Return of the swallows: San Juan Capistrano—usually March 19

April   Cherry Blossom Festival: San Francisco
Ramona Pageant: Hemet—April through May

May   Jumping Frog Jubilee: Angels Camp
Ojai Music Festival: Ojai

June   Highland Gathering and Games: Long Beach
San Diego National Shakespeare Festival—June through September

July   California Rodeo: Salinas

August   California National Sea Festival: Long Beach
Old Spanish Days Festival: Santa Barbara

September   State Fair: Sacramento
Monterey Jazz Festival

October   San Francisco Film Festival

December   Las Posada: Padua Hills

State Tree: Giant Redwood

Glossary

Full Pronunciation Key

The pronunciation of each word is shown just after the word, in this way: **abbreviate** (ə brē′ vē āt). The letters and signs used are pronounced as in the words below. The mark ′ is placed after a syllable with a primary, or heavy, accent, as in the example above. The mark ′ after a syllable shows a secondary, or lighter, accent, as in **abbreviation** (ə brē′ vē ā′ shən).

a	hat, cap	i	it, pin	p	paper, cup	z	zero, breeze
ā	age, face	ī	ice, five	r	run, try	zh	measure, seizure
ä	father, far			s	say, yes		
		j	jam, enjoy			ə	represents:
b	bad, rob	k	kind, seek	sh	she, rush		
ch	child, much	l	land, coal	t	tell, it	a	in about
d	did, red	m	me, am	th	thin, both	e	in taken
		n	no, in	TH	then, smooth	i	in pencil
e	let, best					o	in lemon
ē	equal, be	ng	long, bring	u	cup, butter	u	in circus
ėr	term, learn	o	hot, rock	u	full, put		
				ü	rule, move		
f	fat, if	ō	open, go				
g	go, bag	ô	order, all	v	very, save		
h	he, how	oi	oil, voice	w	will, woman		
		ou	house, out	y	young, yet		

The pronunciation key is from the *Thorndike-Barnhart* Dictionary Series.

---

act (akt), *noun*, a law passed by Congress.

A.D., abbreviation used to label or identify the years after the birth of Christ. (The abbreviation *A.D.* stands for the Latin phrase *Anno Domini*, which means "in the year of our Lord.")

agriculture (ag′ rə kul′ chər), *noun*, the science or art of farming, including the growth of crops and the raising of livestock.

ally (al′ ī), *noun*, a person, group, or nation united with another for some special purpose.

ancestor (an′ ses′ tər), *noun*, family member who lived in the past; a person from whom one is descended.

aqueduct (ak′ wə dukt), *noun*, an artificial channel or large pipe used to transport water.

assembly line (ə sem′ blē līn), *noun*, a row of workers and machines along which work is passed until the final product is made.

atmosphere (at′ mə sfir), *noun*, air or gas that surrounds the earth or other planets.

B.C., abbreviation meaning "before Christ," used to label or identify the years before the birth of Christ.

bill (bil), *noun*, a suggested law presented to lawmakers for their approval.

boom (büm), *noun*, a sudden, fast growth in size or activity.

boundary (boun′ dər ē), *noun*, the borderline of a place such as a country or piece of property.

boycott (boi′ kot), *verb*, to refuse to buy or use a product or service.

canal (kə nal′), *noun*, a waterway dug across land, used for ships or small boats to travel through, or used to carry water for irrigation.

case (kās), *noun*, a matter for a court of law to decide.

civil rights (siv′ əl rīts), *noun*, the rights of a citizen, especially the rights guaranteed to all United States citizens regardless of sex, age, race, religion, or place of birth.

climate (klī′ mit), *noun*, the weather of an area or place over a long period of time.

conflict (kon′ flikt), *noun*, a disagreement or fight about a thing or idea.

conserve (kən serv′), *verb*, to keep from being used up; to save or use wisely.

constitution (kon′ stə tü′ shən), *noun*, a system of laws that tell how a nation, state, or group is to be governed.

contribution (kon′ trə byü′ shən), *noun*, a gift of help or talent used to benefit others.

council (koun′ səl), *noun*, a group of men and women elected to make laws for and manage a city.

county (koun′ tē), *noun*, one of the districts, or areas, into which a state is divided.

culture (kul′ chər), *noun*, the customs, arts, and other ways of life of a nation or people.

custom (kus′ təm), *noun*, any usual action or practice; habit.

decision tree (di sizh′ ən trē), *noun*, a chart used for the purpose of making a decision about the best way to reach a goal. A decision tree examines problems, possible solutions, and the results of the solutions.

deed (dēd), *noun*, a written or printed statement of ownership. The buyer of land receives a deed to the property from the former owner.

delegate (del′ ə git), *noun*, a person chosen to speak or act for others.

depression (di presh′ ən), *noun*, a time when people are out of work, prices are falling, businesses cannot sell goods, and people have little money to save or spend.

discrimination (dis krim′ ə nā′ shən), *noun*, a difference or unfairness in treatment of a group of people.

distribution (dis′ trə byü′ shən), *noun*, the act of dividing and giving out in shares: *water distribution*.

district (dis′ trikt), *noun*, part of a country, state, or city marked off for a special purpose: *school district, election district*.

drought (drout), *noun*, a long period of dry weather; continued lack of rain.

dust bowl (dust bōl), *noun*, an area, especially in the western plains of the United States and Canada, where violent dust storms often happen.

election (i lek′ shən), *noun*, a choosing for an office by vote.

elevation (el′ə vā′ shən), *noun*, height above the earth's surface.

engineer (en′ jə nir′), *noun*, a person whose work is planning and building engines, machines, roads, bridges, canals, railroads, and so on.

environment (en vī′ rən mənt), *noun*, all the surrounding things, conditions, and influences affecting growth of living things.

exploration (ek′ splə rā′ shən), *noun*, a traveling in little-known lands or seas for the purpose of discovery.

export (ek spôrt′), *noun*, a product sent out of one country for sale or use in another.

extinct (ek stingkt′), *adjective*, no longer existing. A kind of animal that has died out is said to be extinct.

financial (fə nan′ shəl), *adjective*, having to do with money matters.

flow chart (flō chärt), *noun*, a chart used to outline the steps of a plan or process and show the order in which they are to be done.

freight (frāt), *noun*, goods transported by train, truck, ship, or aircraft.

generation (jen′ ə rā′ shən), *noun*, all the people born about the same time; one step or level on a family tree.

governor (guv′ ər nər), *noun*, the elected head of a state government.

import (im pôrt′), *noun*, a product brought from a foreign country into a country for sale or use.

independent (in′ di pen′ dənt), *adjective*, not under another's rule or control; ruling or governing oneself.

index (in′ deks), *noun*, a list of what is in a book, telling on what pages to find various topics.

invest (in vest′), *verb*, to put money in a thing or idea in order to make more money.

junction (jungk′ shən), *noun*, a place of joining or meeting. A highway junction is a place where highways meet or cross.

key word (kē wėrd), *noun*, a word in upper corner of dictionary or encyclopedia page that aids in finding information listed in alphabetical order on that page.

labor (lā′ bər), *noun*, workers as a group: *Labor favors safe working conditions.*

landform (land′ fôrm), *noun*, a physical feature of the earth's surface. Plains, plateaus, hills, and mountains are landforms.

latitude (lat′ ə tud), *noun*, distance north or south of the Equator, measured in degrees. (A degree of latitude is about 69 miles or 111 kilometers.)

legislature (lej′ ə slā′ cher), *noun*, a group of people that makes laws for a state or country.

license (lī′ sns), *noun*, permission given by law to do something.

local government (lō′ kəl guv′ ərn mənt), *noun*, city or county government.

location (lō kā′ shən), *noun*, the position or place where something is or can be found.

longitude (lon′ jə tüd), *noun*, distance east or west on the earth's surface, measured in degrees from the Prime Meridian.

majority (mə jôr′ ə tē), *noun*, the larger number or part; more than half.

management (man′ ij mənt), *noun*, the people that manage a business or institution.

mayor (mā′ ər), *noun*, the person at the head of a city or town government; chief official of a city or town.

merchant (mėr′ chənt), *noun*, a person who buys and sells for profit; a storekeeper or trader.

meridian (mə rid′ ē ən), *noun*, an imaginary circle passing through the North and South Poles.

migrant (mī′ grənt), *noun*, a person who moves from place to place in order to find work.

migrate (mi grāt), *verb*, to move from one place to settle in another.

military base (mil′ ə ter′ ē bās), *noun*, a camp or location for housing soldiers or other armed forces.

mineral (min′ ər el), *noun*, a non-living material obtained by mining or digging in the earth.

minority group (mə nôr′ ə tē grüp), *noun*, a group within a country or state that differs in race, religion, or national origin from the larger part of the population.

mission (mish′ ən), *noun*, a place built by Indians and the Spanish friars where people lived, worked, and worshiped.

monopoly (mə nop′ ə lē), *noun*, complete control of a product or service.

natural vegetation, (nach′ ər əl vej′ ə tā′ shən), *noun*, kind of plants that grow naturally in a certain place or climate.

opportunity (op′ ər tü′ nətē), *noun*, a good chance to do something.

orbit (ôr′ bit), *noun*, the curved path of a heavenly body (such as a planet) around another body in space.

ordinance (ôrd′ n əns), *noun*, a city law.

organize (ôr′ gə nīz), *verb*, to form a group for the purpose of working toward a common goal.

overland (ō′ vər land′), *adjective*, on land, by land, or across land.

parallel (par′ə lel), *noun*, any of the imaginary circles around the earth that are parallel to the Equator.

pass (pas), *noun*, a narrow road or path: low place between two mountains.

patent (pat′ nt), *noun*, a government document, or paper, which gives a person or company sole rights to make, use, or sell a new invention for a certain number of years.

patriotic (pā′ trē ot′ ik), *adjective*, showing love and loyal support of one's own country.

pesticide (pes′ tə sīd), *noun*, a chemical used to kill pests that harm crops.

petition (pə tish′ ən), *noun*, a written request from the people for some desired government action or change in law.

pioneer (pī′ ə nir′), *noun*, a person who settles in a part of a country, preparing it for others.

pollutant (pə lüt′ nt), *noun*, something that dirties the environment, especially waste materials.

population (pop′ yə lā′ shən), *noun*, 1. the people of a city, country, or district. 2. the number of a group of animals or people living in a given area.

presidio (pre sē′ dē ō), *noun*, a fort in Spanish California.

prospector (pros′ pek tər), *noun*, a person who explores an area looking for minerals; a miner.

pueblo (pü eb′ lō), *noun*, a Spanish village, or town, built of adobe and stone.

rancho (ranch′ ō), *noun*, a ranch in Spanish California where cattle were raised; the Spanish name for *ranch*.

recreation (rek′ rē ā′ shən), *noun*, play or amusement; something done for fun.

relocation camp (rē′ lō kā′ shən kamp), *noun*, a place where Japanese Americans, taken from their homes, were sent to live during World War II.

representative (rep′ ri zen′ tə tiv), *noun*, a person elected by the people to serve in government; a person chosen to act or speak for others.

reservation (rez′ ər vā′ shən), *noun*, land set aside by the government for a special purpose: *an Indian reservation.*

reservoir (rez′ ər vwär), *noun*, a place where water is collected and stored for use.

resource (ri sôrs′), *noun*, minerals, water, and people are examples of resources.

revolution (rev′ e lü′ shən), *noun*, a war; a complete overthrow of an established government.

revolve (ri volv'), *verb*, to move in a circle; to move in an orbit around something: *The moon revolves around the earth.*

riot (rī' et), *noun*, a wild, noisy, and often violent public disturbance caused by a large crowd or mob.

rotate (rō' tāt), *verb*, to spin around a center or axis: *The earth rotates on its axis.*

secondary reference (sek' ən der' ē ref' ər əns), *noun*, a second source, or place, where information on a subject can be found.

slavery (slā' vər ē), *noun*, the custom of people owning other people; the custom of keeping slaves.

smog (smog), *noun*, dust, smoke, and chemicals that pollute air.

specialize (spesh' ə līz), *verb*, to do and become good at one special kind of work.

stock (stok), *noun*, parts or shares of a company sold to raise money.

stockholder (stok' hōl' der), *noun*, an owner of stocks or shares in a company.

strike (strīk), *noun*, the stopping of work to get higher pay or better working conditions.

style (stīl), *noun*, manner, method, or way.

subheading (sub' hed' ing), *noun*, a small title, usually in dark print, that divides information given in a chapter or article.

survey (sər' vā), *noun*, a formal study or poll.

surveyor (sər vā' ər), *noun*, a person who measures a piece of land to set its boundaries.

tabulate (tab' ye lāt), *verb*, to arrange facts and figures in charts or lists.

telegraph (tel' ə graf), *noun*, a system for sending messages in code by wire.

topsoil (top' soil), *noun*, the upper part of the soil that is rich and good for growing crops.

tourist (tur' ist), *noun*, a person traveling for pleasure.

trailblazer (trāl' blā' zər), *noun*, a person who finds or marks routes through unmapped, or unknown lands.

transcontinental (tran' skon tə nen' tl), *adjective*, crossing a continent.

union (yü' nyen), *noun*, a group of workers joined together to protect workers' rights and to improve conditions.

veto (vē' tō), *noun*, the right of the president or governor to refuse to sign bills passed by lawmakers.

volume (vol' yəm), *noun*, a book forming part of a set or series: *One book in a set of encyclopedias is a volume.*

Index

Acknowledgments

Quoted Material

21 From BULLETIN 78 of the Bureau of American Ethnology of the Smithsonian Institution. Government Printing Office, Washington, D.C., 1925. **51** Prudencia Higuera, "Trading with the Americans." THE CENTURY, November 1890 to April 1891. **65** THE TRAILBLAZERS. New York: Time-Life Books, 1973, p. 91. **67** Elisha Brooks, A PIONEER MOTHER OF CALIFORNIA. San Francisco: Harr Wagner Publishing Co., 1922, p. 23. **72** James W. Marshall, "To J. H. Hutchings, on the Discovery of Gold January 24, 1848." HUTCHINGS' CALIFORNIA MAGAZINE, Vol. 2, No. 5, November 1857. **75** Chauncey L. Canfield, THE DIARY OF A FORTY-NINER. Boston: Houghton Mifflin Company, 1920, p. 82. **88** Mariano Guadalupe Vallejo, CALIFORNIA: A HISTORY by Andrew F. Rolle. New York: Thomas Y. Crowell Company, Inc., 1969, p. 233. **98** One Indian Chief. Quoted in CALIFORNIA—WHERE THE TWAIN DID MEET by Anne Loftis. New York: Macmillan Publishing Co., Inc., 1973, p. 21. **106** From THE PONY EXPRESS: *The Record of a Romantic Adventure in Business* by Arthur Chapman. Copyright 1932 by Arthur Chapman. Reprinted by permission of G. P. Putnam's Sons. **120** "Newsboys of Old: How They Flourished in California Thirty Years Ago" from the SAN FRANCISCO CALL, January 29, 1882. **122–123** Sarah Bixby-Smith, "Watermelons" from MY SAGE BRUSH GARDEN. Cedar Rapids, Iowa: Torch Press, 1924. **122–123** Sarah Bixby-Smith, ADOBE DAYS. Cedar Rapids, Iowa: The Torch Press, 1926.

Illustrations

The abbreviations indicate position of pictures on a page. *T* is top, *b* is bottom, *l* is left, *r* is right, *tl* is top left, *tr* is top right, and *br* is bottom right.

Unit 1 **18** (l) James Russel Stephens/Photo Network. **29** Michael Collier. **31** John Reginato. **32** Photo Network. **34** (l) Photo Network; (r) Robert Eckert/EKM-Nepenthe. **35** Mark E. Gibson/Norcal Graphics. **42** (l) California State Library; (t) The Bancroft Library. **43** Michael Collier. **46** Historical Library First American Title Insurance. **47** Lowie Museum of Anthropology, University of California, Berkeley. **49** California Historical Society/Title Insurance and Trust Co. (Los Angeles) Collection of Historical Photographs. **50–51** James Walker/California Historical Society, San Francisco. **52** James Walker/California Historical Society, San Francisco. **53** (l) James Walker/Bancroft Library; (r) Los Angeles County Museum of Natural History. **54** Chronicle Books.

Unit 2 **58–59** Union League Club, New York, N.Y. Photography by Sandak, Inc. **62** (t) Michael Collier; (b) Photo Network. **64** Photo Courtesy Remington Art Museum, Ogdensburg, New York. **65** (l) Walters Art Gallery, Baltimore; (r) California State Library. **66** Justus Ghormley/Photo Network. **67** (r) The Denver Public Library, Western History Department. **69** California Historical Society, San Francisco. **70** California Department of Parks and Recreation. **74** San Francisco Maritime Museum. **75** The Denver Public Library, Western History Department. **76** California Historical Society, San Francisco. **77** Suzanne Snider. **78** Wells Fargo Bank History Department. **79** Arnold Genthe/M.H. de Young Memorial Museum. **80** John Sanford. **83** California State Capital Museum. **85** John Palmer. **87** California State Library. **88** The Bancroft Library. **89** The San Francisco African American Historical & Cultural Society. **90** California Department of Parks and Recreation.

Unit 3 **94–95** Peters Collection. Photography by Sandak, Inc. **97** Historical Library First American Title Insurance. **99** National Archives. **100** California State Library. **103** (b) California Historical Society/Title Insurance and Trust Co. (Los Angeles) Collection of Historical Photographs; (r) Historical Library First American Title Insurance. **104** The Society of California Pioneers. **105** The Thomas Gilcrease Institute of American History and Art, Tulsa, OK. **107** Wells Fargo Bank History Department. **112** Southern Pacific photo. **114** Southern Pacific photo. **121** (l) California Historical Society, San Francisco; (r) San Francisco Maritime Museum. **122** California Historical Society/Title Insurance and Trust Co. (Los Angeles) Collection of Historical Photographs. **123** John Sanford. **124** California Historical Society Title/Insurance and Trust Co. (Los Angeles) Collection of Historical Photographs.

Unit 4 **128–129** Julien Hutten/Photo Network. **131** (t) Historical Library First American Title Insurance; (r) Suzanne Snider. **132** John Sanford/Photo Network. **135** California Historical Society/Title Insurance and Trust Co. (Los Angeles) Collection of Historical Photographs. **136** Wells Fargo Bank History Department. **137** Michael Collier/Collier-Condit. **138** (b) John Sanford/Photo Network; (t) Sierra Club. **143** Bureau of Reclamation. **144** Southern Pacific photo. **147** Mark E. Gibson/Norcal Graphics. **148** (t) Department of Water and Power, Los Angeles; (b) Bureau of Reclamation. **153** (r) American Learning Corporation; (b) Environmental Protection Agency. **154** James Woodard/Photo Network. **155** (r) Michael Collier; (b) California Historical Society/Title Insurance and Trust Co. (Los Angeles) Collection of Historical Photographs. **156** Michael Collier. **157** California Historical Society/Title Insurance and Trust Co. (Los Angeles) Collection of Historical Photographs. **158** The American Film Institute. **159** (t) Courtesy of Lucasfilm, LTD; (r) Collectors Bookstore.

Unit 5 **168–169** Design by Judith F. Baca/Photo by Linda Eber. **171** Elin Haaga. **173** Library of Congress. **177** Wide World. **178** San Diego Historical Society. **179** (l) Library of Congress. **181** United Press International. **182** United Press International. **183** Jeanne Wakatsuki Houston. **184** San Francisco Maritime Museum. **185** United Press International. **187** Chuck O'Rear/West Light. **188** United Press International. **190** Photo Network. **191** United Press International. **192** (l) James Woodard/Photo Network; (r) John Malmin. **193** Photo Network. **194** (t) John Sanford; (b) James Woodard/Photo Network. **195** (l) Dan McCleery/Photo Network; (r) Photo Network. **196** (l) Dan McCleery/Photo Network; (r) Photo Network.

Unit 6 **202–203** John Sanford/Photo Network. **205** (r) Photo Network; (b) Photo Network. **206** (tl) Photo Network; (tr) Lupe Rodriguez/Photo Network; (b) Jon Dixon/EKM-Nepenthe. **207** Photo Network. **209** James Aurness/West Light. **210** James Aurness/West Light. **212** Teresa P. Hughes. **213** Art Torres. **215** (l) United Press International; (r) United Press International. **217** John Reginato. **222** James Aurness/West Light. **223** James Aurness/West Light. **227** Dan McCleery/Photo Network. **228** Chuck O'Rear/West Light. **229** Rex Malcolm. **231** Larry Dunmire/Photo Network. **232** Greenpeace.

Unit 7 **236–237** John Malmin. **240** John Sanford/Photo Network. **241** (r) Mark E. Gibson/Norcal Graphics; (b) Michael Collier. **242** (t) John Sanford/Photo Network; (l) Photo Network. **243** Justus Ghormley/Photo Network. **244** Diane Feinstein. **245** (t) Lawrence McElrea/Photo Network; (b) Michael Collier. **247** (r) John Dixon/EKM-Nepenthe; (b) John Dixon/EKM-Nepenthe. **248** (l) Photo courtesy of The Experience Center; (b) Photo Network. **249** (tl) Photo Network; (tr) Photo Courtesy of the Pasadena Tournament of Roses Association; (b)© Walt Disney Productions. **252** (l) Allan Berliner; (r) United Press International. **253** (l) Bonnie Schiffman; (c) United Press International; (r) March Fong Eu. **254** (t) R.K. Strite; (b) United Press International. **255** Designed by Judith F. Baca/Photo by Linda Eber. **256** (tr) Jet Propulsion Lab; (tl) United Press International; (bl) United Press International. **257** (tr) Sharyn Warner; (br) John Sanford/Photo Network; (bl) Photo Network. **258** (tl) Photo Network; (bl) Suzanne Snider; (cr) Dan McCleery/Photo Network. **261** John Sanford/Photo Network. **262** Michael Collier. *263* (r) John Sanford/Photo Network; (b) NASA. *264* NASA. **265** John Sanford. **266** Photo Network.